TOWARDS A NEW MUSEUM

TOWARDS A

NEW MUSEUM

VICTORIA NEWHOUSE

THE MONACELLI PRESS

First published in the United States of America in 1998 by
The Monacelli Press, Inc.
10 East 92nd Street, New York, New York 10128.

Library of Congress Cataloging-in-Publication Data
Newhouse, Victoria.
Towards a new museum / Victoria Newhouse.
p.   cm.
Includes bibliographical references and index.
ISBN 1-885254-60-1
1. Art museum architecture.
2. Architecture, Modern—20th century.
I. Title.
NA6695.N49   1998
727'.7'09045—dc21   98-4584

Printed and bound in Germany

Designed by Bureau

Cover: The Guggenheim Museum, Bilbao, Spain,
by Frank O. Gehry & Associates (1997). Atrium.
Credit: Guggenheim Museum Bilbao, 1997. Photo by
David Heald © Solomon R. Guggenheim Museum
Foundation, New York.

Chapter 3 was published in a slightly different version in
Architecture, September 1996, 88–101.
Chapter 7 was published in slightly different versions in
Architectural Digest, July 1995, 34–35, and in
Architecture, December 1995, 39–45.

To Si

Acknowledgments

My first debt in realizing this book is to Adolf Placzek, for his ongoing support and skillful guidance. Robert Gottlieb's editorial suggestions allowed me to focus my ideas and gave me a broader context for them. Terry Bissell's meticulous line editing has made the book more readable. Andrea Monfried has effected important improvements.

For many of the museum typology concepts on which the book is based, I am grateful to Alex Gorlin, whose presence on several research trips and whose critique of the manuscript have made a tremendous contribution to it. My husband, Si, had valuable insights into the art that is the book's raison d'être. Without Joel Honig's masterful help in completing the research, I could never have met the deadline or achieved the scope. Suzanne Stephens has given me useful directives throughout my research and writing. Jean-Louis Cohen provided a critical reading. Gianfranco Monacelli has shown exemplary patience.

There are many others who contributed to *Towards a New Museum*: the museum staffs, whose cooperation has been extraordinary; all those who generously gave their time for interviews; Nora Beeson, who was the first to evaluate and encourage the project; Rosemarie Haag Bletter, whose comprehensive bibliography led my research; Yve-Alain Bois, for his exhaustive El Lissitzky bibliography; Joseph Giovannini, who brought the Atelier Mimesis to my attention; Robert Kahn, who made available material on Frank Stella; Robert Rosenblum, who guided my research of antecedents for artists' museums; Myra Nan Rosenfeld, who provided historical background; Ealan Wingate, who shared his expertise on contemporary art; and Elizabeth Wingate, who helped with ancient art.

Allison Silver facilitated my Los Angeles research; Susan Train's persistence produced material on Lascaux II and several photographs from Paris; Doris Mentrup came to the rescue for many German-based problems; Steven Newhouse gave me information on electronic technology; Mary Lou Selo and Marianne Eggler-Gerozissis translated journal articles from the German; and Linda Johnson offered stalwart assistance in many areas.

PREFACE

The past decade has seen changes in museum architecture as revolutionary as those forecast by Le Corbusier in his 1923 manifesto *Vers une architecture*. His title, in English, *Towards a New Architecture*, thus inspires my title. Le Corbusier compared machine-produced forms favorably with the Parthenon and saw himself as initiating the trends he described. In *Towards a New Museum*, I merely observe and assess what others have done and will be doing to report on the direction museum architecture is taking.

One intriguing aspect of the current proliferation of museums is the "museumification" of seemingly every phenomenon known to humanity, from Sverre Fehn's Glacier Museum in Norway to Hans Hollein's Vulcania, the project for a museum about volcanoes in France's Auvergne region (to open in the year 2000). *Museum* refers here, however, only to art museums, which I have grouped according to their predominant architectural characteristics, although these sometimes overlap. Not only are there more museums than ever before but also more functions for them to accommodate, more range in the kind of art they contain and more rationales to their design.

In visiting new museums in the United States and Europe in the last three years, I was struck by their extraordinary diversity and also by the prevalence of time-honored concepts, sometimes brilliantly reinterpreted. The obvious superiority of some of these buildings spurred me to try to assess why they succeed where so many others fail. I hoped that my conclusions might contribute to the creation of more such places. In this sense the book is intended for architects as well as for all those who are interested in museums: trustees, members, directors, curators and, of course, their vastly expanding audience. I had no intention of compiling a comprehensive survey of the world's new museums, and my choices for inclusion depended on my interest in the buildings in question.

When the term *museum* was first used in the Renaissance in reference to private collections, it evoked a different experience from what we now know. In one of the museum's earliest incarnations, the *Cabinet of Curiosities,* natural and art objects were jumbled together on the walls and ceilings, cupboards and drawers of one or two rooms. Their purpose was to surprise and delight: viewers had to find the special objects that attracted them and then make their own connections, interacting with the art in much the same way that artists were to advocate in the 20th century. Today, private museums often replicate these characteristics by the eclectic nature of their selections and, in many cases, a lack of didactic intent. The dozen updated versions of the cabinet of curiosities described in Chapter 1—from Philip Johnson's innovative painting and sculpture galleries on his Connecticut estate to Erwin Heerich's pavilions on the romantic Insel Hombroich in Germany to Tadao Ando's inclusion of "architecturalized nature" for the Pulitzer Foundation in St. Louis, Missouri—are as much about discovery and joy as were their Renaissance forerunners.

Duty began to outweigh delight with the creation of the public museum, a product of the Enlightenment's self-imposed obligation to instruct. Many critics felt that removing works of art from their original religious or civic settings was equivalent to burying them. (Anyone fortunate enough to have experienced the frescoes of Giotto in the luminous tall aisle of S. Francesco at Assisi before its earthquake damage in 1997, or those of Piero della Francesca in the mysterious intimacy of the choir of S. Francesco at Arezzo, can appreciate the criticism.) Relocation in the 19th century from palaces like the Louvre to structures conceived solely for exhibition purposes compounded the problem: museums increasingly divorced art from a lived experience and elevated it to the status of a secular religion in what I refer to as the *Museum as Sacred Space.* Their connotations as temples of culture notwithstanding, 19th-century museums imitated the palaces for which some of the art had been made: skylit galleries whose proportions, colors, wainscoting and moldings provided a complementary framework for the art on exhibition.

By the early 20th century, new museums were replacing these architecturally articulated rooms with open space in which paintings were hung on flat white partitions, often illuminated only by artificial light. This so-called neutral approach was successful for Modern art, which was by definition self-contained and self-referential; it was much less so for other genres. Now that contemporary art is no longer a secular religion nor living artists the revered demigods they once were, the idea of sacred museum space is obsolete unless it is radically reinterpreted. The four museums discussed in Chapter 2 attempt such a reinterpretation. Steven Holl's new forms for a museum in Helsinki and Peter Zumthor's unique statement for a *Kunsthaus* in a small town in Austria are more successful in this respect than is Mario Botta's Museum of Modern Art in San Francisco or Richard Meier's Museum of Contemporary Art in Barcelona.

Amid the profound artistic and architectural transformations that have taken place during the museum's history, there are also surprising continuities. Still popular is the *Monographic Museum,* devoted to a single artist, a type developed early in the 19th century in reaction against the museum's isolation of objects. The idea of providing a context for art by showing works from every phase of a career, and thereby demonstrating the creative process, was widely adopted, and soon inspired Gustave Moreau and Auguste Rodin, among others, to bequeath their studios for public display. (In a variation on the same theme, Turner specified in his legacy to the London National Gallery that his paintings be exhibited together.) Chapter 3 looks at the way in which this 19th-century model is being adapted to 20th-century requirements in new museums for Andy Warhol, Cy Twombly, Hans Josephsohn, Ernst Ludwig Kirchner, Felix Nussbaum and Constantin Brancusi.

Artists have carried the idea even further by designing their own museums, some of which are discussed in *Artists' Museums and Their Alternative Spaces.* Duchamp's conceptual Boîte en Valise—literally a small box placed in a suitcase—presented replicas of his lifework in relationship to one another and to the container. Claes Oldenburg and Patrick Ireland have followed Duchamp's lead with their own formulas for exhibiting their work, while Donald Judd expanded the concept: physically, by making spaces for art throughout a 340-acre site in western Texas, and ideologically, by presenting the work of other artists as well as his own. Additionally, Chapter 4 explores the scheme for a Jackson Pollock museum and four projects by Frank Stella.

The surprise and delight inherent in most of the museums discussed in the first four chapters are unfortunately not to be found in *Wings That Don't Fly.* These inappropriate additions to existing buildings have transformed architecture like that of New York's Metropolitan Museum into a veritable maze and have severely compromised such important landmarks as Frank Lloyd Wright's Guggenheim Museum in New York and the Louvre in Paris. In New York, the Museum of Modern Art has suffered a similar fate, and the Whitney Museum of American Art has also been threatened. Chapter 5 questions the validity of growth that often strains the very concepts on which a museum was founded and addresses institutional attitudes toward art and architecture that clearly give priority to art, often to the detriment of both architecture and, more important, the relationship between the two. Successful additions are wings that read as separate structures: Louis Kahn's Yale Art Gallery, James Stirling's Staatsgalerie in Stuttgart, Venturi, Scott Brown and Associates' Sainsbury Wing in London and Rafael Moneo's project for the Audrey Jones Beck Building in Houston.

With its expansion to a variety of media that includes installation, video and performance, art has become theater, a development paralleled by the emergence of the *Museum as Entertainment.* Upon its inauguration 21 years ago, the Centre Pompidou in Paris, designed by Renzo Piano and Richard Rogers, signaled a message with its instantly successful plaza and lively street life. With all of its innovations, the Pompidou returned, broadly speaking, to the pleasure principle of the first Renaissance museums. Chapter 6 explores the far-reaching repercussions of toppling art off of its pedestal and presenting it as just one of several cultural attractions offered by the museum for an easily accessible metropolitan experience. Shopping, eating, performances, along with fund-raising and urban renewal, now vie with the preservation and exhibition of art as museum mandates. One consequence is the substitution of high-profile architecture for art when no collection is in place—a sure way to shortchange art. And Piano himself warns that within the museum itself "too much public appeal results in profanation that can destroy a museum." On the positive side, incorporating exhibition spaces into the facilities of large commercial complexes (as in Turin and Lyons) enlivens art, as artists for two centuries have demanded. In competing with other forms of entertainment, museums are looking to the architecture and techniques of theme parks, themselves an outgrowth of the 19th-century International Exhibitions that figure prominently in the Pompidou's lineage. The Groninger Museum in Holland and Richard Meier's Getty Museum in Los Angeles both recall this precedent.

Two decades before the Centre Pompidou began to change the social implications of art, the New York Guggenheim laid the groundwork for a new way of looking at it. By his replacement of the traditional box with a continuous spiral in the Guggenheim, Wright prepared the way for the creation of the *Museum as Environmental Art.* Following Wright's lead in calling white the loudest color (he compared its use as a background for painting with "taking a high C in music as the background for orchestral tonality"), architects have increasingly realized that there is no such thing as neutrality. Every space has its own distinct identity that affects the contents: without a harmonious relationship between the two, museum architecture fails. Chapter 7 describes designs that restore the historic connection between container and content in uniquely contemporary ways: those by Peter Eisenman, Wolf Prix, Rem Koolhaas, Daniel Libeskind and Frank Gehry.

The architecture of each era reflects the taste of its time. Just as the World Trade Center and AT&T Building define New York City for today's 30-year-olds, the city's Art Deco skyscrapers epitomized it for a previous generation. The first museums—in the late 18th century—were likened to "graveyards" when they opened; now they appear as models of contextualism. Conversely, current interpretations of the modern, flexible space that was championed in the first half of the century are often lifeless. Of all building types, the art museum remains the most resistant to a common denominator and consequently allows architects unusual freedom to reflect their period.

If for Le Corbusier the 1920s were characterized by the promise of mass production, the 1990s are marked by the explosion of an electronic revolution; the afterword addresses the impact of this revolution on museums. Now technology can extend an institution far beyond its physical confines, bringing information and original computer art into homes worldwide. Additionally, virtual reality provides a strong context for art and a greater possibility of viewer interaction than any other means yet devised.

While 5,000 museums have sites on the Internet, and video artists are devising ways to bypass museums altogether, the institution continues to enjoy a proliferation of facilities unequaled at any other time in history. In the United States alone 600 new art museums have opened since 1970; in France 400 museums were built or renovated during the 14 years of François Mitterrand's presidency (1981 to 1995). When I began work on this book, I picked up more or less where Douglas Davis left off in his thought-provoking publication *The Museum Transformed* (1990), and numerous projects have arisen since I completed my research. Among them are renovations and additions: the Milwaukee Art Museum by Santiago Calatrava, the Tate Bankside in London by Herzog and de Meuron and New York's MoMA by Yoshio Taniguchi. There are new buildings as well, such as the Modern Art Museum of Fort Worth by Tadao Ando, the Samsung Museum at Seoul National University in South Korea by Rem Koolhaas and many other museums and exhibition spaces in countries outside the European and North American confines of *Towards a New Museum*.

Chapter 1

The Cabinet of Curiosities: An Update

Museums satisfy . . . a deep natural want . . . as deep and as natural as sex or sleeping.

Philip Johnson

Most major art museums are based on private collections that were assembled long before these public institutions came into being. Louis Palma di Cesnola's collection of Cypriot antiquities formed the nucleus of the Classical collection for the Metropolitan Museum of Art in New York, as the Lizzie P. Bliss bequest initiated the holdings of that city's Museum of Modern Art (MoMA). In Europe princely collections are the core of today's great public museums: to wit, Francesco de' Medici's holdings now at the Uffizi Gallery in Florence and the Hapsburg treasures at the Kunsthistorisches Museum in Vienna. From the first Renaissance acquisitions of antiquities and art for their own sake, collectors have felt the need to exhibit them in specially established spaces.

The grouping together of precious objects has gone on since antiquity: Egyptian tombs, ancient temples and medieval church crypts and royal treasuries—the *Schatzkammern*—all sheltered such collections. But the attractive presentation of these pieces, including art, as opposed to their secretive storage, marked the beginning of what we know as the museum. At the beginning of the 16th century, in English country houses and French castles, painting collections, at first confined to portraits, were shown in long, connective corridors. Referred to as galleries, these passageways were widely used as places to take exercise, and art was hung on their walls to distract, much as television does today for people on treadmills.

In early-16th-century Italy the *studiolo* provided an accessible, art-oriented version of the *Schatzkammer*. Whereas the small study was the privilege of a few prominent palaces, by midcentury there had developed a variant of it that swept Europe in a veritable craze. The cabinet of curiosities, or *Wunderkammer*, was a room whose walls and ceilings, cupboards and drawers, housed collections that included a bizarre spectrum of natural curiosities as well as art objects: one Venetian cabinet displayed corals, crystals, oysters with two pearls, horns, teeth and claws along with antiquities and paintings. In contrast with the devotional and didactic purpose of religious collections, these cabinets were intended primarily to "entertain and amuse" and only secondarily to instruct or uplift. Exhibits randomly juxtaposed what were considered to be scientific objects and art; there was no attempt at specialization or classification in what was an encyclopedic approach meant to create a miniature cosmology.

Cabinets of curiosities were so popular throughout Europe that even members of the bourgeoisie—pharmacists, for instance—created them. Art, however, remained for some time the purview of the aristocracy, who from the early 16th century on had turned to gardens as settings for art structures: in England summerhouses—and in Italy loggias, pavilions and grottoes—were used to exhibit antique sculpture. (Bramante's Belvedere sculpture court at the Vatican, begun in 1503 for Pope Julius II, is the first and most famous example of such an installation.) By the end of the century several aristocratic collectors had separated art from their other holdings in *Kunstkammern*, usually in independent structures. One of the first to do so, the Hapsburg archduke Ferdinand II, both constructed new buildings and renovated a corn silo for this purpose at his castle of Ambras in the Tyrol, thus establishing a precedent for adaptive reuse that is still followed. Soon the Hessian landgraves in Kassel, Emperor Ferdinand I in Munich and Emperor Rudolph II in Prague were among those creating private museums.

Besides the additional space they provided, these buildings may have reinforced the prestige attached to important collections, visits to which were routinely requested by foreign dignitaries, ambassadors and heads of state.

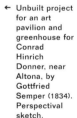

← Unbuilt project for an art pavilion and greenhouse for Conrad Hinrich Donner, near Altona, by Gottfried Semper (1834). Perspectival sketch.

As new collections were put together in the 19th and 20th centuries, private individuals also began to commission architecture for them. One of the most remarkable designs was Gottfried Semper's for Conrad Hinrich Donner near Altona, Germany (1834), which returned to the association of sculpture and gardens by combining a neoclassical art pavilion with a greenhouse and a small orangerie. Semper later applied ideas he had used for Donner to his famous Picture Gallery in Dresden. The

← Glorietta, Baron Heinrich Thyssen-Bornemisza Museum, Lugano, by Giovanni Gerser (1937). Gallery enfilade.

Glorietta (1937)—a gallery in Lugano for Baron Heinrich Thyssen-Bornemisza by Giovanni Gerser—featured enfilades based on the galleries of 17th-century Italian palaces like the adjacent Villa Favorita (which the baron inhabited). Marble door jambs and rich damask and velvet wall coverings were meant to evoke the periods of the Old Masters that the Glorietta houses.

Dear to most collectors is the idea that what they have assembled will be kept together even after their death, in perpetual tribute to their distinctive taste. In some instances—the Isabella Stewart Gardner Museum in Boston, the Frick Collection in New York and Sir John Soane's Museum in London (whose eclectic collections recall those of the cabinets of curiosities)—this has been accomplished by the bequest of a home for their treasures. In others, as with the Robert Lehman wing at the Metropolitan, the collector stipulates to the recipient museum that the gift must be displayed separately (see Chapter 5). For this kind of separate display, however, collectors now more than ever before are building their own museums. Alan Turner, for five years the president of Chicago's Museum of Contemporary Art, feels that "to put a private collection in a museum is to lose it, because it is buried in a place that is too big." (In a historical throwback, Turner will use his weekend farm's corn silo, currently being renovated by Stanley Tigerman, as one of several pavilions for his contemporary collection.)

Some of these galleries were designed for private enjoyment, accessible only to the owners and their friends; others were designed for public attendance. Many start as the former and end up as the latter. A strong incentive for opening a private museum to the public is the owner's wish to provide an alternative to institutional settings. The collector's reaction against art's institutionalization is frequently as decisive as the artist's (see Chapters 3 and 4). Repeatedly, collectors say they want their holdings to be seen in a setting that is more like a home than a museum. And even a consummate museum professional like William Rubin, the curator of MoMA's Department of Painting and Sculpture from 1967 to 1988, asserts that art is ideally viewed in a domestic setting. For Rubin:

> Museums are essentially compromises . . . Their weakness
> is that they are necessarily homogenized—emptied
> of all connotations other than art. And that is, finally, an
> artificial situation.

With a single client and no board of trustees or staff to deal with, the architect's task is simplified; the existence of a strong collection to which the architect can design is also an asset. Where no such collection is in place, museum architecture almost always fails. Clearly formed ideas—usually one person's—of what and how art should be viewed, and reaction against operational aspects of public museums, have generally resulted in private museums' matching art and architecture most successfully. In that they are usually produced by a single person, private collections have a strong identity—unlike the more anonymous museum collections amassed by many. This holds true especially for the Menil in Houston and the Insel Hombroich near Düsseldorf, which present unorthodox combinations of disparate art objects—as do the Beyeler in Basel and the Pulitzer in St. Louis, with their juxtapositions of tribal and Modern art. Unusual also are the Saatchi's in-depth holdings of contemporary artists and the Rubell's cutting-edge selections, in London and Miami respectively.

Several of these museums entail a physical challenge: at the Insel Hombroich, visitors have to walk considerable distances over uneven terrain; at Philip Johnson's compound in New Canaan, they cross a precarious bridge; at a private gallery in Montana, they must pass through a deep berm (the gallery is remote in the first place). The importance of effort in connection with viewing art was understood early on by museum architects: stairs were monumental; doors had to be opened (as exemplified in Vienna by the Kunsthistorisches Museum's enormously tall and heavy portals to the gallery enfilades). By having to overcome obstacles (like the need to find the hidden treasuries of ancient times), the viewer earns a privilege, something that is increasingly rare in new museums where escalators move people like packages and a combination of audioguides and labels tells them what they are supposed to be seeing. In the words of Dominique de Menil, whose museum is discussed below: "The great things are those you discover."

PHILIP JOHNSON PAINTING GALLERY

New Canaan, Connecticut

by **Philip Johnson**

1965

3,150 square feet

2,990 square feet of exhibition space

$215,000

One of the first Modern designs for a private museum was by Philip Johnson for his own collection of contemporary art. In addition to satisfying his need for more space, there were a number of related motivations for the painting gallery Johnson built on his 40-acre Connecticut estate. The architect professed dissatisfaction with the way pictures looked in the museums he had designed in the late 1950s and early 1960s, asserting that "Big museums are a bore." In addition, he anticipated the problem of growth that would soon lead to innumerable—and in many cases problematic—museum expansions (see Chapter 5). His gallery, in which the viewer can sit while paintings move past on panels, addressed the issues of both viewer fatigue and storage.

It is typical of Johnson, whose long career has been marked by an uncanny sensitivity to new trends, that he chose to put the gallery underground at just the time when artists attempting to escape the gallery system were making their first earthworks. Not wanting his new gallery to compete with his famous Glass House, he left only the entrance exposed in a grassy mound that has been compared with "a cross between a Mycenaean beehive tomb and an atomic shelter." Johnson calls it his *Kunstbunker,* and it is reached by a footbridge he describes as made of the thinnest possible layer of steel, with a high camber and no handrail, "so that it would be springy—and precarious, with the uneasy feel of a rope bridge!"

Interior. ↑

Plan. ↓

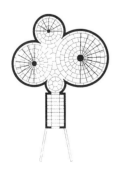

Within, a long, low entrance hall leads to four tangential circles of varying diameters; three of these contain swiveling newel posts to which off-white carpeted panels, like postcard racks, are attached. The different diameters—the largest is 40 feet—are meant to accommodate a range of painting scales. The gallery's organization derives from Sir John Soane, but it is also a fact that Johnson had recently completed the Museum for Pre-Columbian Art at Dumbarton Oaks, which was based on a circular motif punctuated by wide cylindrical columns.

The arrangement has worked well for Johnson's art, but its applicability to a public museum is questionable. Security is one concern, since the way in which the paintings are exposed would necessitate an escorted system of viewing them. Even more restrictive is the large amount of space required by the circles' radii, and these in turn limit the size of the paintings that can be shown.

PHILIP JOHNSON SCULPTURE GALLERY

The *Kunstbunker* presented problems for Johnson as well: he had to move sculpture out of the way of the pivoting racks. This practical issue, together with his feeling that the outdoor sculpture he had placed on the property distracted from the landscape, gave him a welcome excuse to build another gallery: he chose a site west of the painting gallery to which a row of old maples leads like an allée. The sculpture gallery's simple white-brick exterior is barnlike, but its interior has been described by the architectural historian John Coolidge as "one of the most artfully intricate of twentieth-century buildings."

New Canaan, Connecticut

by **Philip Johnson**

1970

5,000 square feet

4,900 square feet of exhibition space

$383,000

In plan, a square and a pentagon are twisted at a 45-degree angle to one another. The resulting forms are identified by Johnson as his first break with the geometrical tradition of the International Style, which eventually led to the radical, free-form "Monsta" gatehouse he built on the property in 1995. It also influenced his designs for the Art Museum of South Texas at Corpus Christi (1972) and for the angular, prismatic office buildings he was constructing at the time. At the periphery of this complex container, a stair with a ten-inch parapet spirals down around

a central courtyard to connect five alcoves, or "shelves," as the architect calls them. These pivot out from the stair and satisfy one of Johnson's main concerns, that "each sculpture should have its own background" without the conflict of one work being seen behind another. The glass ceiling rising in two slopes to an 84-foot ridgepole fulfills his wish to provide the natural light he feels is ideal for sculpture. The cathode tubes attached to the rafters do not effectively soften shadows as they were supposed to, and Johnson laughs off the much-admired striated patterns cast by the roof structure as a "happy accident."

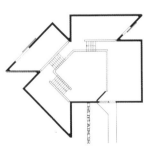

↑ TOP: Interior.
BOTTOM: Plan.

Three shelves identical in plan and area have ceiling heights that range between six and twenty-five feet; their walls relate differently to the slanted roof; and access to each one varies. Thus, not only is each sculpture—those by Robert Morris, Claes Oldenburg and Frank Stella, among others—given its own background, but these backgrounds are themselves distinct from one another.

Johnson's individual presentation of both sculpture and painting—one to each shelf for the former, a single painting on a single panel for the latter—ties in with William Rubin's belief that "it is not such a good idea to hang a lot of paintings on a wall; ideal is one painting at a time." Still, the juxtaposition of the three painting racks in the underground gallery and the overall view available everywhere in the sculpture gallery allow a dialogue between the artworks.

THE MENIL COLLECTION

Houston, Texas

by **Renzo Piano Building Workshop and Richard Fitzgerald and Partners**

1987

100,000 square feet

24,000 square feet of exhibition space

$24 million

When Philip Johnson was designing his sculpture gallery he said he wanted a building that looked small on the outside and big on the inside. This was exactly how Dominique de Menil described the museum she wanted. Both collectors envisaged buildings with exterior modesty and interior intimacy that at the same time accommodated as much material as possible. Although Johnson had thought of the application of his painting gallery design to institutional storage, it—and the sculpture gallery—was never meant to serve the public until after his death. The de Menils (who preferred to drop their name's particle for the American institution) had other ideas. Conceived with her house in mind, the museum was meant to convey to the visitor the excitement felt by a collector in the presence of her acquisitions.

Dominique de Menil, an heir to the Schlumberger oil-field services fortune, has lived since 1941 in Houston, where she (with her late husband, Jean) has made a considerable impact on the city's culture. In 1949 Johnson built a home for the de Menils that was the city's first example of International Style Modernism. By 1971 the couple had inaugurated their Rothko Chapel, designed by Johnson and constructed by the Houston architect Howard Barnstone, in which fourteen of the artist's somber late works are shown in a suitably contemplative ambience. Father Marie-Alain Couturier, a Dominican priest who was a factor in Le Corbusier's commission for the Monastery of La Tourette, encouraged the de Menils in their first acquisitions and may have influenced the spiritual atmosphere of the collection's settings: two chapels—the Rothko and the recent Byzantine Fresco Chapel by Dominique de Menil's architect son, François—and the ethereal Cy Twombly Gallery.

Disenchanted with their relationship with existing institutions in Houston, in 1973 the de Menils approached Louis Kahn about building their own museum. Jean de Menil's death, later that year, followed by Kahn's in 1974, put an end to these discussions. The formality of Kahn's scheme—so different from what was eventually built—suggests that the client might not have proceeded with it in any case. Dominique de Menil subsequently discussed her project with other architects, including Luis Barragán, until 1981, when Pontus Hulten, director of Paris's Centre Georges Pompidou, introduced her to Renzo Piano, primarily known for his part in designing that building. By then the de Menil collection included more than 10,000 paintings, sculptures, prints, drawings, photographs and rare books, from the Paleolithic to the present. Over the previous 20 years the de Menils had also acquired 12 acres in the Montrose suburb of Houston where the museum was to be located. The houses near the museum are in wood, painted a uniform gray with white trim, and are used for related activities: auditorium, bookstore, services and guest quarters. Unlike the

monumental museums that had been built in Texas during the preceding decades—Mies van der Rohe's in Houston, Louis Kahn's in Fort Worth and Edward Larrabee Barnes's in Dallas—the Menil echoes Montrose's vernacular scale and materials. At the same time, in deference to Mies's presence in the nearby museum district and to Johnson's adjacent International Style St. Thomas campus, the Menil museum is a Miesian rectangle, with one entrance set back in a configuration reminiscent of Kahn's Kimbell. Its single-story wood-and-exposed-steel exterior is in the tradition of the Case Study Houses, the influential southern California experiments in low-cost residential architecture of the 1950s and 1960s.

To ensure an intimate setting, Dominique de Menil decided to show only 10 percent of her collection at any one time, with art rotating to the galleries for limited periods. The bulk of the art was housed in a structure running the entire length, and over a third of the width, of the building. This windowed penthouse, more like a crowded gallery than most museum storage, which is never meant to be seen, is accessible and inviting to curators and scholars. By calling the area her "treasure chamber," Dominique de Menil evokes the medieval treasury; the heterogeneity of the collection, with its filing cabinets full of Joseph Cornell boxes and exotic objects, including one from Captain Cook's inaugural voyage, relates it also to the cabinet of curiosities.

↑ Exterior with
  "treasure chamber" above.

↓ Ceiling diagram.

Of equal importance to context, domestic scale and the "treasure chamber" concept was the client's insistence on what she termed "living light": illumination that would vary with weather and time of day. This request inspired the platform roof, with its leaf-shaped light diffusers, which Piano designed with engineers

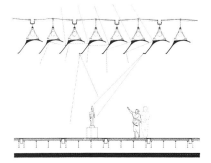

Peter Rice and Tom Barker. Having just constructed a yacht in reinforced concrete, the architect decided that the fine texture and thinness of this material would adapt well to the leaves' organic form. They are held by ductile iron trusses revealed on the exterior as a white colonnaded roof. Each of the massive, fixed, 40-foot-long leaves incorporates natural and artificial light, spatial definition, ventilation, weatherproofing and drainage.

The formal, recessed entrance from the park and a more modest access from the street are joined by a broad cross-axis. It, in turn, is intersected by an east-west promenade almost 320 feet long, with the galleries fronting the park on one side and service areas facing the street. Glazing at the ends of both circulation spines allows views to the surrounding neighborhood. The exhibition space is divided into six rooms, several of which can be further partitioned; they have white walls just over 16 feet high and black-stained pine floors more typical of a manufacturing environment than of a gallery. The black and the rough finish provide a rich contrast with the smooth white wall surfaces in an interesting departure from the light-colored wood or stone floors of most museums.

Interior. ↑

Plan. ↓

Twentieth-century art (up to the time of Jean de Menil's death), and particularly Surrealism, constitutes the largest, most inclusive part of the collection—and this is what is best served by Piano's loftlike, naturally lit spaces. In a direct reference to the de Menil home, the art of tribal cultures is installed in galleries with glass-enclosed garden courts that give it an appropriate context. The less cohesive grouping of antiquities, Byzantine and medieval art fares somewhat less well in darkened rooms: without the natural light and the ceiling articulation provided by light baffles, the building's character is obscured.

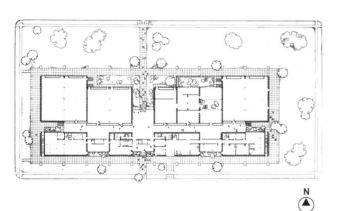

N

Unique to this private museum and visible to the public are its extensive facilities for exhibition planning and conservation. As someone who has curated her own scholarly exhibitions, Dominique de Menil understandably wanted what she called "a working museum," and she has achieved this admirably. The accessibility of the treasure chamber and the openness of areas for support services are constant reminders of the uniquely art-related activities that animate this sophisticated version of an art barn.

BEYELER FOUNDATION MUSEUM

Basel Riehen, Switzerland

by Renzo Piano Building
Workshop with
Burckhardt+Partner AG

1997

71,200 square feet

29,170 square feet of exhibition space

$37 million

← Western facade.

When Ernst Beyeler, one of Europe's leading dealers in Modern art, decided to create a museum near his hometown of Basel, he intended to select an architect through a competition. Precious time was lost in discussions with the conductor and philanthropist Paul Sacher, who wanted Beyeler to build next to the Tinguely Museum he was planning (see Chapter 3), before the dealer opted for Piano simply because he liked the Menil museum. More uniform than the Texas collection, the 20th-century masterpieces acquired by Beyeler and his wife, Hildy, are housed in homogeneous spaces that have none of the dichotomy in ceiling treatment of Piano's earlier museum. Beyeler played an active role in developing the design, stating his program as "a museum where one can find *luxe, calme, et volupté.*" The architect/client relationship flourished. "Without a good client, the architecture is nothing," according to Piano. "It becomes just an academic exercise."

Two museums completed by Piano in the decade between his work on the Menil and the Beyeler use natural, zenithal light as the guiding design principle. For his Cy Twombly Gallery across the street from the Menil in Houston and his Brancusi Studio in Paris (see Chapter 3), new technology helped to refine complex ceiling systems that, in contrast to the earlier leaves, are hidden. In both a flat metal-and-glass roof appears to float above masonry walls. The Beyeler Foundation is a continuation of Piano's development of the theme: in this case, he pulls the glazed roof beyond its masonry supports. He completely concealed the mechanical systems in all three museums, whose serene spaces represent a dramatic switch from the exposed trusses, columns, cross-bracings and brightly painted ductwork of his Pompidou.

Beyeler's collection of some 160 objects represents his vision of Modernism, beginning with Monet, ending with Warhol, and excluding major movements like German Expressionism. In a gesture popular with many collectors, tribal sculpture—in this case from Alaska, Africa and Oceania—is scattered among the Modern art. This integration of separate categories of objects is another reminder of the cabinet of curiosities, which constitutes an important part of Basel's history. Indeed, the legacy of Erasmus (who died in Basel in 1536) was preserved in a cabinet whose acquisition by the city in the mid-17th century made it the first civic community to support a public museum.

The site of Beyeler's museum is in a narrow 19th-century park that runs north-south parallel to a highway in Riehen, a suburb two miles outside Basel. An existing structure on the property, the historic Villa Berower, will be used for offices, a library and a restaurant, thus reserving the museum primarily for the exhibition of art (with books related to it available in the bookstore). Picking up on the street walls of local red sandstone, Piano has enclosed the eastern edge of the building with a wall of a similar but richer stone, a red porphyry from Patagonia that he used throughout. This wall and glimpses of the diaphanous glass roof are all that is discreetly revealed to the roadway. A narrow lobby runs from the main, south entrance to the north, garage access. On one side of the lobby, built into the protective street wall, are the ticket counter, bookstore and service facilities.

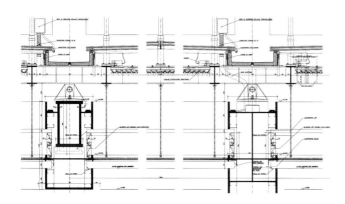

Ceiling diagram. ↑ At the south of the old estate a gate in the wall opens to a sloping hill. Because Beyeler wanted level space, the entrance is almost seven feet below the grade level of the site's highest point. It is reached by gentle terraces that end in a pool beside the glazed south facade. Views into this southernmost gallery reveal a huge Monet that harmonizes with the landscape it overlooks.

The street wall is the spine, in front of which four load-bearing walls, each nearly 400 feet long, run parallel, forming the lobby and three rows of gallery space. Lateral divisions are flexible. All the galleries are approximately 23 feet wide with 16-foot-high ceilings and will usually be partitioned into lengths of 36 feet, ideal dimensions for the various scales of work exhibited. A basement space with lower ceilings, which receives some natural light, will be used together with one main-floor gallery for temporary exhibitions of contemporary art. Beyeler rejected the stretched fabric ceilings of the Twombly and Brancusi museums in favor of white steel screens that diffuse light evenly and allow occasional views to the sky. Above them is a 5.25-foot space for mechanical

equipment, electronically controlled louvers and incandescent light (used only at night), topped by the roof of tilted brise-soleils, whose glass is partially silk-screened to make it opaque. Most walls are white with some individualized color schemes—as in the case of a pale gray gallery for works by Giacometti. Light French oak floors, in which air vents run laterally, are uniform throughout. Tiny reveals at the bottom of partitions and window frames embedded within the walls dissolve the distinction between exterior and interior and further enhance this architecture of space and light.

↑ Galleries.

↓ Site plan.

The museum's walls are intended to rise from the earth like old ruins, and indeed its trabeated architecture recalls the temples of antiquity. A winter garden parallels most of the museum's western facade, which faces a large grazing meadow, one side of which extends into France, the other into Germany. The incongruity of this protected farmland juxtaposed with the museum's sophisticated forms and content lends a special charm. Only from this side, where the entire length of the building is visible, can the extension of the glazed roof beyond its two supporting columns at each end be appreciated. (An earlier design with a second pair of end columns projected the roof further into the landscape, even more gracefully.)

Piano's statement that "the collection governed the forming of space, the circulation and the light" explains the complementary nature of this building to its contents. The architect's classic Modernism is perfectly matched to the museum's Modern masterpieces.

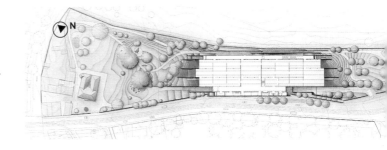

MUSEUM INSEL HOMBROICH

Düsseldorf, Germany

by **Erwin Heerich**

1987

280,000 square feet of park and pavilions

39,400 square feet of exhibition space

cost undisclosed

The guiding philosophy for this museum in the German Rhineland is surprisingly similar to the cabinet of curiosities' mixture of natural and artificial. At Insel Hombroich, nature is represented by the landscape rather than by a rare object, as it would have been in the cabinet of old, but the visitor's immersion in the natural environment is so intrinsic to viewing art that it becomes part of the display, and handmade objects are as unexpected as those in any *Wunderkammer*.

In 1982 the real estate developer Karl-Heinrich Müller bought Hombroich Island in the small Erft River between Düsseldorf and Cologne. While sowing 150 different kinds of plants, Müller at the same time insisted that vegetation be allowed to grow freely, in accordance with his philosophy that "nature helps itself, we don't need to interfere." Consequently, the site's three topographies— a cultivated 19th-century park, the woods, meadows and marshes of a flood-plain and agricultural fields—grew together into a single, seemingly natural landscape. The island shelters a variety of wildlife, and birdcalls and the croaking of toads mix with the far-off sound of cars on a country road. Along with the scent of wildflowers and marsh waters, the odor of manure is a surprisingly pleasant aspect of the experience of this unusual museum. The incorporation of smell and other senses—sound, touch—in what has come to be the exclusively visual experience of art raises interesting possibilities.

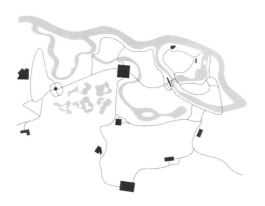

For Müller, Bonn's museums are "like cemeteries," and he states that it was not a museum that he wanted to found but "a living place for artists to interact without any bureaucracy, where nature is as important as art." To accomplish this, Müller asked the Conceptual sculptor Erwin Heerich to design a series of pavilions for exhibiting collections that randomly juxtapose art from widely different periods and places. Identifying labels, acoustiguides and signs are banned: "After all," says Müller, "you carry no label, why *should* you or I? When people listen to an acoustiguide they only remember what it says—[they think] everything must be explained, but love, life, your kids, can't be explained." Müller's personal take on how art should be experienced extends to air-conditioning (which he doesn't tolerate), light and restoration. Because the artists he consulted favored lots of natural light, the objects at first had almost no protection from it, and Müller was subsequently forced to install ultraviolet screens. He has been criticized for the light damage sustained by some of the work exhibited, but he responds that "nothing is forever" and feels that it is preferable to enjoy art in natural temperatures and light

even if damage ensues. As for restoration, for Müller "it is like a face-lift: everything accomplished in a lifetime is taken away in a moment." (In this, Müller's ideas are similar to those of the great Impressionist collector Albert C. Barnes.)

The 12 new pavilions are similar in their highly textured, recycled-Dutch-brick cladding; their 20-inch-thick exterior walls; their hot-dip galvanized skylights and window frames; their white walls and light-colored marble or basalt floors. But each pavilion combines different geometrical forms and distinct interior arrangements.

The L-shaped ticket building has been compared with a small border station, so like entering another country, or even another world, is the visit it introduces. The absence of signs or any directionals creates a sense of mystery that is compounded by the way some of the pavilions are hidden behind hedges or reached by means of narrow wood footbridges.

To emphasize the pavilions' presence as sculpture, two of them—the Turm (tower) and Vitrine—have been left empty, to be enjoyed solely in and of themselves. A counterpoint is the large outdoor sculpture: works by Mark di Suvero, Alexander Calder and others. Six of the seven pavilions where art is shown depend entirely on natural light, which in all but two is provided by skylights. One of the most effective exhibits is at the edge of a small wood: the single-space Orangerie is rectangular, with one side entirely glazed in a central, rectilinear section and the roof at each end pitching up sharply to make angled facades. Within, giant Khmer heads on individual pedestals gaze impassively toward one of the island's many small ponds.

The Lange (long) Galerie, used mainly for sculpture, is small in comparison with the island's two largest art pavilions, the square Labyrinth and the rectangular Große Galerie. Different types of skylights and different positioning of

↑ Orangerie.
LEFT: Exterior
RIGHT: Interior.

← Site plan.

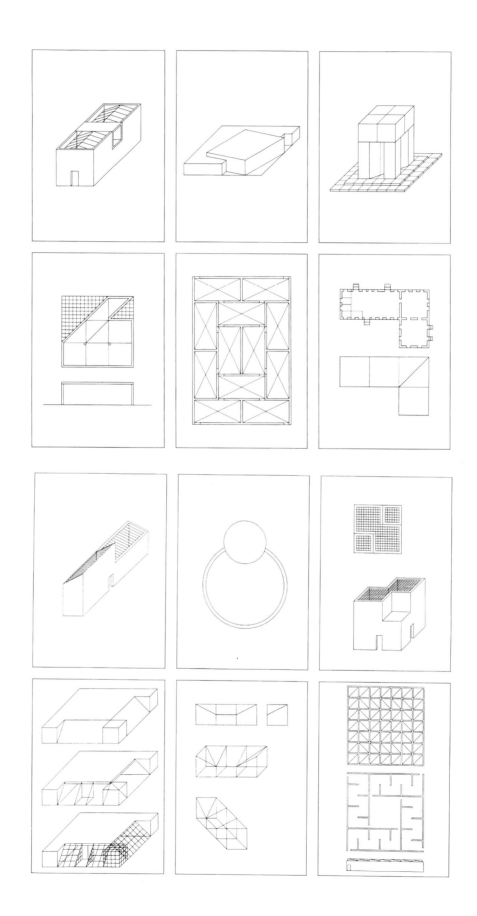

their entranceways, room arrangements and interior partitioning distinguish one from the other. In both, however, there is a disorienting, mazelike effect that lends an element of surprise to displays that include archaeological objects; African, Oceanian and Pre-Columbian art; Egyptian sculpture; Chinese glass; and 20th-century work by, among others, Kurt Schwitters, Yves Klein, Jean Arp, Francis Picabia, Ellsworth Kelly and Gotthard Graubner, a German artist responsible for all the museum's installations.

With no openings in what appears to be a continuous brick facade, the Schnecke (snail) is the most austere of the Insel Hombroich galleries. The entrance is hidden behind the longest side of its triangular-prismatic form, repeated within by a mirrored-glass and metal atrium open to the sky. It is reserved primarily for works on paper, which cover a spectrum from Rembrandt to Cézanne and Matisse.

The gallery that is most ambitious architecturally, the Tadeusz, named after the representational painter Norbert Tadeusz, is the only two-story building. Its tall rectangular volume is separated into two distinct spaces by a wide drop in the ceiling that expresses the cubic room inserted above. The awkward division of the lower space is justified by the serene upper room, with its floor-to-ceiling windows at both ends overlooking the landscape. Reached by a steep double stair and a precarious catwalk, the meditation room has cushions strewn over the floor, offering a restful interlude.

One generously fenestrated pavilion is occupied by a cafeteria that offers an un-museum-like fare of black bread, boiled potatoes, hard-boiled eggs and plum jam. Another serves as a studio/residence for Graubner. The Art Brut sculptor Anatol Herzfield also works on the island, using an old log cabin for his studio. Additional buildings that predate the museum include a barn converted for concerts and a 19th-century house in which Müller lives.

Müller cites as his models two other private museums: the Kröller-Müller in Otterlo, the Netherlands, by Henry Van de Velde (1938–53) and the Louisiana in Humlebæk, north of Copenhagen, by Jørgen Bo and Vilhelm Wohlert (1958–82). Like Insel Hombroich, these museums enjoy bucolic settings taken into account by their architecture, especially at the Louisiana, where Miesian pavilions are connected by glass corridors.

Müller's museum also invites comparison with Donald Judd's arrangement of discrete structures for the display of art at Marfa, Texas (see Chapter 4). In both cases, architecture is determined by an artist rather than by an architect: each conveys a sense of discovery to art presented in a contemplative, spiritual environment enlivened by the presence of ongoing studio work.

In 1994 Müller acquired a former NATO rocket-launching station adjacent to the island, where he has converted existing structures and plans to use several well-known architects to build facilities for scientists and artists. For this "cultural laboratory" he would receive outside funding for the first time and would solicit art from other collectors to exhibit in a new space. Expansion could bring about the institutionalization this passionate collector has tried so hard to avoid.

← Pavilion plans and isometrics.
FIRST ROW: Tadeusz,
Graubner studio/residence, Turm.
SECOND ROW: Schnecke,
Große Galerie, ticket building.
THIRD ROW: Lange Galerie,
Vitrine, Turm.
FOURTH ROW: Cafeteria, Orangerie,
Labyrinth.

PRIVATE MUSEUM IN MONTANA

by Emilio Ambasz
& Associates
1993

1,200 square feet

cost undisclosed

If in Müller's museum the equation of art and nature recalls the cabinet of curiosities, Argentinian-born architect Emilio Ambasz has more recent antecedents that closely link the two. For many years Ambasz has taken his inspiration from earthworks; instead of creating forms he buries his buildings, giving nature clear precedence in its relationship to architecture. For a collector who shares her husband's passionate commitment to land cultivation and preservation, Ambasz seemed the ideal person to design a gallery separate from a new house on a vast property in western Montana; Ambasz's concept for a gallery related so intimately to the residence that he ended up designing both.

Within a spectacular east-west valley filled with cottonwood trees whose green leaves shimmer to silver in the wind, Ambasz has placed the two structures with exquisite sensitivity. Running through the valley is a creek that feeds a small lake: to the north of it, at the foot of the pine-covered mountainside, is the south-facing house; south of the lake and about a half mile upstream is the north-facing museum. Siting reflects the architect's intention that the museum appear as a neighbor in the wilderness to an otherwise lonely house. To emphasize further the relationship between the structures, in plan the convex gallery fits perfectly into the concave villa; even the gallery's small central recess corresponds with the villa's central bay. Both are partially sunken, leaving prominent facades—in the Western tradition—higher and longer than their respective buildings. Typical of Ambasz's work, the facades' identical materials combine high-tech and natural—in this case, white metal lattice for ivy to cover and, in a further allusion to the vernacular, wood logs. In a series of classical references the colonnades of rough-hewn logs are in turn tipped with metal that simulates capitals, and they lean against facades crowned by bronze cornices.

The museum's private nature is emphasized by its secretive entrance through a bermed back wall, a configuration similar to Frank Lloyd Wright's semicircular Second Jacobs House, in Middleton, Wisconsin (1948). An enclosed circular sculpture court precedes this entrance through a constricted corridor that leads to the single exhibition space. The detached building came from the clients' wish to see only parts of their contemporary collection at one time. Since they intended to rotate pieces that would otherwise be stored, relatively little space was needed. Even so, a free-standing wall was added to compensate for the lack of hanging space on the glazed north side.

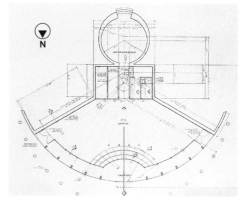

↑ Plan.

The dialogue the museum sustains with both the natural and the built environments is as important as the exhibition space itself. When the facade is approached from any direction, the tension between museum, nature and villa builds up one's anticipation of the art. For two unbuilt projects Ambasz designed in the 1980s—one for the New York art dealer Leo Castelli, the other a residence in Córdoba, Spain—he envisioned stark, angular forms that appear surrealistically aloof from their proposed sites. In Montana the architect has moved away from the geometric simplicity of these earlier houses in favor of a theatrical, baroque image reinforced by the simulated rocks in which both structures are carefully positioned. This stage-set quality is particularly appropriate to art that in several cases is performance-like: Tony Oursler's audio-video of an animated figure could not wish for a more dramatic setting.

↓ View from residence to gallery.

Gallery interior. ↑

Gallery exterior. →

ART PAVILION IN LOS ANGELES

Los Angeles, California

by **Franklin D. Israel**

Design Associates

1991

7,000 square feet

2,500 square feet of exhibition space

$2 million

In the late 1960s Count Panza di Biumo adopted the High Renaissance idea of a rustic building as art repository by converting the stables that adjoin his 18th-century house in Varese, northern Italy. Some two decades later a Los Angeles businessman decided to build his own art barn for a collection of Modern and contemporary art that in both scale and aesthetic did not fit into his traditional home.

The architect he contacted, New York–born Frank Israel, had settled in Los Angeles early in his career and was soon associated with several local architects of the same generation—including Thom Mayne, Michael Rotondi and Eric Owen Moss—all of whom were influenced by Frank Gehry. Their use of raw, industrial materials and their skewed geometries and overlapping planes are, like Gehry's, strong and innovative.

The Art Pavilion was conceived by Israel as a great ark, a recurring motif in his architecture. Sited at the top of a steep hill on a three-acre lot with a stream and a dense eucalyptus grove, the building is defined on the park side by a large steel-and-wood boat-shaped balcony. Intended originally as an elevator with solid metal panels, the balcony underwent changes that resulted in its visual overload. The simpler facades of fiberglass-reinforced-concrete panels framed in Honduran mahogany resemble shoji screens: split scuppers and balcony railings in lead and hot-dipped galvanized steel are also of Japanese derivation. To placate the concerns of neighbors in Mediterranean-style houses, the pavilion was given a gabled tile roof, hidden by a low parapet of the concrete wall panels.

Interior stair. ↑

Large timber trusses and a pitched roof set the barnlike tone for this 40-foot-high exhibition space (the walls are 25 feet high). Its two long sides open to the exterior by means of large sliding doors, achieving an outdoor-indoor effect. Tall corner windows recall Frank Lloyd Wright's and Rudolph Schindler's mitered corner glazing, a device that brings in ample light and provides a rhythmic break in the interior where art cannot be hung. Linking this space with a lower gallery is a free-floating stair in sandblasted steel with a clear-coat finish, whose materials, design and detailing are typical of Israel's style—as is the unexpected incorporation of a wet bar into its top part.

The Art Pavilion has been called a combination "high-tech Japanese tea house, California dwelling of the 1920s and renovated industrial warehouse." These elements fit, respectively, a client enthralled by images from many trips to Japan, an architect inspired by early Californian Modernism and a collection of Modern and contemporary art best viewed in loft spaces typical of utilitarian structures.

↑ Exterior, park side.

← Interior.

THE SAATCHI COLLECTION GALLERY

**98A Boundary Road,
London**

by **Max Gordon**

1984

30,000 square feet

27,000 square feet of exhibition space

cost undisclosed

Considering how many alternative spaces for art there were by 1984, Charles and Doris Saatchi's conversion of a garage and motor-repair shop in London into a private museum has received an inordinate amount of attention. The renown of 98A Boundary Road as a gallery for painting and sculpture since the 1960s was due partly to Charles Saatchi himself, a partner with his brother Maurice in one of the world's largest advertising and public-relations agencies. But it was also due to Saatchi's high profile as a collector of international avant-garde art and the atypical nature of the space he commissioned for it. In their emphasis on neutrality, Saatchi and the late Max Gordon, the friend and architect he chose to design the space (which became Gordon's best-known work), created galleries more like those of a public than of a private museum. In contrast with most projects of its kind for which the collector personalizes the architecture, 98A Boundary Road is remarkably anonymous. An obsessively shy man, Saatchi more than made good his assertion that "the art is what deserves all the attention."

To provide the plain space requested by his client, Gordon designed a container within the container of the original trapezoidal structure, a concept the architect also applied to the Fisher Landau Center (1991) in New York. Between the lining and the periphery are spaces for an office, workshop and services. Gordon used light to unify the galleries, and indeed the only feature of the original building left intact is the steel-trussed shed roof, whose exposed electrical trunking and pipes were removed to enhance its lightness. Fluorescent tubes were installed in metal troughs within the roof structure to help avoid shadows. Below the trusses, partitions that conceal structural columns were built for five galleries, and the floor of the largest gallery was excavated four feet to achieve a 14-foot wall height, slightly higher than the other spaces. Within these windowless, relentlessly white galleries (with light gray floors) that incorporate no seating or any other element that might detract from the art, the exhibitions take on a didactic quality unusual for a private museum. Only 98A Boundary Road's half-hidden gate and mysteriously high gray-walled entrance yard seem private.

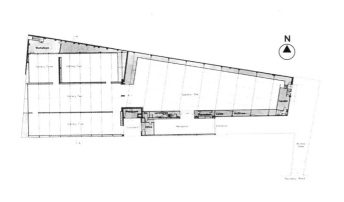

Plan. ↑

Interior. →

Shortly after the gallery was installed it was opened regularly to the public two afternoons a week. Now open four days a week, some of its special exhibitions attract as many as 100,000 visitors during their two-and-a-half-month runs. Saatchi remarks that for more obscure shows, "no one comes. But we aren't influenced by this—we want to please ourselves. The thing we like doing best is to present art not seen elsewhere." In its anonymous setting Saatchi's exhibition program serves the public in its own distinct way. His description of the experience captures what private museums, essentially, are about:

> The whole advantage in being a private collector is that
> I don't have to think like a museum. No museum curator in his
> right mind would want to get lumbered with twenty Schnabels
> or fifteen Morleys, because it would throw the collection
> completely out of balance. But you're free to make harebrained
> decisions if you're not thinking in museum terms.

FISHER LANDAU CENTER

**Long Island City,
New York**

by **Max Gordon**

in collaboration with

William Katz

1991

25,000 square feet

12,000 square feet of exhibition space

cost undisclosed

Gallery. ↑

Sitting area. ↓

Because she liked the Saatchi Gallery, Emily Fisher Landau chose Max Gordon as the architect for a museum to house her growing collection of contemporary, Native American and tribal art. But the result is quite different from the Saatchi, perhaps partly because of Landau's use of the artist William Katz as a consultant. Located in a four-story former parachute-harness factory, Gordon's museum unified interiors and reduced the building's extensive fenestration by lining each level in the same manner as 98A Boundary Road. For the Landau, however, he left openings in the lining for natural light and views to the exterior. Vertical fluorescent tubes at each side of the windows disguise their position behind the periphery. Spotlights and wall washers light the displays. No attempt was made to conceal structural columns, their flared capitals recalling those of Frank Lloyd Wright's Johnson Wax Building. (Ceilings were dropped nine inches in exhibition spaces to hide plinths above the capitals.)

Not only did Landau choose to have columns and windows articulate the exhibition spaces of her museum, she also made small rooms into homey sitting areas. Outfitted with pieces from her extensive collection of 1930s tubular aluminum furniture by Warren MacArthur, these rooms emphasize the personal and private nature of the center, which is open by appointment only.

RUBELL FAMILY COLLECTION

Miami, Florida

renovated by **the Rubell Family**

1992

36,000 square feet

30,000 square feet of exhibition space

cost undisclosed

The Rubells' conversion of a two-story warehouse is an extreme example of a collector's decision to focus on art rather than on architecture. Having acquired over 900 objects within two decades, many of which are installation pieces that require spacious rooms of their own, the Rubells had in mind only their need for more space when they bought the warehouse. With the help of their son, Jason, a collector in his own right who has run two art galleries, the couple designed their conversion as economically as possible, dividing open spaces with temporary partitions. Basically they left the building intact.

The ground floor's lofty 20-foot ceilings temper the space's raw quality, which is more persistent on the 13-foot-high second floor. With almost no natural light or views to the exterior, the expanses of untreated concrete and plasterboard could be oppressive; in fact they are well suited to the contents. Described as "raw, obscene and nightmarishly immense," the collection features young artists, many of whom were unknown when the Rubells acquired their work. This was the case with the now established sculptor Charles Ray, whose *Oh! Charley, Charley, Charley . . .* consists of eight life-size casts of the naked Ray arranged in an orgiastic circle. Correspondingly, the 70-foot trains of Beverly Semmes's three waterfall-like gowns have all the height they need in a ground-floor gallery.

Located in a working-class residential neighborhood of North Miami, the museum has attracted considerable interest. It is now open to the public three days a week, with a monthly attendance of about 150.

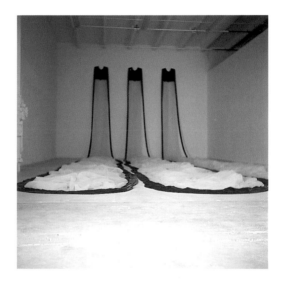

TOP: Ground floor → with *Blue Gowns* by Beverly Semmes. BOTTOM: Second floor with *Oh! Charley, Charley, Charley . . .* by Charles Ray.

GOETZ COLLECTION

Munich, Germany

by **Jacques Herzog and Pierre de Meuron** with **Josef Peter Meier-Scupin,** site architect

1992

7,530 square feet

2,920 square feet of exhibition space

cost undisclosed

Jacques Herzog and Pierre de Meuron, the two Swiss architects of this refined small museum in Munich, have been in partnership for two decades (they were joined in 1991 and 1994 by Harry Gugger and Christine Binswanger, respectively). Their recent success has prompted numerous publications of their work and interviews in which Herzog and de Meuron liberally express their opinions on architecture, planning and occasionally clothes. Characterized as the "new simplicity," their boxlike architecture relies for expression on inventive cladding materials, which include their signature copper wrapping of a railroad signal box (designed in 1988 and now a prototype for the Swiss railroad system) and a floral motif silk-screened on translucent polycarbonate panels for the Ricola Europe factory and storage building in Mulhouse, France.

For the exhibition of art they share with a number of artists they have worked with a deep-seated belief in unintrusive, nonhierarchical space—what they call "anonymous architecture." Outspokenly critical of spaces for art designed by their peers, including Frank Gehry, Hans Hollein, Jean Nouvel, James Stirling and Venturi, Scott Brown and Associates—as well as the earlier solutions of Louis Kahn, Alvar Aalto and Le Corbusier—the two Swiss are convinced that artists have keener perceptive abilities than architects. Consequently, they have used artists as consultants for many aspects of their work: for the Goetz galleries, the Austrian abstract painter Helmut Federle served in this capacity. Herzog and de Meuron also count Donald Judd and Agnes Martin as important influences; the affinity is established with the Goetz Collection, whose focus is Arte Povera and abstract monochromatic painting.

This private museum was built in a residential district of Munich for a former art dealer, Ingvild Goetz, who wanted "to have a space where you can only be with the art and not disturbed by the normal inventory of a house." Although it was intended solely for Goetz's use, requests for access were so persistent that she now regularly opens the gallery, for which there is no outside financial support, in the late afternoon. Its site is the parklike garden of birches and pine trees where her 1960s house is located, and one of her requests was for a structure that would be subordinate to the landscape. Local building regulations limited the height and footprint of the new structure, thereby suggesting the partial burying of one level, which is the basis for the design.

The building consists of a reinforced-concrete tub (26 by 79 by 10 feet) dropped into the ground to its upper edge; across its width two 8-foot-high reinforced-concrete tubes carry a wood-frame box that rises 54 feet above the tub. Translucent glass fills the perimeters between the tubes, one of which ends in transparent glass, the other in an aluminum door. The same milky glazing is used for a rectangular crowning form that repeats the dimensions of the

↑ Northern, entry facade.

← Railroad Engine Depot,
Basel, by Jacques Herzog
and Pierre de Meuron
(1989, project built 1995).

↑ Gallery.

Plans. ↓

↓ Sections.
TOP: West-east.
BOTTOM: North-south.

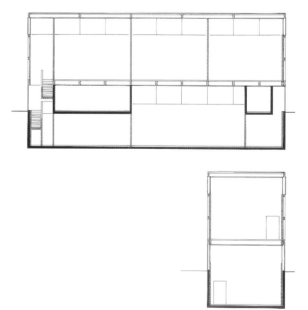

ground-level glass box. These two glazed elements provide clerestory light for the two levels of exhibition space. A gap between the outer skin and the free-standing building allows air flow and houses all the mechanical systems so that no technical apparatus mars the purity of the viewing spaces. As ingenious as the structure is, it takes second place to surface materials, the architects' prime concern. Typically for them, the envelope's birch plywood, matte glass and untreated aluminum were chosen for their sensuality and ambiguity. With changes in light, the wood resembles concrete and the matte glass is used like other materials rather than as glazing, revealing only shadowy images of what is behind. Herzog and de Meuron's emphasis on surface is part of an attitude that rejects architecture as construction, theory, process, symbolism or narrative in favor of creating specific objects that have their own autonomous reality. In this respect it resembles much of the work in the Goetz Collection.

The larger tube serves as the museum's lobby, office and library; the smaller one houses mechanical and storage. Entrance is therefore through a work space, beside which a narrow double stair leads down to the basement and up to the first-floor galleries. The underground level contains a low, artificially lit room that precedes a larger rectangular space with natural light from the same nearly five-foot-high clerestories as above. On the upper level, three almost square spaces differ only in that one has windows on three sides, the others on two. Ceiling height throughout the non-axial enfilade is 18 feet; walls are an off-white hand-troweled plaster; floors are oak with no baseboards. Deemed a distraction from the art, views to the exterior have been ruled out.

The gallery's exterior seems to play on the relationship between glass, concrete and steel panels in the flat, structural bay system of Kahn's Center for British Art at Yale University in New Haven. In reality, it derives from the firm's own 1989 design for a Basel railroad engine depot, where the roof lights of vehicle-repair shops prefigure the Goetz's glass volumes and an administration building sits on U-shaped wedges reminiscent of the later structure. In line with the partners' interest in repetitive themes, the same glass volume appears in their winning entry for the Tate Gallery's competition (1994) for the conversion of London's Bankside Power Station into a gallery of Modern art. There, occupying the full length of the roof, and one story high, the "light beam" signals the museum's presence. The Goetz gallery's clerestories and ceiling light strips will also serve as a model for the Tate Bankside.

PULITZER FOUNDATION FOR THE ARTS

St. Louis, Missouri

preliminary project by **Tadao Ando**

2000

25,600 square feet

11,450 square feet of exhibition space

cost undisclosed

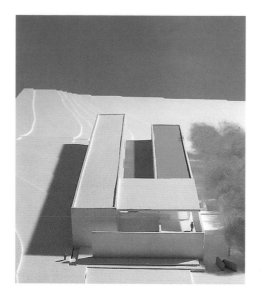

← Model with northeast entry at left.

Joseph Pulitzer was the editor and publisher of the St. Louis *Post-Dispatch* and chairman of the Pulitzer Publishing Company; his wife served from 1964 to 1973 as the curator at the St. Louis Art Museum. Collectors of Modern and contemporary art, the Pulitzers initially wanted a building for large pieces that were difficult to place in their home. They were attracted to the work of Tadao Ando, who was strongly endorsed by artists in their collection; they were also influenced by the architect's design of the gallery for Japanese screens at the Art Institute of Chicago.

After Joseph Pulitzer's death in 1993, Emily Pulitzer developed the idea of a building that would be more than a private art repository. She envisioned something that would contribute to the architecture of the city's midtown Grand Center Arts and Entertainment District, a gallery in which a variety of spaces would offer different contexts for an eclectic mix: African art next to a Cézanne, which in turn might be next to an Ellsworth Kelly. The museum would be available to the public—by appointment only in order to avoid the crowding that could disrupt its contemplative mood. Unlike the usual impetus, there was no wish to immortalize a collection; Emily Pulitzer describes the foundation rather as "an alternative viewing possibility to what municipal museums, as they grow bigger and more institutional, can provide; neither institutional nor domestic, it will be something completely different."

This first semipublic building in the United States by Ando (who recently won the competition for a new museum for Modern art in Fort Worth, Texas) will embody his characteristic themes: geometric forms, unified material and the presence of nature. The north-south structure consists of two two-level boxes, both 24 feet wide but with unequal lengths (204 and 216 feet) and heights: the eastern wing's greater height is designed to block unsightly views at this side; the western wing adapts to a drop in the land. The two long, parallel rectangles are separated by a reflecting pool of the same width. A modest entranceway, tucked into the leftover 12-foot space at the building's northeast corner (a second access is being considered for the northwest corner), opens to a lobby facing the pool; from here visitors may proceed to the main, double-height gallery in the eastern wing, to the offices, library, storage and services in the western wing or to the roof garden, on one side of which stands a Miesian glazed pavilion in which there is a sitting area.

Eight-foot-high windows allow light to reflect from the pool into the main gallery, which also has a small skylight above the south wall. A stairway leads down from this exhibition space to two other galleries without natural light, support services and areas for future expansion. As with the Menil Collection, daylight here is diffused but not stabilized, so there will be variations according to time, weather and season. In the main gallery certain conditions will allow for the focused rays of daylight that Ando has used in the past to define space. The building will be primarily in concrete and glass with painted plaster interiors.

The series of structures at Museum Insel Hombroich and at the Chinati Foundation at Marfa (see Chapter 4) convinced Emily Pulitzer that a break in looking at art enhances one's experience of it, prompting her request for views to the exterior and ample relaxation space. Her desire accords with Ando's belief in the need to combine nature and architecture; nature is provided here by water in the largely open-air pool and by greenery on the roof terrace. Ando has stated that it is to such "an architecturalized nature . . . that a sacred space must relate." While the Pulitzer Foundation excludes urban realities, and in this sense is a sanctuary for art, its openness to the exterior and its varied spatial experiences promise to make the best kind of sacred space.

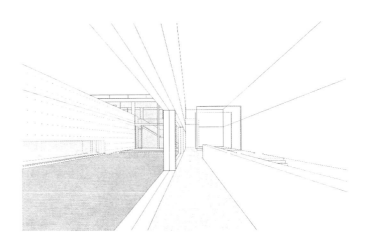

↑ Interior perspective.

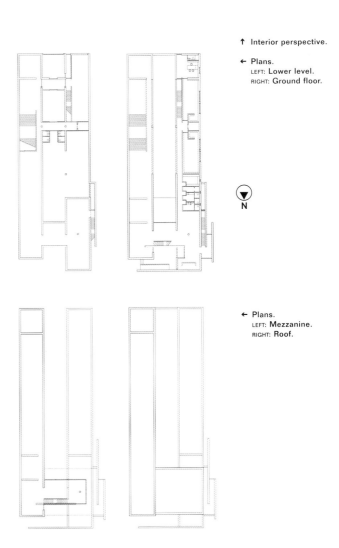

← Plans.
LEFT: **Lower level.**
RIGHT: **Ground floor.**

N

← Plans.
LEFT: **Mezzanine.**
RIGHT: **Roof.**

The construction of a special structure for art still has the same connotations of power and prestige that were historically associated with such projects. The New York–Los Angeles gallery owner Larry Gagosian states that in addition to the tax advantages it offers in the United States, a private museum announces to the art world that its owner is "a collector to be reckoned with." This is a very real consideration for, among others, Los Angeles–based businessman Eli Broad, who considers himself "a kind of evangelist" in lending the art he displays privately in a converted industrial building to institutions around the country.

Whatever the secondary motives for making a private museum might be, at the top of the list is a passion for collecting. Like the creators of the *Kunstkammern*, the person establishing his or her own gallery today is unfettered by didactic concerns, the need for publicity and the internal politics of public museums. That person is also free to indulge any acquisition whim and to commission architecture appropriate to it.

These highly personalized choices are not without their detractors. The exhibition of unrelated individual historic objects at the Menil Collection has been criticized for its lack of context. Müller's unconventional handling of climate control and conservation at Insel Hombroich has been denounced as destructive. What is more, the cabinet of curiosities' contents were routinely dispersed upon their owner's demise, and the ability of today's private museum to survive beyond the original founder's lifetime is questioned; the death of the Los Angeles collector, whose name has been withheld, has left his art pavilion with no leadership and facing the possibility of a neighborhood-enforced move that would endanger the character of the enterprise. Many private collections are so personal that even if their owners wanted to donate them to an existing museum, it would be difficult to integrate them with an established program. Whereas individuals were formerly a source of important material for public museums, they are now in competition with them: private museums are generally regarded as threatening by institution directors who see coveted work being channeled outside the established culture industry.

None of these objections overrides the visual richness and successful architecture achieved by the museums discussed here. Their relatively small size is a prime asset, in that exhibition areas can be scaled like domestic space; without actually being residences—arguably the optimum place for viewing art—they approximate residences. As with the highly entertaining cabinet of curiosities, the architecture of many of today's private museums addresses the problems of exhibiting art specific to them, fulfilling Father Couturier's belief that "a museum should be a place where we lose our head."

Chapter 2

The Museum as Sacred Space

The noted historian Nikolaus Pevsner dates the word *museum* in its modern sense to the Italian collector Paolo Giovio in 1539, though it did not enter the English language until 1683, in reference to the Ashmolean in Oxford. The early museums, unlike today's, were not open to the general public; only patrons deemed acceptable by the collectors, and the occasional artist, could gain access. The guiding principle of the collections was aesthetic: they were meant to entertain.

The Enlightenment belief in reason changed all this. Specialization and classification brought a didactic approach to art, which was newly expected to instruct rather than primarily to please. Together with a faith in art's ability to improve humankind, there developed a sense of public entitlement to culture. Among the first of many rulers throughout Europe to open their collections were the electors of Saxony; and in Paris in 1750 part of the royal collections was made available to the citizenry for three hours twice a week in rooms arranged for this purpose in the Luxembourg Palace. By the time these galleries reverted to a royal residence in 1779, plans had been under discussion for several years to transform the Louvre's Grande Galerie into a public museum. The Revolution allowed the project to be realized, and in 1793 the Louvre became the world's first national collection.

Making art accessible to the public in palaces adapted for it was soon standard procedure. Beginning in the 1820s this development was paralleled by a wave of new, purpose-built museums that symbolized yet another way of thinking about art. No longer meant to be merely pleasurable, or primarily didactic, art became a secular religion. Gradually, museums built for the worship of art replaced churches built for the worship of God.

Architecture reinforced the sacred message: neoclassicism was the style of the time, and the dome and colonnade for a museum project in 1803 by the French teacher and architect J.-N.-L. Durand established a typology for the exterior, as his gallery enfilades did for the interior. Soon Christian imagery—cathedral and church domes—was added to the pagan imagery of Greece and Rome for these 19th-century temples of art. In the same way that sacred space in the service of a deity excludes exterior distractions in order to focus on worship, museums were isolated in parks and their main rooms sealed from views of the world around them. (However, unlike church chapels and altars, modern museums eventually banned all architectural articulation for fear that the eye might stray from the art; also frequently banned was natural light—so often inspirational in its effect in religious buildings.)

In the second half of the 19th century picturesque architectural styles continued to treat museums as secluded and revered bastions of culture. The Wadsworth Athenaeum in Hartford, Connecticut (1844), introduced the fortress as a model whose influence was still being felt more than a century later in Marcel Breuer's Whitney Museum of American Art in New York (1966). The exclusionary stance failed, however, to deter the public. Museum attendance in the 1850s was such that even in French resort towns summer hours had to be extended and upholstered furniture provided. By then monumental museum architecture was established across Europe—London, Berlin, Munich, Dresden and St. Petersburg all boasted grand structures built specifically for the exhibition of art—with similar buildings being erected in the eastern United States.

Despite their popular appeal, from the beginning public museums were criticized. In his *Lettres* of 1796 the critic and theoretician Quatremère de Quincy contrasted the pleasure of viewing art in Italy, where it was part of everyday life, with viewing it in a museum, a place he described as a "waxen desert, which resembles a temple and a salon, a graveyard and a school." Particularly in Italy many of the greatest works of art were to be found in sacred spaces—in cathedrals, churches, even small rural chapels—where they were an integral part of daily life. By exhibiting works confiscated from religious institutions by the revolutionary government and, subsequently, objects plundered by Napoleon's armies, the Louvre established the precedent of taking artworks out of their lived settings and isolating them in museums. Great altarpieces that for centuries adorned the churches for which they had been painted became showpieces in galleries. The Elgin marbles—a frieze from the Parthenon, a caryatid column from the Erechtheum—were hacked from the Greek temples they were part of and made into artifacts for the British Museum. For those, like Quatremère and later critics, concerned with contextualism, even the elaborate decors of palace-museums and of Beaux-Arts purpose-built galleries provided insufficient compensation for the original settings of these objects.

While museum attendance increased in Europe and in a few major American cities, the early 20th century's political and cultural revolutions produced detractors of the institution who sounded surprisingly like those of over a hundred years earlier. In his first *Futurist Manifesto* (1909) the Italian poet Filippo Marinetti expressed the feelings of many of his fellow artists when he called museums and libraries "cemeteries" that should be destroyed. The Russian painter and architect El Lissitzky echoed this sentiment in describing exhibition spaces in 1923: "We no longer want the room to be like a painted coffin for our living body." Pinpointing the rationale behind these criticisms, the Swiss-French architect Le Corbusier, like Quatremère, wanted to see objects in their natural settings. For him Pompeii was "the only true museum worthy of the name" (even though by the time he visited the site, the best frescoes had been removed). The French symbolist poet Paul Valéry treated the subject in his 1925 essay "The Problem of Museums":

> Painting and sculpture . . . are orphans. Their mother is dead, their mother, Architecture. As long as she was alive, she gave them their place, their function, their constraints.

↑ Museum of Modern Art, New York City, by Philip Goodwin and Edward Durell Stone (1939). Galleries.

↓ Unbuilt project for a Museum for a Small City, by Mies van der Rohe (1942). Plan.

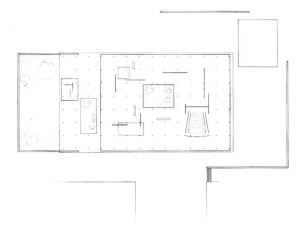

Despite the outcry, museum interiors became even less contextual than they had been earlier. At the time of its inauguration in 1939, Philip Goodwin and Edward Durell Stone's six-story Museum of Modern Art in New York City looked more like a small apartment building than a museum, squeezed as it was between existing buildings instead of grandly residing in a traditional park setting. But its interior spaces were more abstract and more awesome than anything yet seen: loftlike floors inspired by commercial architecture were divided by unarticulated, predominantly white partitions in what a critic described as an "artificially lighted world, confined and remote" (see Chapter 5). Abstraction was carried to the extreme by Mies van der Rohe's 1942 Museum for a Small City project in which universal open space replaced any semblance of rooms: walls were freestanding within a glass box. His Neue Nationalgalerie in Berlin (1968), which was based on these same principles, further contributed to the whitening of museum space, space that seemed ever more anonymous. What would Quatremère—critical of the Louvre, a palace at least similar to those for which some of its art was originally made—have said about exhibiting Impressionist works in such galleries? The artist Eric Fischl's reaction is similar to Valéry's:

> Museums are about dead things; there is no optimum space for living painters because art is no longer connected with living institutions like the church or government as it was historically, or with the life of the bourgeoisie, as it was in the 19th century.

Fischl points out that today's art museums do not replace these historic settings: removed from the architecture they were created for, works are organized according to an established hierarchy of artists. "We don't have allegories or myths that are tacitly agreed to; we only have heroes like Pollock," he says. For Fischl, decontextualized paintings become collage, the 20th century's equivalent to Renaissance perspective, but whereas "perspective was about seeing, collage is about thinking."

Over twenty years ago, the critic Brian O'Doherty (who as an artist uses the name Patrick Ireland) applied the indelible label "the white cube" to spaces that exert a two-fold alienation: depriving art of an architectural context and isolating it in what he described as a "timeless, limbo-like gallery constructed along laws as rigorous as those for building a medieval church." In her book *Civilizing Rituals* (1995), Carol Duncan compares the role of a museum curator with that of a medieval high priest of art responsible for planning the iconographic program of a cathedral:

> Just as images of saints were, by example, supposed to trigger in the initiated a quest for spiritual transcendence, so in the museum, art objects focus and organize the viewer's attention, activating by their very form an inner spiritual or imaginative act. The museum setting, immaculately white and stripped of all distracting ornament, promotes this intense concentration.

The analogy of the museum as the cathedral of the 20th century has become a given. But instead of evoking the church's role in life the museum turned instead to an association with death: the museum as mausoleum. The white cube's "limbo" soon became the "graveyard" deplored by earlier critics. In reaction to this, in the 1970s attempts to make museum boards more democratic and the appearance of a new, less authoritarian breed of directors and curators accompanied a physical opening up of museum buildings: large glazed areas allowed welcoming glimpses inside as well as views out to their surroundings. By the end of the decade Paris's Centre Culturel Georges Pompidou's panoramic views of the city had eliminated the visual separation between exterior and interior, while the activity of its entrance plaza and the movement of its glazed escalators and in its corridors signaled the restoration of entertainment as one of the museum's basic purposes (see Chapter 6). Postmodernism brought a more inclusive approach to exhibition spaces, with Hans Hollein, James Stirling and Robert Venturi, Denise Scott Brown and their various associates among those who tried to restore a visual context to art (see Chapters 5 and 7). They in turn were followed by Frank Gehry and others who sought to create a dynamic interaction between art and architecture (see Chapter 7). Yet despite these changes in attitude the idea of the museum as sacred space—now "immaculately white and stripped of all distracting ornament"—retains its appeal.

In his lecture "Four Walls and Light from Above or Else No Painting on the Wall"(1979), the German artist Georg Baselitz rejected the connection between artist and architect and the attempts to integrate their respective work in favor of nonintrusive galleries:

> high walls, few doors, no side windows, light from above,
> no partitions, no baseboards, no base molding, no paneling,
> no shiny floors and finally, no colors either.

William Rubin expresses similar feelings. Known for his landmark exhibitions of work by modern artists, he insists that architecture should impinge on these objects as little as possible. The abstract artist Dorothea Rockburne shares Rubin's attitude: she wants architecture that will provide "a pause for art," during which she can respond to "a challenge that is almost divine." It was exactly the kind of space described variously by Baselitz, Rubin and Rockburne that MoMA initially provided.

In 1939 MoMA's reconceptualization of the museum was revolutionary and perfectly timed to meet the needs of the new art of the 20th century. Movable partitions could be tailored to fit each exhibition, thereby providing a flexibility unknown in conventional galleries with fixed walls. And despite the starkness that startled critics when the museum opened, its galleries were anything but dead: walls were canted, in some cases colored and in others softened by curtains. The scale was domestic, with 12-to-14-foot-high walls and relatively small rooms that were modeled on the proportions of the New York apartments for which the work was made. In their original state many of the galleries had daylight, and throughout, track lighting was a novel improvement over the lighting in other art venues. Large windows allowed ample views to the exterior. Cézanne, Matisse, Picasso and Miró looked as at home in MoMA's galleries as Manet, Monet and Renoir did in the intimate, light-filled spaces of Paris's former court-tennis club, the Jeu de Paume, when it became a museum for Impressionism in 1947. But with the steady erosion of its architecture to a bland, repetitive circuit, MoMA became a pastiche of its former self and the prototype of the deadly white cube (see Chapter 5). Lifeless imitations of the modified version of MoMA's sacred space, often blown up to grotesque proportions, distort the original in the same way that crude imitations of Mies's steel-and-glass skyscrapers are a travesty of his elegant schemes.

Architects continue to design museums as sacred space with mixed results: attempts to remove everything extraneous to the viewing of art often produce anonymous spaces that fail. The handling of light, scale and texture plays a part in determining the fine line between a museum that works and one that doesn't, and nowhere are these more important than in museums created as sacred space. For a number of reasons scale is particularly important: relatively modest private and monographic museums tend to be more successful in achieving this kind of space than are larger institutions for diversified collections in which galleries lack a sense of place (see Chapters 1 and 3). Sacred museum space originated in another era for a different kind of art from today's: it is difficult to resurrect a style that belongs to the past.

Four new museums for contemporary and Modern art—all conceived as temples of art—are considered here. Steven Holl's nearly completed museum in Helsinki comes closest to an effective reinterpretation of sacred space. Peter Zumthor's Kunsthaus in Bregenz is the most strictly "sacred" in its exclusion of everything unrelated to the viewing of art, thereby raising questions as to its adaptability. Both architects manipulate natural light skillfully, and Holl additionally uses unusual forms to animate interiors. Art is less well served by Mario Botta's museum in San Francisco, whose role he compares to that of a cathedral, and Richard Meier's Barcelona Museum of Contemporary Art, which the architect envisions as "a cathedral of light."

KIASMA MUSEUM FOR CONTEMPORARY ART

Helsinki, Finland

by **Steven Holl Architects**

1998

140,000 square feet

75,350 square feet of exhibition space

$40 million

Promising "a serene religiosity of space" for a museum in Helsinki that will contain art from the 1960s to the present, Steven Holl tries to strike a balance between the white box's neutrality and interiors that interact with their contents. He has opted for what he calls silent and serene architecture, because he feels that the more expressive artists—Bruce Nauman and Vito Acconci, for example—can adapt to this kind of environment, whereas it is more difficult for artists who require calm surroundings to show in expressive spaces. What saves this design from the deadening effect of large neutral space is a variety of shapes and proportions together with natural light caught in an unusual system of scoops.

Site photomontage. ↑

Holl's scheme—the winning entry in a 1993 competition for which there were 500 contestants—is based on the concept of kiasma (or chiasma), a biological term for the intersection or crossing over of two tracts, like nerves or ligaments, in an X shape. For the architect, the museum's intersections are with culture, nature and the urban grid. Culture is represented by the surrounding landmark buildings: Eliel Saarinen's railroad station to the east, Alvar Aalto's Finlandia Concert Hall to the north and the national parliament to the west. Nature is the water of Töölö Bay, which Holl wishes to extend south from its edge at Finlandia Hall through the museum. Inside, the bay is recalled by a rectangular pool whose contents are recirculated to project the sound of moving water to certain areas of the museum; in winter the pool will freeze over, and at night it will reflect light radiating from the building. A pedestrian path cuts through the structure, linking its east and west sides: the east side sheared off to align with the city grid, the museum's curved shape embracing the triangular park at the west.

Rather than follow the Nordic tradition of pastel exteriors that contrast with the region's gray skies and wintry landscapes, Holl's materials reflect these natural tonalities: cladding strips of matte gray zinc in some areas and a brighter hand-sanded aluminum in others. Structural glass planks evoke the ice of Töölö Bay. The extensive glazing of the western facades alternates frosted and clear glass, the latter used for the galleries. Only the acid-reddened brass window frames and mullions on the north facade and the south entrance facade are in a darker color.

Channeling water from the bay may be stymied by abutting railroad tracks and loading facilities in an area for which the city has been trying, unsuccessfully, to devise a master plan through most of this century. Furthermore, a ten-story office building currently under construction threatens to crowd the

← Exterior with entry. Model.

↓ Entrance foyer.

museum and interrupt its relationship to the low-rise buildings at the east. In fact, the most functional example of kiasma is the building's two interlocking masses: a five-story curved structure that opens like the mouth of a great horn toward Finlandia Hall and, within it, a smaller, four-story rectangle containing offices and a cafeteria as well as galleries. Between them a dramatic skylit entrance atrium follows the inflection of the larger structure to a narrow vanishing point. Ramps on one side, reminiscent of Frank Lloyd Wright's Guggenheim Museum and Le Corbusier's Villa La Roche–Jeanneret, and a stunning twisting stairway beyond the atrium connect the two structures. This layered circulation system adapts, in a simplified version, that of Rem Koolhaas's Rotterdam Kunsthal (see Chapter 7). As in the New York Guggenheim, the atrium provides central orientation; additionally, it allows independent access to the ground-floor café, bookstore and 240-seat auditorium.

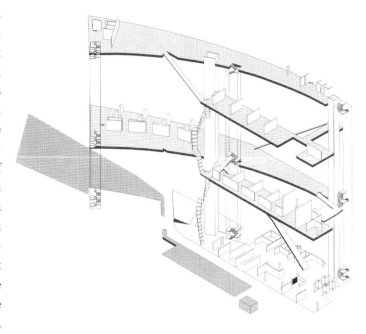

↑ Isometric.

← Gallery with bow-tie skylight.
  Model.

The museum's curve plays an essential role in the distribution of natural light. In Helsinki's northern latitude the sun never rises above 51 degrees. Holl explains that the glazed western facade acts like a catcher's mitt, catching the sun's horizontal rays and deflecting them through the central section to the galleries below, while the curved roof allows for secondary skylights. The system provides variant natural illumination to galleries at every level.

As with most sacred space, interiors have been stripped of all distracting details such as moldings, door frames and light fixtures. Gallery walls are white sand-finished gypsum plaster, hand-troweled to create a rough texture; floors are blackened concrete. But important differences among the spaces individualize them. Ceiling heights range from 14 to 30 feet. One of the 30-by-30-foot galleries in the rectangular segment is double-height with both a skylight and a window, and two have clerestories to the atrium; a diagonal enfilade slightly varies the configuration of each room. The subtly inflected walls of other galleries allow for yet another kind of space, with distinctive bow-tie skylights atop the double-curved walls promising a particularly interesting illumination. An enormous loft area (82 by 148 feet) shares the top floor with an artist's studio and a conference room.

From the moment one enters the museum's white concrete-walled reception atrium, the mystery of its receding curve and diffused skylight arouses a sense of excitement and anticipation. Holl promises to satisfy these expectations with equally challenging sacred spaces.

KUNSTHAUS BREGENZ

Bregenz, Austria

by **Atelier Peter Zumthor**

1997

30,000 square feet

15,000 square feet of exhibition space

$30 million

For a museum that will be used only for changing exhibitions of contemporary art in Bregenz, western Austria, Peter Zumthor presents a box that connects ever so subtly with the world around it. The architect's pared-down style conforms to the mandate for sacred space: nothing will be allowed within this small building but art. The product of six years' collaboration between the architect, a strong director (Edelbert Köb) and many of the Austrian artists whose work will be exhibited, the museum's windowless galleries reject scenic views of the nearby lake and all interior articulation. But the building's etched-glass skin does allow an awareness of outside traffic at ground level, and of sun and clouds on the upper floors, which acknowledge, without actually revealing, its setting.

Born in 1943 in Basel, where he trained as a cabinetmaker, Zumthor beat out 80 other entrants to win the 1990 competition for the Kunsthaus. His daring proposal was for a compact building that rises just above the old town's roofline in defiance of municipal height limitations. The museum stands between an Art Deco theater and a Beaux-Arts museum in a small park on the eastern shore of Lake Constance. The lake's opposite side borders Germany and Switzerland, whose eastern areas are expected to provide an audience for the Kunsthaus beyond the local population of 27,000 (already augmented in summers by the 180,000 visitors to its musical comedy festival).

Zumthor has applied complex concepts of controlling daylight and temperature modulations to a ghostly box of a building. Approaching the museum's entrance at the east, facing the park, the visitor sees a cube whose sides are enclosed by an armature of large etched-glass panels barely overlapping, but not touching, one another to create an effect that the architect describes as that of slightly ruffled feathers or fish scales. The panels are attached by metal clamps to a steel frame standing three feet past the building's faintly visible concrete structure; this curtain wall acts as a protective skin, light modulator and thermal insulator. The silhouetting of stairs and structure behind the translucent outer wall recalls both Herzog and de Meuron's Goetz Collection and Gigon and Guyer's Kirchner Museum (see Chapters 1 and 3). (Laurids and Manfred Ortner's unbuilt 1990 proposal for a museum of Modern art in Vienna was an early example of glass juxtaposed with concrete to this purpose.)

To the right of the cube is a small building that houses offices, the museum's library and store and a café-restaurant. Its black concrete walls are honed so smoothly that at first they appear to be steel. Early on in the project the artist Donald Judd was asked to design this annex, but Zumthor rejected the vaulted form he proposed. It is no wonder that Judd was attracted to the undertaking: Zumthor's geometrical forms and refined surfaces have much in common with Judd's minimal aesthetic (see Chapter 4).

← View from Lake Constance.

↓ Kunsthaus with administration, restaurant, and shop building at right.

Detail of etched-glass → armature.

Entry area. ↓

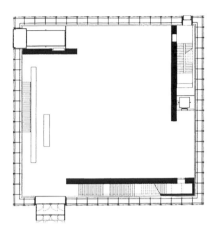

Within, three asymmetrical concrete slabs, continuous from two levels below grade to the roof, support four square horizontal boxes: a ground-level entrance foyer and galleries above. A lecture hall and services occupy two basement floors, one of which is partially illuminated by a light ditch. The three galleries have uninterrupted over-six-foot-high spaces that act as light collectors for each level. Tucked between the slabs and the outer wall are exposed air-system ducts, passenger and cargo elevators and, at the entrance facade, an elegant, long, narrow staircase. A prefabricated system of water and air pipes that uses one-sixth the energy of a conventional climate-control system is embedded in the walls and ceiling.

The entrance area is approximately 79 feet square and 14 feet high—a room of such perfect proportions that it takes one's breath away. This free-span space is repeated on the three upper floors (the top level is slightly higher) but with open-jointed etched-glass ceiling panels, smaller than those on the exterior, hung from the concrete ceiling on hundreds of thin steel rods. Filtered daylight from the light collector above each floor reflects from concrete ceilings that rake down toward the middle and penetrates the galleries as diffused light; a grid of daylight neons on the structural ceiling mixes artificial and natural light. The raw-concrete walls have a flawless, velvety quality, while the floors of seamless gray terrazzo are polished and become lighter in color on the upper levels.

Overall plan of ↑ museum and administration/ restaurant/ shop building.

Museum section. ↓

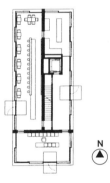

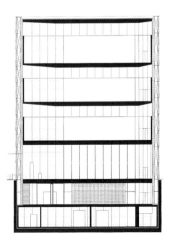

Zumthor combines carefully crafted textures, luminous diffused natural light and small scale to make his ephemeral statement. However, the galleries' puritanical quality is both an asset—in its strong identity—and a liability—in its suitability to a limited number of art forms. Particularly appropriate work figured in the institution's inaugural exhibition: James Turrell placed a series of floodlights in the space between the museum's structural concrete and its glass facade, illuminating its entire height with changing colors. Within the galleries a variety of light sculptures materialized light and space in a stunning dialogue between art and architecture.

← James Turrell,
night installation.

↓ TOP: Group show.
BOTTOM: Per Kirkeby
installation.

SAN FRANCISCO MUSEUM OF MODERN ART

San Francisco, California

by **Mario Botta**

in association with

Helmuth, Obata

and Kassabaum

1995

225,000 square feet

50,000 square feet of exhibition space

$62 million

← Entry facade.

The Ticino-born, Lugano-based Mario Botta has described his San Francisco Museum of Modern Art (SFMOMA) as "a space dedicated to witnessing and searching for a new religiosity." Indeed, the museum's central, truncated cylinder comes directly from the architect's church designs.

When SFMOMA (housed since 1935 in part of the War Memorial Veterans Building) was ready to select a site for its own building in 1987, space where it really belongs—in Yerba Buena Gardens, San Francisco's new downtown cultural center—was no longer available. Designated an urban redevelopment area in 1966, the 22-acre Yerba Buena Gardens encompasses streets adjacent to its three consecutive pedestrian-only blocks; the museum settled on Third Street, one of these adjacent streets but on the far side of a busy four-lane throughway, which effectively cuts it off from the cultural district. Accentuating this separation, when Botta received the commission in 1988 the architects Fumihiko Maki and James Stewart Polshek were already in the working drawings stage for, respectively, the Galleries and Forum Building and the 750-seat Arts Theater to be constructed across the street from the museum. Neither of these facilities acknowledges the more commanding SFMOMA; in fact, both turn their backs on Botta's building.

Given the museum's less than ideal placement and its stated competition with Los Angeles's well-known Museum of Contemporary Art by Arata Isozaki (1986), it needed to have a strong visual impact. The three massive setback volumes in Botta's signature red-brick patterns, penetrated by the sliced-off circular skylight clad in equally characteristic white-and-black-striped granite, respond to this need, but with an insensitivity to neighbors that is surprising for an architect known for the contextualism of his work. The museum's near-windowless monumentality appears heavy in front of the slim Pacific Telephone and Telegraph Building behind it, while it overshadows the smaller structures in the park before it. Its fortresslike facade is not made more inviting by the low height and shallow depth of its entrance portal.

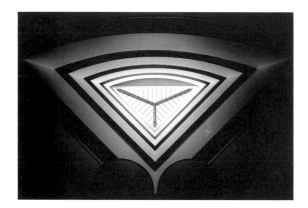

At the time that Botta began to design this, his first freestanding building in the United States, he had already started to develop a series of religious structures. A church for the small town of Mogno in his native Ticino (1986–96) is a cylinder with an elliptical glazed roof. He enlarged the Mogno design for a cathedral at Evry (1988–95), a new town near Paris, using the same glazed truncated cylinder that became the San Francisco museum's identifying feature. Despite his repeated use of the form—and his bathing of both interiors in natural light—Botta was unable to translate Evry's intense spiritual quality to San Francisco.

The effectiveness of Botta's religious architecture is affirmed by the number of commissions he has received—five churches and a synagogue to date. But it was none of the architect's church designs that decided the trustees in his favor. Rather, it was his skillful handling of light in the skylit, triangular entrance atrium of the Gotthard Bank in Lugano (1988) that was the determining factor in the selection.

The antecedent is appropriate in relation to the museum's entrance lobby, whose function is distinctly revenue producing in that it provides access to a bookstore and a cafeteria (both of which also have street entrances), the 299-seat Wattis Theater and a large multipurpose events room that is rented out as well as used for museum activities. The architect calls the lobby a "piazza," comparable to a town square—a metaphor he also applies to the main exhibition space in his Tinguely Museum in Basel (see Chapter 3). Yet many of the museum's features are derived from the temple or the church that was the basis of classic museum typology. The skylit, 135-foot cylinder rising within the rectilinear lobby replaces the dome that traditionally marks a main orientation space. Three structural columns are placed in a configuration reminiscent of Bernini's altar baldachin at St. Peter's Basilica in Rome. The monumental stairway's square balconies are like pulpits; the large circular openings at either side of the

shaft have cruciform bracing. Conversely, the area's surfeit of surface materials—gray and black stripes of granite that alternate rough and polished surfaces, white plaster, arctic birch and metal—recalls "a great Art Deco department store," as critic Herbert Muschamp put it, while the gimmicky bridge that spans the top of the shaft seems more appropriate to a fun fair.

↑ Entrance lobby.

← Cathedral, Evry, by Mario Botta (1995). Exterior.

← Gotthard Bank, Lugano, by Mario Botta (1988). Skylight.

There is nothing intrinsically wrong with today's museums providing commercial and fund-raising amenities—if they do not become the dominant image. Despite the shortcomings of a recent renovation, for instance, the Metropolitan Museum of Art's bookstore and gift shop do not detract from the dignity of its grand entrance hall. The huge main floor of Paris's Centre Georges Pompidou is designed in the same vocabulary as the library and museum above it: even with commercial functions and heavy traffic, a balance between culture and entertainment is maintained by the exhibition spaces. In San Francisco there is no art in the lobby, and the profane altogether outweighs the sacred.

The building has two outstanding exhibition spaces, only one of which succeeds in creating a context for the art. The majestic scale and diffused daylight of the top-floor Fisher Gallery are sympathetic to the contemporary work it is primarily intended for. The clear-span space resembles the loft architecture that is so well suited to current large-scale multimedia work. By contrast, the skylit 210-foot-long enfilade that occupies the second floor's entire width is dramatic architecture, but it singularly lacks drama as a place for paintings. At either side

of its central passageway, seven 16-foot-high galleries are identical except for a window in the central bay: white walls are marked only by a thin reveal at the floor and at the channel-vaulted ceiling. In these repetitive spaces, the museum's strongest holding—a comprehensive collection of Clyfford Still, Richard Diebenkorn and other San Francisco Bay area artists and selections from the New York school—appear to be stored in a beautifully lit filing cabinet.

The other rigorously neutral galleries conform to many of the rules for good museum space: different ceiling heights on each floor, a variety of room sizes and natural light made possible—through coffered vaults expressed on the exterior as lanterns—in areas where the building is set back. With so much going for it, why, with the exception of the Fisher Gallery, is the art experience in this museum so unsatisfying? Perhaps it is precisely because too many rules have been followed. There is a formulaic impersonality to galleries that, though of various proportions, seem to have been designed to accommodate anything that might go on their walls—a one-size-fits-all approach—rather than for specific types of art or photography. William Rubin says of exhibition installations, "You have to design the interior walls to the story you're telling." The problem with Botta's San Francisco museum is that there is no story: the galleries (except the Fisher) relate neither to the art they exhibit nor to the city.

Unlike the Helsinki and Bregenz museums, where entrance areas are of a piece with the galleries, SFMOMA presents a disjunction between the atrium's mixed metaphors and the rest of the structure. The ambivalent imagery of the entrance piazza is immediately confusing in terms of what it introduces. The disjointedness follows through to the galleries, whose lack of identity deprives them of a vitality that is essential to successful exhibition space.

← Second-floor enfilade.

↓ TOP: Second-floor plan.
CENTER: Ground-floor plan.
BOTTOM: Longitudinal section.

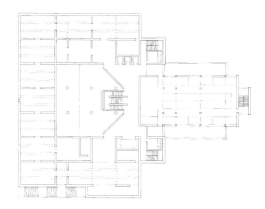

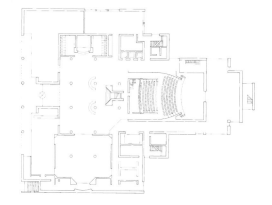

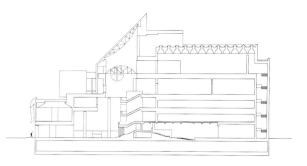

MUSEUM OF CONTEMPORARY ART, BARCELONA

Barcelona, Spain

by **Richard Meier & Partners**

1995

150,000 square feet

60,000 square feet of exhibition space

$35 million

In a process that has been compared with the surgical excision of deteriorated organs, Barcelona—like several other historic European cities—is currently being renewed through limited interventions into the fabric of its older neighborhoods. The Centre Georges Pompidou provided a model for this approach in the 1970s (see Chapter 6). And like the Pompidou, Barcelona had neither a collection nor a director in place at the time the building was being designed. (Not until June 1995 was Miguel Molins appointed director; the museum is now run by an unusual consortium of the Catalunya and Barcelona governments and a private foundation that provides acquisition funds.) In the absence of a client for the architect, the Barcelona museum also resembles the Galician Center of Contemporary Art at Santiago de Compostela (1993) by Alvaro Siza. Both buildings suffer from the problems of the Pompidou, problems endemic to museums designed with no specific contents in mind. More farsighted was the Basque government in its arrangement with New York's Guggenheim Museum for the selection of art and a staff for Frank Gehry's Bilbao museum (see Chapter 7).

Of these three Spanish cities, Barcelona, with its 1.7 million population, is the largest, and its program of urban renewal the most substantial. Barcelona undertook plans for self-improvement shortly after the country's return to democracy in 1976 and eventually allocated $7.5 billion to redesigning infrastructure, parks and neighborhoods in a massive effort stimulated by its selection as the site for the 1992 Summer Olympics. Like most of the urban plans discussed here, Barcelona's relates to an extensive region, in this case stretching from Marseilles to Valencia. As a much-publicized element in this greater whole, the Museum of Contemporary Art (Museu d'Art Contemporània de Barcelona, or MACBA) is especially significant in the way it will influence future projects in an increasingly city-oriented Europe.

Barcelona's then mayor, Pasqual Maragall, met Richard Meier during a visit to New York in 1984 and invited him to join a group of international architects working on Olympics-related projects. Meier accepted on the condition that he could eventually design a museum for the city. At the time, the Picasso Museum and the Tàpies Foundation were Barcelona's only institutions devoted to 20th-century works, and sites were being considered for a museum of contemporary art. Meier chose the location in the medieval Raval, a densely populated, working-class neighborhood with narrow, dark streets just west of the lively boulevard Las Ramblas. Maragall, who had not yet visited any of Meier's museums, was delighted that an architect he regarded as "a symbol of light and air" would be working in a neighborhood where these elements were of major concern.

↑ Entry facade fronting Plaça dels Angels.

Renewal called for the demolition of several apartment blocks, the construction of new residential and commercial facilities, the adaptive reuse of old religious buildings primarily for cultural activities and the creation of open public spaces. For all the good intentions, the museum has been successful only in establishing the popular new Plaça dels Angels by marking the square's north side. But it bears no relation to the 16th-century Convent dels Angels that borders its southern and western sides or to the neighborhood generally.

Conversely, for the High Museum of Art in Atlanta (1983) and the Museum für Kunsthandwerk extension in Frankfurt (1985), Meier successfully dealt with the existing context. At Frankfurt in particular the grid on which his design is based gracefully incorporates the 19th-century Villa Metler that it supplements. Echoing the villa's form, the addition's three cubic pavilions fit into a park, leaving a north-south pedestrian path from the riverside entrance to the street behind, thereby contributing a new connection with that part of the city on the other side of the river. In Barcelona Meier's massive white building does not address either the smaller scale or the earth colors of its surroundings. Unlike Siza's Santiago museum, whose uncompromisingly modern form fits discreetly into its awkward historical site, Meier's building looks out of place. MACBA might be regarded as an elegant exoticism were it not for the voyeuristic position in which visitors are placed in relation to the laundry-strung balconies of its underprivileged neighbors.

Galician Center of ↑ Contemporary Art, Santiago de Compostela, by Alvaro Siza (1993), in center rear.

Lobby and ramp. →

Rising from a gray-granite podium, the museum's facade consists of a stuccoed entrance screen to the west of a large area of horizontal fenestration, with brise-soleils that project in front of lacquered aluminum panels. Balancing the opaque screen, at the eastern side of the windows is an Aalto-like stuccoed form that Meier calls the Peanut.

Immediately inside, a passageway leads around a single-story circular lobby to the north facade. Here, in the sole acknowledgment of its surroundings, is a link to a courtyard the museum shares with Casa de la Caritat, a 13th-century church, and later convent, occupied by the Centre de Cultura Contemporània, a new university building and, from the courtyard north, other cultural institutions. This entrance passageway divides the building into its two distinct parts: to the east, three stories of exhibition and circulation; to the west, seven stories of offices and a nonpublic library.

It is in the eastern part of the building that Meier gives full range to his design pyrotechnics. He has used a longitudinal circulation spine with a cylindrical form before but not with the same complexity and drama as here. The

glazed southern facade initiates a series of parallel incidents: continuous ramps; the 125-foot-long atrium; two balconied, glass-bricked passageways; and the galleries, all of which seem to be suspended in space, thanks to the play of light from the facade and skylights. The ramps stop short of the end walls as do the gallery levels, so there are light-filled slots between the third- and second-floor galleries, which indirectly light the latter. A series of steel-railed balconies provide views to the ground level. Daylight also washes the walls of the cylinder and the Peanut galleries, a result of the glazed openings around their inner perimeters.

Philip Johnson described his experience of the great atrium by saying, "You seem to float in light." In the tradition of sacred space, its pervasive natural illumination and soaring scale do indeed recall the magic of Baroque church architecture. But does the building work for art?

Ironically, the very light that defines and animates the architecture so successfully poses a problem for viewing the museum's contents. The brise-soleils do not effectively control the bright southern sun that pours through the facade, penetrating the partially open galleries. The high levels of sun also make air-conditioning prohibitively expensive.

These are not new issues for Meier. A similar situation at the High Museum necessitated replacement of the atrium's glazing with glass that reduced light levels, covering of vertical windows with fiber screens and addition of interior screens to the two top floors. At the Frankfurt museum and the Des Moines Art Center addition completed the same year, window coverings had to correct excessive light.

Except for the Des Moines addition, where intimately scaled galleries are enlivened by balconies and ramps, and the Getty Center Museum in Los Angeles (1997) with its classic design, Meier's crisp white interiors all inevitably relate to the white cube's sacred space. But MACBA's long, open galleries (23.5 feet high on the top level, 14.75 feet high on the other two levels), divided by movable partitions placed on brushed stainless-steel blocks, are more anonymous than the roomlike spaces of the architect's Atlanta, Frankfurt and Des Moines museums; they might work as a *Kunsthalle* in which temporary exhibitions would demand specific installations. The Peanut and circular galleries are Meier's nods to the need for specially shaped galleries with which artists might interact, but his heart does not seem to be in the effort: the Peanut is an unresolved space. With no specific program, the architect had to guess what he was designing for; the result is a brilliant spatial exploration that gives little context to the art exhibited in it.

Despite the cost of MACBA, almost double its original estimate, the five years—instead of an estimated twenty months—it took to build and its various functional difficulties, there is general satisfaction with the result. Meier is one of the world's most glamorous architects, and the glamour of his MACBA is already bringing to a deteriorated section of the city the hoped-for renewal. But architecture, not art, is what his museum is about.

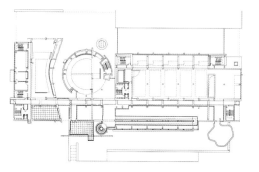

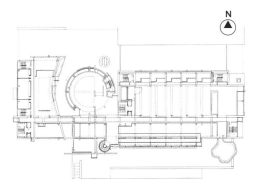

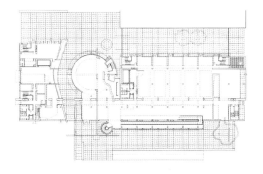

Plans. →
TOP: **Second floor.**
CENTER: **First floor.**
BOTTOM: **Ground floor.**

In its original state, New York's MoMA was a model of so-called neutral, sacred space that worked well for the art shown in it. Today's museums too often are a tame, dumbed-down version of what once was, and they frequently suffer from a lack of attention to the kind of art for which they are intended. Pop art, for example, with its dependence on everyday objects, is, like many contemporary art forms, antithetical to the abstracted nature of sacred space. Furthermore, the days of the sequestered temple of culture are over; late-20th-century museums that ignore the hurly-burly of today's world impart a feeling of unreality to their contents.

Interactive museum interiors such as that of the New York Guggenheim and those of museums as "environmental art" influenced by it can be attacked on many grounds, but supposedly neutral galleries can be just as problematic. At San Francisco and Barcelona, Botta and Meier, both of whom think of museums as cathedrals of culture, have created architecture that fails to enhance the art it is meant to serve. Most of the exhibition spaces in each structure lack a sense of place, and neither museum achieves an integral relationship with its site.

Zumthor's Kunsthaus is suitable only for contemporary art capable of animating its severe setting. In this it may prove to be as limited in what it can successfully exhibit as Peter Eisenman's Wexner Center (see Chapter 7). The strong character of the Kunsthaus's interiors and their discreet connection with the exterior save it from the mediocrity that threatens so many attempts at neutrality. Of the four museums discussed here, Holl's can most satisfactorily accommodate the widest range of art in its diversely shaped spaces, with natural illumination that is also varied. His individualized galleries demonstrate the possibility of lively, art-enhancing sacred space that is not neutral.

Reviewing the relatively short history of the museum, it would appear that there is no such thing as neutrality. There is bland architecture that isolates and deadens art, and there are expressive spaces that point up, elevate and animate art to make it part of our lives.

Chapter 3

The Monographic Museum

There is nothing that quite equals the museum of a single artist; the experience is like being spellbound in a magical play.

Mark Rosenthal,
Curator of 20th-Century Art,
Guggenheim Museum Soho,
New York City

The homes and studios of artists such as Peter Paul Rubens, one of the great artist-collectors of the Baroque period, were early models for the museum. More common art repositories were artists' workplaces with solely their own output, an example that was adapted early in the 19th century as the single-artist museum. Conceptually, these museums enshrine an individual artist, but recent interpretations of the type aren't necessarily sacred spaces as defined here: abstracted spaces meant to disappear in relation to their contents. On the contrary, the Warhol Museum's renovated factory spaces, the Felix-Nussbaum-Haus's dramatic non-Euclidean geometries, the Brancusi Studio—within its formal pavilion—and the Atelier Mimesis are anything but abstract, their architecture interacting strongly with the art they contain. The Tinguely Museum attempts, not altogether successfully, a similar interaction. Even when monographic museums do approximate sacred space, as with the Twombly, Josephsohn and Kirchner museums, the breadth of their presentation—work from different periods of the artists' production, supplemented for Twombly and Kirchner by art in different mediums, including prints, engravings, drawings, paintings and sculpture—conveys an exciting sense of the artistic process. These sacred spaces are also animated by skillful manipulation of natural light.

Dorothea Rockburne refers to drawings as "the bones of thought . . . the hinges" that allow the viewer to understand the paintings they lead to. She is critical of blockbuster exhibitions as they were in the late 1970s: shows like

"The Treasures of Tutankhamun" and various Van Gogh exhibitions that concentrated on masterpieces and ignored the creative process that produced them. Rockburne also cites the problem presented by enormous museums that make it difficult to exhibit works of different scales together. The curator Mark Rosenthal goes further, pointing out that certain artists die when only one of their works is shown: to understand the mystery of Robert Ryman's minimalist white paintings, for example, the viewer must be surrounded by them, and the small scale of Paul Klee's and Agnes Martin's paintings puts them at a disadvantage when shown with those of other artists. Displaying different aspects of a single artist's production in what is, or approximates, his or her working environment is the purpose of the monographic museum. If successful, this museum type enshrines the artist and illuminates the output, providing a chapel-like setting animated by the dynamic relationships between objects.

Historically, the existence of this kind of museum depended on an artist's gift or legacy of major work plus a variety of related materials. The oeuvre being too extensive for an existing, more general institution to display, the bequest dictates that the artist or the artist's collectors, admirers or heirs find a museum for it. In the late 1990s, however, a number of monographic museums are opening regardless of the availability to them of prime works. Furthermore, concern that the content is too limited and fixed and does not offer enough to entice visitors back can cause the name artist to be supplanted as the museum's main focus by changing exhibitions and other attractions.

One of the first monographic museums was Francesco Lazzari's Gipsoteca Canoviana (1836), which was dedicated to the neoclassical sculptor Antonio Canova. Shortly after Canova's death in 1822, his half-brother and heir, Monsignor Giambattista Sartori, decided to build a museum to exhibit what the artist had left in his Rome studio. Dissatisfied with existing displays of single works, he wanted to provide a background of plaster casts, clay models and other preparatory material that would help viewers appreciate the isolated, finished marble sculptures with which they were more familiar.

↑ Antonio Canova Gipsoteca, Possagno, by Francesco Lazzari (1836). Interior.

To hold these materials, a museum in the neoclassical style, the architectural equivalent of the work it was to contain, was built in the garden of the house where Canova was born, in Possagno, northern Italy. The possibility that too elaborate a building would overshadow its contents resulted in a skylit, rectangular room nearly 100 feet long, whose austerity was attenuated by a large raised niche at one end, coffered vaults and three short partition walls. Bas-reliefs were installed on the upper part of the dark walls, busts and portraits on the shelves below, funeral stelae on the partition walls. Individual statues and statue groupings were placed on the floor in a profusion that was meant to compensate for the absence of the specific architectural setting for which each sculpture was conceived. Even though it is in a Modern idiom, Carlo Scarpa's 1,500-square-foot expansion (1957) of the Gipsoteca is in complete harmony with the original building. By angling out the exterior wall of the added wing, Scarpa created a forced perspective that makes the area appear larger than it is. Bringing some glazed corners into the structure and popping others out, adding clerestories and opening one wall to the exterior, he achieved dramatic plays of light that complement the work as effectively as does the building's neoclassical architecture.

Influenced by the Gipsoteca, a younger contemporary of Canova's, the Danish sculptor Bertel Thorvaldsen, began to discuss a museum (1848) for his own work with the architect Gottlieb Bindesbøll. It was the first of many institutions devoted to a single sculptor—such as the David d'Anger Museum in the town from which he took his name and the Musée Rodin in Paris—that were modeled after the Gipsoteca. Also a romantic classicist, whose influence in Italy is said to have exceeded Canova's in the mid-19th century, Thorvaldsen donated his life work together with his collection of antiquities to his native city of Copenhagen. To display this magnificent gift, the king offered a former coach house next to his 18th-century palace, Christiansborg. Bindesbøll added barrel-vaulted porticoes at the front and back of the building and enclosed its courtyard. Particularly in his polychromatic exteriors and interiors that highlight the white sculpture he was influenced by the works of several German architects—Franz Christian Gau, Karl Friedrich Schinkel, Leo von Klenze and Gottfried Semper. Bindesbøll may even have known Semper's colorful private gallery for Conrad Hinrich Donner's Thorvaldsen collection.

The artist wanted small, domestically scaled rooms, lit as his studio was, both horizontally from one side and vertically. In 1814 the architect John Soane had incorporated into his Dulwich College Picture Gallery a mausoleum for Sir Francis Bourgeois, the creator of the collection, and the dealer Noel Desenfans and his wife. This model could have influenced Thorvaldsen's decision to be buried in the courtyard, adding a mausoleum/monument significance to the museum's inherent nationalist symbolism.

From museums built in the spirit of the artist's studio it was a short step to institutionalizing the studio itself. In 1862, spurred by the death of the woman he loved, the French symbolist painter Gustave Moreau began to plan for the preservation of his oil sketches, drawings and watercolors, which he feared might otherwise be lost. By 1895 Moreau had transformed the two top stories of the Paris townhouse he shared with his parents into exhibition spaces, for which

↑ Addition to Gipsoteca, by
Carlo Scarpa (1957). Interior.

← Thorvaldsenianum,
Copenhagen, by Gottlieb
Bindesbøll (1848). Interior.

he bequeathed the initial funding. Moreau's museum opened to the public in 1903, three years after his death.

The two floors are joined by a spiral stair, and the high-ceilinged, spacious rooms with their studio windows have an irresistible charm. Large oil paintings are double-hung on the upper walls; drawings and other smaller works are displayed below them on movable screens and in freestanding armoires. The system recalls the one designed by Soane for his house in London (1813), now Sir John Soane's Museum.

The Gipsoteca, built posthumously; the Thorvaldsenianum, an existing building adapted according to the artist's specifications; and Moreau's institutionalized studio established three basic formats for the monographic museum, which are still imitated. One of the most successful recent examples is the Pablo Picasso Museum in Paris (1985). In 1975 the French government designated a 17th-century mansion to house works by Picasso—"Picasso's Picassos"—as well as the artist's collection of contemporary art, historical paintings and ethnic art, which the authorities had acquired in lieu of inheritance taxes. The large array of Picassos gives a good overview of his life's output even without great examples of his cubist and late paintings, which the museum does not have.

Picasso had lived for many years in Paris, which is therefore an appropriate location for the museum, and Jean Boullier's Baroque Hôtel Salé, like the palatial homes Picasso preferred to live and work in, is a fitting setting for his art. Dominique Bozo was appointed curator of the project, and in 1976 five architects were invited to compete for the commission, eventually awarded to Roland Simounet.

The success of Simounet's project lay in his ability to retain the atmosphere of a historic mansion in an up-to-date museum. He did this by keeping parts of the structure—rococo door frames, flooring, stucco and stone ornamentation—in some rooms, interspersed with new rooms in gutted spaces. Climate control and illumination are hidden: the light of concealed neon uplifters is reflected onto the walls from chamfered recesses around the edges of suspended ceilings. Only in the rooms that retain their stucco ceilings is there a visible source of artificial light; the chandeliers were designed by Diego Giacometti, whose tables, chairs and other furnishings contribute to the museum's domestic setting. Filtered daylight comes from existing windows on both the garden and court sides of the building. Ramps in a skylit ground-floor gallery constructed outside the hôtel's walls lead to exhibition spaces in the basement; the descent offers multiple viewing levels and vistas through interior windows that are particularly interesting for sculpture and that help to animate the space.

A clear path is indicated by the grand stair—preserved, together with the entrance hall, in its entirety—which is the major point of orientation. The visitor is guided by a series of subtle details, such as the different shades of white walls, the direction of the parquet floor and Scarpa-like angled vitrines slipped into corners or alcoves. A devoted Corbusian, Simounet credits the Modern master's example for the "unraveling thread" of the itinerary. Architects Steven Holl and Wolf Prix both cite the example of Simounet's concealment of technology and his use of ramps in their recent museum designs (see Chapters 2 and 7).

The homes and workplaces of a number of 19th-century American artists are today open to the public. But the construction, or adaptation, of a building for a single-artist museum is rare in this country compared with the proliferation of such monographic museums in Europe, where they have enjoyed great popularity from the start. The opening in 1993 of a Norman Rockwell Museum in Stockbridge, Massachusetts, designed by Robert A. M. Stern, followed in 1994 by Richard Gluckman's Andy Warhol Museum in Pittsburgh, in 1995 by Renzo Piano's Cy Twombly Gallery in Houston and in 1997 by Gluckman's Georgia O'Keeffe Museum in Santa Fe may signify a new direction.

← TOP: Gustave Moreau Museum,
Paris (1895). Interior.
BOTTOM: Picasso Museum, Paris,
renovated by Roland Simounet
(1985). Ground-floor gallery.

ANDY WARHOL MUSEUM

Pittsburgh, Pennsylvania

by **Richard Gluckman Architects**

1994

73,000 square-foot existing building

15,000 square-foot addition

35,000 square feet of exhibition space

approximately $12 million

↑ Gallery.

The 1920s warehouse, clad in terra-cotta tile, that houses the Andy Warhol Museum looks to be the polar opposite of the Picasso Museum's refined *hôtel particulier.* In fact, Richard Gluckman's adaptation of this commercial space is as appropriate to the pop artist as Simounet's historic mansion is to Picasso. Given that Warhol used mass-production techniques and called one of his studios the Factory, the warehouse museum is an apt replication of his famed workplace.

The Andy Warhol Foundation was established two years before the artist's death in 1987. After the work was inherited, attempts to obtain permanent exhibition space for it in New York were unsuccessful, so the foundation's directors turned to Pittsburgh, Warhol's birthplace. The city had lost the collections of two of its most famous citizens—Henry Clay Frick and Andrew Mellon—to New York, and a combination of civic pride plus the tourist possibilities of a Warhol museum made it determined not to let this collection get away. Braving the state legislature's distaste for the artist's lifestyle, the Carnegie Institute obtained state funding, an accomplishment that the institute's current director, Phillip M. Johnston, described as most unusual "for something as untried in this country as a single-artist museum."

A covered bridge enclosed by dark-blue mottled walls leads to the museum entrance. The bridge's aluminum-leaf ceiling recalls the silver-painted factory, and the large, "living room" exhibition space it introduces, furnished with commodious leather couches, is modeled after the English country-house look

Warhol favored in the 1970s. From this reception area the visitor can go to the small theater, filled with vintage Marcel Breuer movie-house seating, to offices and archives in the four-story addition or to the old building and its seven floors of exhibition space. The warehouse was stripped of everything except its concrete, space-defining structural columns and beams. Daylight from a rare window, and on the top floor from light scoops, supplements lighting that is deliberately old-fashioned: spotlights highlight the paintings rather than the whole wall. The galleries' crude, commercial character, so appropriate to this artist, is further emphasized by the contrasting smooth, colored, unarticulated surfaces of the horizontal hallways that meet the backlit main stairway. From the hallways extend variously proportioned white-walled galleries. Replicas of some of Warhol's own environments—cow- or Mao-papered rooms and *Silver Clouds*, his 1966 installation of helium-filled, metalized plastic balloons—contribute to the Warholian ambience.

The museum's success in conjuring Warhol's spirit compensates for its not having examples from every aspect of his oeuvre. Despite the large number of works shown, none of the museum's founders—the Dia and Warhol foundations and the Carnegie Institute—owned such important pieces as the early, hand-painted comic book characters, the paintings by numbers or a major canvas in the Marilyn series. Like the Picasso, the Warhol is a monographic museum that evokes a strong image of the artist despite an incomplete representation of his work.

← Stairway and corridor.

THE CY TWOMBLY GALLERY

Houston, Texas

by **Renzo Piano Building Workshop**

1995

11,000 square feet

6,400 square feet of exhibition space

$4.2 million

In contrast to the Warhol's industrial setting, and incomplete collection, the Cy Twombly Gallery, located across the street from the Menil Collection to which it belongs (see Chapter 1), closely follows historical models. The artist donated major works of art (from 1954 to the present) and participated in the museum's design. Even the Genoese architect Renzo Piano's Modern evocation of a column-and-lintel entrance to this pink concrete box refers to the architectural tradition of the first monographic museums.

Twombly's refined scribbles and abstract calligraphy are grounded in the Classical past: the artist has spent a major portion of his life in Rome, and for this building Piano employed an Italianate vocabulary that is quite different from the American syntax he used for the Menil's gray, wood-frame structure. The Twombly consists of eight 28-foot-square windowless spaces, one of which is a double gallery, 16.5 feet high. The plan, the seamless, hand-troweled white plaster walls and the frameless doors all derive from Italy. These characteristics, together with proportions dictated by the paintings and a special system for diffused natural light, make it an ideal place for Twombly's art. No changing shows are planned for the Twombly, for which there is a formal commitment to display the present exhibition permanently.

Piano's "leaf" roof for the Menil Collection marked the beginning of the architect's series of innovative museum roofs and ceilings. At the Twombly a four-part system consists of a steel grid that contains the mechanical systems and supports a layer of angled aluminum louvers; beneath these are a glazed skylight with a panel of motorized louvers and, finally, a tautly stretched canvas ceiling. The result is an otherworldly luminescence worthy of work that has been described by the French theorist Roland Barthes as producing an experience comparable to a Buddhist awakening. Filtered, the powerful Texas sun enlivens Twombly's baroque pastel palette without glare or shadows; only for pale monochromatic paintings like *Lexington Suite* (1959) does the lighting seem harsh. In the absence of sun, however, the galleries lose some of their interest; artificial illumination is reserved for the rare occasions when the gallery is open at night. For light-sensitive pieces, the large central gallery (a space that resembles the inner sanctum of a pagan temple) has an opaque ceiling.

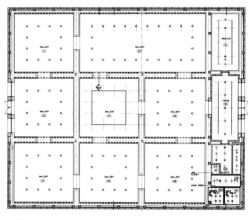

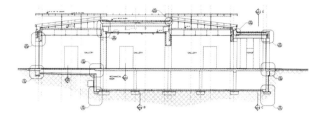

↑ LEFT: Plan.
  RIGHT: Section showing ceiling system.

← Entrance facade with Menil Collection at right.

↓ Galleries.

HANS JOSEPHSOHN: THE CONGIUNTA FOUNDATION

Giornico, Switzerland

by **Peter Märkli**

1992

2,420 square feet

$332,650

For its architect, Peter Märkli, the Congiunta Foundation is "just a house for reliefs and half figures." Indeed, Märkli doesn't think of the Congiunta Foundation as a museum, and of all the enterprises discussed here it is the least museumlike: built of raw concrete, it is without electricity and water or the standard museum amenities of climate control, security or social and commercial facilities. No entrance fee is solicited.

Sculptor Hans Josephsohn, the subject of this museum, was born in 1920 in Königsberg, then in East Prussia. A Jew whose parents were exterminated by the Nazis, he took refuge in Zurich in 1939. His life is reflected in the alienation of his bronzes: human figures that convey a sense of metaphysical discomfort.

Entrance facade. ↑

The foundation was created by several art lovers particularly interested in Josephsohn's work; the group included Märkli, who discovered the site for the project in Switzerland's upper Ticino district. The Alpine foothills are a rugged prelude to the picturesque grandeur of the taller peaks; small mountains crowd in on both sides of the valley, casting long shadows as soon as the sun passes its apex. The rocky terrain gives the setting an even darker cast. Although the museum sits in an open, sunlit field, the surrounding landscape is well suited to its stark architecture, which in turn relates to Josephsohn's rough-surfaced, existential figures.

The Congiunta Foundation could be described as a simple raw-concrete box, but it is simple in the way that a Barnett Newman painting is simple. Its architect is a theoretician who works from a complex dimensional module, leaving the realization of his buildings to a colleague. Even the exterior formwork has meaning: its pattern of normal, and what has been called "leftover," lengths characterizes the difference between the building's artistic concept and its technical actualization. Because the sculpture doesn't need to be seen in the round, the museum's narrow spaces are uniquely suited to it—but lest his own intentions compete with the artist's, Märkli asked the mason to determine the formwork for the interior rather than dictate it himself. While the artist and architect have known and admired each others' work for many years, Märkli specifies that Josephsohn did not participate in the design process.

Like the nearby Romanesque church of San Nicolao, the museum turns its back on the town. No path leads to it. The building is sited at the end of a hayfield, and its strict linearity continues that of the vineyards it abuts. Without base, crown or windows, the 138-foot-long museum appears from the exterior

Western facade. ↑

Third gallery, with →
small rooms at left.

as a stone monolith. Within, however, it provides four different spatial experiences dependent only on changes in height and length and firmly punctuated by the awkwardly high thresholds that separate the three main rooms. The first space—almost square and relatively lofty—presents Josephsohn's early (1950s) abstract reliefs. The second gallery is low and therefore receives more intense light; it leads as if it were a corridor to a third space equal to it in length but almost twice as high, where four separate entrances open at one side to skylit, chapel-like rooms that provide yet another kind of space. The soaring third gallery achieves the monumentality of a great church apse. Light penetrates the three main galleries through translucent Plexiglas clerestories that form the sides of a lantern running the length of the sheet-metal roof; steel I-beams support a plywood ceiling that opens into the lantern.

The building's off-center entrance door marks an axis for the clerestories and for the frameless openings between the three large rooms. The north-south orientation ensures either direct illumination of the bas-reliefs that hang on the deeper walls of the second and third galleries, where there are also freestanding bronzes, or reflected light from the wall facing them.

Conceived by its founders as a rural shrine, the Congiunta Foundation requires a pilgrimage: located in the small town of Giornico, it is over 100 miles north of Milan and even farther from Zurich, the two major cities closest to it. This unusual enterprise has been widely praised in the architectural press, and even without publicity, people are finding their way here: at the local café, where the museum's key can be picked up, the owner reports an average of three hundred visitors a month, consisting largely of European and American student groups. What is remarkable about this is that Josephsohn is not a world-class artist, nor is Märkli's architecture, on its own, so extraordinary. Rather, it is the two together that provide the powerful aesthetic—even spiritual—experience.

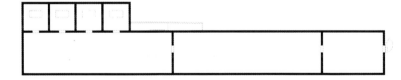

Ground-floor plan. ↑

Longitudinal section. ↓

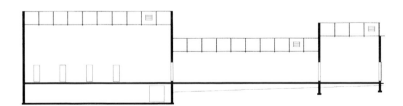

THE ERNST LUDWIG KIRCHNER MUSEUM

Davos, Switzerland
by **Annette Gigon and Mike Guyer**
1992

23,680 square feet

10,440 square feet of exhibition space

$7.5 million

← Exterior with entry.

Like Märkli, Annette Gigon and Mike Guyer are thought of as minimalists, yet nothing could be more different from the Congiunta Foundation than their Kirchner Museum. Märkli's architecture is truly minimal in its bare-bones construction and lack of all amenities, whereas Gigon and Guyer achieve minimal effects by means of sophisticated materials and structural techniques. In both museums, the architects defer to the artists with interiors that, in the manner of sacred space, focus attention on the object. But while the Congiunta's narrow galleries, rough textures and diversified light effects relate specifically to its contents, only the views to the spectacular mountains that Kirchner painted tie his namesake museum to the art it houses.

The Kirchner Museum is a startling presence, perched as it is like an ice cube on the Davos hillside, an elegant addition to the famous ski resort's surprisingly dowdy architecture. Its glazed surfaces reflect light in a dialogue with the surrounding snow and ice, and its flat roof, surfaced with crushed glass instead of pebbles, shimmers in the crystalline mountain light. Upon closer inspection, the glass cube reveals its different components: transparent glazing for the entry pavilion and at the ends of the corridors, and frosted insulating glass that appears opaque before the high concrete walls of the ground level but is translucent in the upper lanterns (where structural elements can be glimpsed). As does Gigon and Guyer's 1995 addition to the Winterthur Museum of Fine Arts (see Chapter 4), the Kirchner explores glazing's versatility.

The main level contains three galleries that measure 29.5 by 59 by 15.5 feet, a smaller rectangular gallery and the circulation areas. The library, bookshop and support functions are located on the lower level, which faces the southeast on the

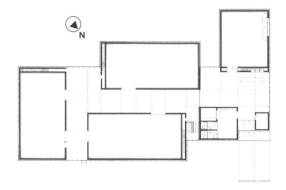

site's slope. The museum is entered via a rising ramp; the low ceilings and raw-concrete surfaces of the entrance foyer and adjoining corridors evoke industrial spaces. Galleries do not adjoin one another but must be entered individually from the corridor. The deliberate crudeness of this interconnection makes the extraordinary refinement of proportion, detailing and light in the exhibition spaces all the more captivating. In contrast with the rough corridors that look to the exterior, these sublimely lit, ethereal spaces are impervious to the outside world.

Because snow often covers alpine roofs, the architects devised opaque lanterns to crown each gallery: their insulating glass walls admit daylight only laterally. Dependent on this lateral light, the galleries had to be located in discrete volumes separated by low, wide corridors. The influx of natural light is regulated by louvers adjusted either by a sun-sensitive computer program for each of the spaces or, in the absence of sun, by an electrical or manual system. Within the lantern spaces, in which some thermal energy is stored, special neon tubes are directed upward and reflect from the glass sheathing. Matte-glass ceilings diffuse natural and artificial light in the galleries, whose plaster walls are painted a luminescent beige.

Ground floor plan. ↑
Galleries and corridor. ↓

A founder of the bold, often brutal art movement die Brücke, Ernst Ludwig Kirchner lived from 1917 until his suicide in 1938 near Davos, the Swiss cure-and-resort town in Thomas Mann's *The Magic Mountain*. In 1982, mindful of a vast potential audience in Davos's 2.6 million visitors a year, the town's director of tourism opened a small Kirchner display at the local post office. The exhibition was a modest success, but by the time it took place the artist's major works were elsewhere. The subsequent donation of 500 Kirchner objects by Roman N. Ketterer, the artist's executor, together with important loans provided substantial material, but as with the Warhol, many of the masterpieces were missing. Still, the gift justified the creation of a space to hold it, implemented in 1989 by a competition. In planning a Kirchner museum that also had to be able to accommodate borrowed exhibitions, the architecture committee wanted to have its cake and eat it too. One has only to see Kirchner's easel painting and hand-carved furniture—the latter inspired by South Sea island sculpture—in the two nearby farmhouses in which the artist lived and worked to understand the issue of showing similar works in the museum's pared-down galleries. The houses now belong to Eberhard Kornfeld, an art dealer and benefactor of the museum, who has kept the interiors much as they were when Kirchner lived there, although neither is open to the public. The houses' smaller walls provide a framework for the paintings and even more so for the graphic work that is lacking in the larger museum. Wood-beam ceilings add texture against which the sensual furniture plays. Even the houses' spotlights are more appropriate than the museum's diffused light for work made in somber interiors.

Annette Gigon began her career with Herzog and de Meuron (Mike Guyer with Rem Koolhaas), and for the Kirchner the example of her former office was followed: influencing the design was Rémy Zaugg, a Swiss artist who is committed to the importance of serenity in the viewing of art. Kirchner's work, a large portion of which was created for the ornate rooms of middle-class households in the early part of the century, is not best served by this kind of self-effacing setting. Informed by an ingenious handling of natural light, the Kirchner would be ideal for certain Modern and contemporary art, but it provides an insufficient context for the powerful German Expressionist works. The museum's programmatic insistence on neutral architecture and changing exhibitions shifts its focus away from the artist to whom it is dedicated.

 Gallery.

THE JEAN TINGUELY MUSEUM

Basel, Switzerland

by **Mario Botta**

1996

65,200 square feet

30,850 square feet of exhibition space

$23 million

Basel appears to be the ideal place to display the work of the sculptor Jean Tinguely (1925–91), who grew up there and whose work has been a street presence since the 1977 installation of his *Carnival Fountain* in front of the centrally located municipal theater. Tinguely lived from the age of two in Basel where, reportedly, his observations of nature in the surrounding woods inspired his first *meta-mécaniques*—hydraulic wheels with sound. But the artist was born in Fribourg and in his last years made his studio in a large bottle factory in a remote rural area of that canton. He installed exhibition spaces in his workshop at La Verrerie, which was considered the logical place for a museum by those close to Tinguely. It was here that 55 works were stored, which his longtime companion and collaborator, the sculptor Niki de Saint Phalle, donated to the new museum in Basel, a gesture criticized by some as wresting Tinguely away from his friends. There was, however, no structure or financial support for La Verrerie.

Tinguely described himself as an artist of movement, and taken to its extreme, "movement" predicates works that by their built-in self-destruction avoid the "museumification" rejected so emphatically by the confirmed political, social and artistic rebel. Though tempered toward the end of his life, Tinguely's attitude is in fact hard to reconcile with the formal building designed for his work by Mario Botta.

The museum was initiated by Paul Sacher, an orchestral conductor whose sculptor-collector wife, Maja Oeri, was active in Basel's cultural life. Oeri, who died in 1989, had been acquiring Tinguely's work since the 1960s. Realizing that their Tinguely collection was too large in number and scale for any existing museum, Sacher arranged for financing of the new facility by the Basel-based Hoffmann–La Roche drug company, founded by the father of Oeri's first husband.

Entrance facade. ↓

The city's requirement of a 10-foot-high sound-barrier wall along the museum's street side explains the blandness of that facade, constructed in the same local red limestone as the Basel Cathedral. Only a small area of Botta's typical patterned brickwork articulates the wall, described by him as "une vibration de la pierre" (a vibration of stone). In contrast are the five glazed bays of the Solitude Park facade, which are crowned by a lozenge-shaped white metal framework roof reminiscent of Botta's celebration tent in Bellinzona (1991) and his shopping center in Florence (1992). A covered entrance arcade to the museum and the park on the broad Grenzacher Street connects with a diagonal path to the park's farthest entrance.

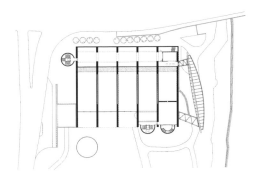

Park facade. ↑

Plans. →
TOP: **Upper floor.**
CENTER: **Mezzanine floor.**
BOTTOM: **Ground floor.**

Sections. ↓

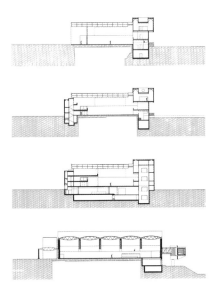

N ◀

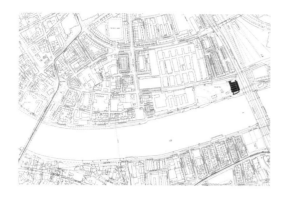

Site plan. ↑

Botta's selection of historic Solitude Park as the museum's location extends neighborhood activity to the river's edge, but he has missed the potential of this beautiful bankside site. A complicated entrance circuit passes from a ticket lobby and museum shop, with no access to the interior, to the real access—a glazed, curved terrace whose supporting columns mar scenic views from the museum's riverside café. The terrace gives visitors only a transitory glimpse of the environment that nurtured the artist, whereas the existing café could have provided a more leisurely experience of it.

Interior circulation is equally controlling. The terrace leads not to the main gallery but to a mezzanine gallery overlooking it. Passage through its bays brings visitors to a stair and elevator, both of which appear insufficient for the expected attendance, and up to a five-part, Schinkel-inspired enfilade that is illuminated by chamfered clerestories. Upon reaching the end of this top gallery, visitors must retrace their steps to the stairs or elevator and down to a series of artificially lit basement galleries before reaching the climactic main gallery.

Rising to a height of 33 feet and extending the full length of the building and over two-thirds of its width, the vast skylit space facing Solitude Park is likened by Botta to a *place couverte* (covered town square). It can be divided into smaller areas by lowering four wide partition walls from bridge beams that support the roof's metal framework, a solution made necessary by the five-story underground Rhine-water treatment reservoir directly below the building. The museum's director, Pontus Hulten, who was long associated with the Centre Pompidou, served as principal client for the project. He encouraged the large scale of the main space and its position at the end of the trajectory on the theory that "if people come to small galleries after big galleries they think they are too small."

The Tinguely fails on several counts. Unlike the Picasso and Warhol museums, this building does not compensate for gaps in the collection. Despite the inclusion of evocative objects from the artist's life, such as his racing car as part of a piece by Eva Aeppli, the rigid circulation and formality seem antithetical to Tinguely's work and personality. His clanking sculptures, made of rusted, found parts look out of place in this pristine setting. They are further diminished by conspicuous black light fixtures on the ceiling that bear an unnerving resemblance to components of the sculpture. In its similarity to an open loft space, the expansive main gallery is the only area that relates to the spirit of Tinguely, but even it will be compromised if it is divided for temporary exhibitions.

← Upper floor onfilado.

↓ Main gallery,
  looking toward mezzanine.

THE BRANCUSI STUDIO

Paris, France

by **Renzo Piano Building
Workshop**

1997

4,500 square feet

1,880 square feet in the original studio

$7.8 million

↑ Entrance facade.

↓ TOP: Ceiling detail.
BOTTOM: Plan.

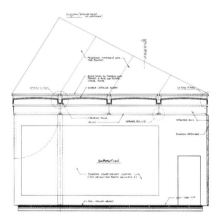

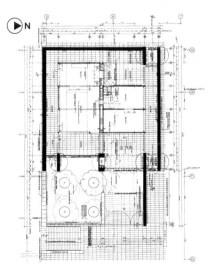

A curious combination of museum and artist's studio, Renzo Piano's pavilion housing the reconstructed work and living space of Constantin Brancusi (1876–1957) stands on the plaza in front of the Centre Georges Pompidou. The sculptor had stipulated that his legacy to the state depended on its display within a replica of his studio, one of several artists' studios on the impasse Ronsin in Paris; the area was requisitioned in 1952 to make way for a hospital. Litigation over control of the estate delayed until 1962 the studio's first reconstruction in Paris at the Musée National d'Art Moderne on the avenue du Président Wilson. When that museum's contents were moved to the newly inaugurated Pompidou, the Brancusi studio was duplicated in a prefabricated structure that was closed in 1990 due to maintenance and security problems. The current reconstruction, as before at the north side of the plaza fronting the center, enjoys a more elegant container than the previous two, but visitors are no longer allowed inside.

Encased in a climate-controlled, travertine and glass mini-museum inset in a granite podium, the studio is reached via a stairway that rises from the plaza to the top of the podium. From here, visitors turn ninety degrees and descend broad, shallow stairs beside a small

← Interior.

formal garden to a reception area that provides a transition between the boisterous plaza and the serenity of Brancusi's world. They then proceed counterclockwise through an ambulatory surrounding the studio. Brancusi's spaces are meticulously re-created to approximate the original, but they are effectively sealed by floor-to-ceiling glazing that replaces windows, doors and most of the east and south sides, where just enough wall remains to provide a background for the *Endless Column*s. In a gesture toward the parent museum, the glazed entrance wall allows tantalizing glimpses into the studio from the Pompidou. The asymmetry between the studio's three-bay display area and two-bay living/storage area leaves an extra bay, which is used to exhibit material related to Brancusi.

Evocatively, the very jazz and folk music that the artist listened to on his record player is audible as one passes through this luminous pavilion. Above the studio north-facing light sheds replicate original ones; the viewing corridors have flat roofs made of slightly curved glass panels overlaid with perforated stainless-steel panels that are also used for the sheds' opaque parts. A simplified version of his roof for the Cy Twombly Gallery, Piano's layered roof here consists of an exterior shading device, a middle glass panel and an interior vellum ceiling. The diffused light of the viewing corridor is subordinate to the brighter light of the studio, which highlights the art within it.

The skillful modulation of natural light, the unity of the dark concrete floor in the studio and corridor and the floating quality—created by reveals at the ceiling and floor—of the corridor walls are seamless and help to mitigate the studio's inaccessibility. Looking at a space, however, is not the same as being in that space. Instead of the original studio having been turned into a museum, a replica of it has become a museum artifact. But circumstances dictated this, and preservation of the artist's working methods within a facsimile of their context honors the basic concept of the monographic museum.

FELIX-NUSSBAUM-HAUS

Osnabrück, Germany

by Daniel Libeskind

1998

27,000 square feet

10,700 square feet of exhibition space

$7.8 million

If, in concept, the monographic museum emphasizes the artist, it is the architect of the repository for Felix Nussbaum's work who has put that building on the map. Nussbaum (1904–44) was a secondary artist whose portraits of alienation and suffering were heavily dependent on Giorgio de Chirico; his name was virtually unknown until it came to be associated with the Deconstructivist architect Daniel Libeskind.

Born to a wealthy Jewish family in Osnabrück, Germany, Nussbaum lived in exile in a number of European countries from 1933 until 1939, when he was arrested in Paris and detained as an enemy alien in the south of France. He escaped and survived in hiding until 1944; tracked down by the Gestapo in Brussels, he was sent to Auschwitz, where he was killed. In the last decade, Wendelin Zimmer, an art critic, and Peter Junk, a librarian, two non-Jewish inhabitants of Osnabrück, have endeavored to recover Nussbaum's art and to publicize his life as emblematic of the fate of the city's Jews in the Holocaust.

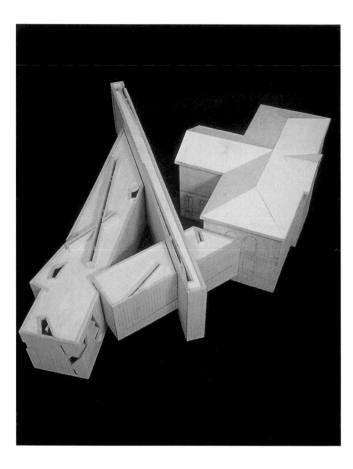

Exterior with Cultural History ↑
Museum at right. Model.

The local savings bank, Nussbaum's principal collector, and the municipal government initiated a museum project with an open competition for which there was the surprisingly high number of 296 submissions. In response to the program's call for an enlargement of the existing Cultural History Museum, Libeskind designed a dramatic new entrance to that museum, using forms that express Nussbaum's role as historic symbol as much as artist.

Like his Jewish Museum in Berlin (see Chapter 7), but on a much smaller scale in size and budget, Libeskind's building is charged with the content of memory. Sited in a park that faces the town's former city wall, the tripartite structure consists of a long, narrow (7.25 feet) concrete Gallery/Corridor, whose claustrophobic space evokes the conditions in which Nussbaum worked while in hiding. A ramped floor adjoins the rectangular wood House containing galleries, an auditorium, a café and the zinc-clad Bridge leading to the older museum. The House is aligned with a former neighborhood synagogue. As at the Berlin museum, window slits that appear to have been slashed at random are dictated by spatial and functional references—in this case, to places within the town (school-

house, home, shops) as they intersect an axis drawn from Auschwitz. After the design was completed, excavation of the site revealed three intact arches from the Peace Bridge, part of the city's ancient fortifications. The symmetrical relationship of the old structure and Libeskind's new Bridge enriches the project's imagery and historical significance.

The concrete walls of the Gallery/Corridor will be used to exhibit work that Nussbaum painted in various prison camps and holding stations. The House and the Bridge will give corresponding space to the city's temporary exhibitions and to the permanent collection: in the plaster interiors of the House, pre-1933 works that represent illusory normality; in the metallic interiors of the Bridge, later works.

← Two levels of Gallery/Corridor. Model.

↓ Plans.
TOP: **First floor.**
CENTER: **Mezzanine floor.**
BOTTOM: **Ground floor.**

Libeskind's design is a study in diagonals. The oblique angles where the segments meet; the asymmetry of the House's auditorium, cafeteria and mezzanine; the way in which the stairwell is wedged partially into one side; the placement of the skylights in all three segments, with the Gallery/Corridor's roof appearing to have slipped sideways; and even the ramps and the House's gently sloping ground floor all contribute to a feeling of unease suitable to this museum's subject matter. At the same time, the design enlivens the viewing spaces.

The Nussbaum museum's double agenda of art and social consciousness should be well served. Only the narrowness of the Gallery/Corridor poses the question of whether this particular area can fulfill its function as an exhibition space as effectively as it will call forth the horror of persecution.

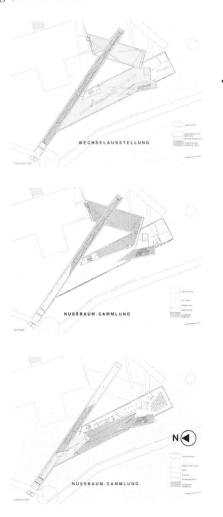

ATELIER MIMESIS

**Munich-Ottobrunn,
Germany**

by **Peter Haimerl,
Ralph Feldmeier** and
Maria Laurent
1993

1,100 square feet

$135,000

A small, futuristic workplace and display area near Munich for the sculptor Beate Schubert is a thoroughly contemporary reinterpretation of the artist-collector's studio of old. Inspired by her childhood memories of playgrounds, tents and the circus, Schubert commissioned three architects who worked with a supplier known for the fabric structures seen widely in Africa and the Middle East. The young architectural team, two of whom trained in the office of Peter Eisenman, actually did much of the construction, which they liken to "an erector set, for which no pencils or drawings were used."

An angled tailgate that looks like the back of an aircraft carrier opens to an 18-by-38-by-18-foot exhibition area that is joined to a slightly larger studio; the two volumes rest on a concrete slab. They consist entirely of prefabricated materials, with standard scaffolding providing the structural framework for the aluminum sandwich plates, Plexiglas sheeting and huge air-inflated Teflon pillows (the studio roof and two of its walls). The Teflon foliate is almost transparent, and delicate, electrically operated aluminum louvers on the interior adjust incoming light. Garage doors at each of the studio's three levels allow airflow for this space, which is also air-conditioned. Volumes can easily be opened, closed or expanded, and the structure's adaptability fits into the architects' concept of a flexible city, in which low-cost housing, for example, is easily assembled and dismantled.

Schubert uses the studio's three levels for the plaster figures she creates and the partially opaque exhibition area for work by herself and by other artists. Displays silhouetted against the studio's translucent walls are more dramatic than those in the exhibition area. Both rooms can accommodate a variety of functions by the simple rearrangement of their lightweight partitions.

Like the Goetz Collection in another Munich suburb (see Chapter 1), the Atelier Mimesis is located near the client's home, in this case an old barn, and is open to the public. Here all parallels end, since the formality of the former and flexibility of the latter are in total contrast with each other. Moreover, Schubert's exhibition of work by a range of artists also sets her gallery apart from other single-artist museums.

↑ Exterior with entry.

← Studio.

Today's monographic museums diverge widely from their 19th-century antecedents. Even when limited to preparatory work (the Canova Gipsoteca's plaster casts, for example), the forerunners of this building type convey every aspect of the artist's oeuvre. Inclusive representation is no longer considered essential, however, in establishing a museum for the artist. Whereas the neoclassical Canova and Thorvaldsen museums were stylistically the architectural extension of both artists' work, monographic museums now do not necessarily relate to their contents.

With incomplete representations, the Picasso and Warhol museums nevertheless call up a picture of the artist. Libeskind has produced a similar effect at the Felix-Nussbaum-Haus, in which the work of a secondary painter is strengthened by powerfully evocative architecture. In the Tinguely Museum, conversely, shortcomings in the permanent collection are compounded by architecture that is antithetical to the sculptor's work and personality.

The Kirchner Museum's attempt to accommodate temporary exhibitions as well as a large permanent collection also poses problems. While the accomplished architecture of this museum is perfectly suited to some art, it relates only marginally to Kirchner's and fails to convey a sense of the artist's spirit and working conditions. Changing exhibitions planned for the Tinguely also threaten that building's best space.

If the Kirchner is a monographic museum in which the dominant spirit has been sacrificed to versatility, the Brancusi is even more of a duality. In order to convey a sense of process, several new museums—the Aristide Maillol in Paris and the J. Paul Getty in Los Angeles, for example—now include re-creations of artists' studios in large vitrine-like settings. However, to apply this format to the reconstruction of an actual workplace that the artist expected viewers to walk through transforms his intentions. As discreet as Piano is with the Brancusi, the program he had to deal with creates a disjunction between art and architecture, whereas the singularly dynamic Atelier Mimesis is today's high-tech interpretation of the artists' studio and collection.

Of the museums discussed in this chapter, the Hans Josephsohn and the Twombly approximate most closely the classic monographic prototype. Both benefit from first-rate collections, to which they are devoted exclusively, with no provision for temporary exhibitions. In each case, the artist himself exerted some influence on the design—although more so with the Twombly.

Even when aspects of the 19th-century models are not emulated, monographic, like private, museums tend to have distinctive architecture closely linked to their locales. The Kirchner Museum makes the visitor acutely aware that it is sited in the area where the artist worked, as do most of the other museums included here. Furthermore, their focused contents have stimulated architects to imaginative responses that contrast with the sameness of so many recent large art institutions. Because the monographic museum is limited in scope and size and tends to enjoy strong local support, it continues to be a viable art venue. That private funding alone sustains most of these museums is one of the most persuasive endorsements of their validity.

Chapter 4

The Museum as Subject Matter: Artists' Museums and Their Alternative Spaces

Artists have always been of two minds about public institutions for the exhibition of their work. The founding by Louis XVIII in 1818 of a museum for living artists—at Paris's Palais du Luxembourg—immediately prompted Théodore Géricault and a few years later Eugène Delacroix to make huge canvases apparently intended for it. Conversely, later in the 19th century, artists rebelled against the prime venue for mass exposure of contemporary art, the Salon. Far more popular than museums, these government-sponsored annual or biennial exhibitions were controlled by a jury. Lasting from a few weeks to several months, they were first held in the Louvre's Salon Carré, then in its Grande Galerie and from 1855 onward in the

Palais de l'Industrie (replaced in 1900 by the Grand Palais): paintings were hung cheek-by-jowl from floor to ceiling, with works by individual artists often separated from one another. The Salons were a powerful factor in determining the fate of a career, and submissions far exceeded available space. When in 1855 the jury rejected three of Gustave Courbet's entries, he constructed his own temporary exhibition pavilion, possibly the first artist-designed exhibition space. Courbet repeated this procedure in 1867, at which time Edouard Manet followed his lead and built a pavilion of his own. Courbet, Manet and later the Impressionists created alternatives to the official Salon just as contemporary artists have found alternatives to museums and commercial galleries. In the 19th century, however, dissatisfaction targeted institutional practice rather than the viewing conditions that are so important today.

By the early 20th century, it was the space itself and the ability to alter the viewer's perception of it that had captured the attention of artists. The Russian Constructivists Vladimir Tatlin, Alexander Rodchenko and Georgy Yakulov built fabrications in wood, metal and cardboard for the Café Pittoresque in Moscow (1917) that were meant to destroy the idea of a room as an enclosed space with solid walls. Another such endeavor was made by the collagist Kurt Schwitters in his Merzbau (in progress from 1923). Some artists used only planes of color to control space: van Doesburg at the Café de l'Aubette in Strasbourg (1928), Mondrian at his Paris studio in the 1920s and in several subsequent experiments. At approximately the same time, El Lissitzky and Frederick Kiesler applied the idea of three-dimensional interactive space to exhibition rooms (see Chapter 7). All of these efforts were limited to interventions within existing structures, and it appears to have been Marcel Duchamp—arguably the century's most innovative artist—who was the first artist actually to design a self-contained museum, though a conceptual one.

Duchamp's implied criticism of the museum as an institution has had many imitators. Among Conceptual artists the most notable is Marcel Broodthaers, whose homage to and parody of the museum extended over time from a display of 19th-century postcards in his townhouse in Brussels (1968)—"Museum of Modern Art, Department of Eagles, Nineteenth-century Section"—to an exhibition of 300 objects at the Kunsthalle in Dusseldorf (1972). Other artists have addressed the museum as a design problem, making, or envisioning, structures that could provide alternative ways of presenting art.

Given the opportunity to create a museum, artists have almost always produced an extension of their own work—what the MoMA curator Kynaston McShine calls "the museum as subject matter." Ellsworth Kelly affirmed the rationale: "What artist," he asked, "would want to exhibit in another artist's museum?" Indeed, several of the designs discussed here were made solely for the art of their creators, two of these—Jackson Pollock's and Patrick Ireland's—within shells designed by someone else. But all of them provide the kind of keen insight into the problems of viewing art that might be expected from the makers of that art.

THE BOÎTE-EN-VALISE

by **Marcel Duchamp**

1936–41

16.125 by 14.125 by 5.4 inches

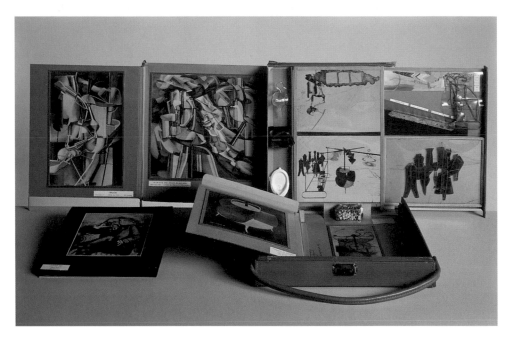

← Boîte-en-Valise, open.

Duchamp likened the exhibition of a single work to the amputation of an arm or a leg. His museum, the Boîte-en-Valise, gave him a special framework in which to show his oeuvre, progressing from one work to another within an enclosure whose proportions, colors, textures and relationships were determined solely by the art. The Boîte has been called a catalogue raisonné, but as Ecke Bonk points out in his monograph on it, rather than having the linear sequence of a book, Duchamp's mini-museum simulates the horizontals and verticals of a room, reflecting in its spatial construction and arrangement of reproductions the overlaps and cross-references of the artist's production. And like most artist-designed museums, the Boîte does not allow for expansion.

The project's roots go back to 1914, when Duchamp photographed some of his notes and one drawing, reproduced them at full scale and assembled them in what is thought to have been five boxed sets. Twenty years later he elaborated this format for notes related to his masterpiece, *The Bride Stripped Bare by Her Bachelors, Even (The Large Glass)*. The artist then decided to apply the same methodology to a reference work of his entire output, reproduced in miniature.

In the mid-1930s Duchamp traveled from Paris to Connecticut, California, Cleveland and back in order to document his work, which was mostly in private collections. He then started the painstaking job of replicating each object by hand, basing the replicas on photographs by such masters of the medium as

Man Ray and Alfred Stieglitz. For two-dimensional objects Duchamp used arcane collotype printing, hand-colored through stencils. The actual execution of these multiples was delegated to a workshop, just as the miniature urinals for *Fountain* were made by a ceramicist. He also designed labels that established a graphic continuity.

Originally conceived as an edition of 300, the Boîte went through three decades of editions, the first of which (1941) consisted of 20 copies, every one inscribed to its owner and including an original drawing. Each box was placed in a traveling salesman's sample valise. Each was fitted with guide rails for the two sliding pullouts and contained 69 reproductions: 17 formed a mobile part of the box itself, the rest were unmounted in loose black four-page foldouts. Three-dimensional replicas such as *Fountain* were attached vertically to the inside of the lid. These various elements would unfold, slide and overlap in specific spatial arrangements that determined the meaning of the objects through their relationship to each other.

The Boîte furthered Duchamp's lifelong preoccupation with the nature and relationship of art and reproduction and provided yet another way for him to blur the boundaries, as he always had, between conventional art and ready-made objects, between the sexes and between words: he signed the Boîte and other works RROSE SELAVY (life is eros), a fictitious twin. The mini-museum also embodied one of Duchamp's most enduring concepts—that the artist is not alone in performing a creative act but needs an interpreting spectator to bring the work into contact with the external world. In her book *unpacking Duchamp: art in transit* Dalia Judovitz explains how the process of manually taking out the contents of the valise removes art from what Duchamp regarded as the museum's sacrosanct precinct and makes it part of a larger reality. Thus, the Boîte "replaces the museum's authority as an institution mediating our perception of art with a valise, a portable 'museum' in miniature." The Boîte, in fact, approximates all the museum's functions: validating objects that have been removed from their context and deprived of their intended role, preserving them and disseminating their abstracted meaning.

THE MOUSE MUSEUM AND RAY GUN WING

by **Claes Oldenburg**

1965–76

respectively 400 square feet

60 square feet

respectively $24,500

$12,500

Like the Boîte-en-Valise, Claes Oldenburg's Mouse Museum and Ray Gun Wing were motivated by mistrust of existing museum practices, and like the Boîte, they are autobiographical, process-conscious and paradoxical. Based on a canvas mouse mask (made to slip over the head) that Oldenburg designed in 1965 after the profile of a movie projector—the reels are the ears, the nose is the lens—the geometrical Mouse Museum is both sculpture and architecture: although built inside existing structures in different locations, it is freestanding and can be entered. The right-angled Ray Gun, added as a wing to the Mouse Museum in 1976, is one-half the mouse: the barrel is half of the head, the handle one ear. Derived from the Buck Rogers comic strip, the image was used by Oldenburg in 1960 to advertise "The Ray Gun and Spex Show" in New York City, in which his *Street* and Jim Dine's *House* installations appeared. Two years later the Ray Gun Mfg. Co. Store was the name the artist gave his studio at 107 East Second Street, when he transformed it into what eventually became known as "The Store," his popular alternative to both the art gallery and the bourgeois institution of the museum. The Store was to provide a number of the Mouse Museum's displays.

Every element of Oldenburg's museum is part of his ongoing attempt to fuse art and life, fantasy and reality, by using the most ordinary, everyday subject matter, and to free objects in space. Stating "I'm the *Mouse*," Oldenburg identifies with both the mouse head and the Ray Gun: the head refers to his thinking processes, including those of organization and classification that make a collection; the phallic gun represents the artist's fantasy of himself as the all-powerful creator and destroyer. Oldenburg's constant manipulation of scale—most typically his monumentalizing of trivia like a clothespin or lipstick—makes the Mouse Museum's downscaling of concepts that are of great importance to him all the more poignant.

↑ Ray Gun Wing (left) and Mouse Museum. Models.

↑ Mouse Museum.
Exterior.

Theater contributed to Oldenburg's museum. The form-giving canvas-and-wood mouse mask and a number of the displays were used as props in Happenings that he participated in during the late 1950s and early 1960s. His installation of the museum is like a one-person performance done within a strict time limit fixed by the artist to ensure a sense of spontaneity. Visitors line up to enter the museum's darkened space as they had for Oldenburg's performance art, and their behavior is considered part of the event. Coosje van Bruggen, Oldenburg's wife and collaborator, describes the ambience of the Mouse Museum and Ray Gun Wing as "somewhere between that of a small scale panorama such as those found in a historical or technological museum and the window of a shop or the stage of a theater."

Mouse Museum. ↑
Interior.

The artist's first plans for a "museum of popular objects" in the mid-1960s included a parody of conventional museum procedures, with an acquisition committee, a bulletin and a filmed "Tour Through the Museum," which made the objects appear life-size. Oldenburg made a pun of the Swedish words for mouse—*mus*—and museum—*museet*. At Documenta 5 in 1972, with the help of the architects Bernhard Leitner and Heidi Bechinie, the rectangle and two circles of the Mouse Museum were constructed in cardboard within a boxlike enclosure, from which an organic nose appendage protruded at the entrance. About 367 objects from Oldenburg's collection were catalogued for display, and the freelance curator Kasper Koenig was designated director of the museum. Four years later the Chicago Museum of Contemporary Art agreed to build the Mouse Museum in a new design proposed by van Bruggen that eliminated the protective box so that the shape could be seen from the outside as well as the inside. The exterior was fabricated in corrugated aluminum facing, imitating the cardboard of the original, and painted black in a nod to Thomas Edison's first film studio, the Black Maria. It was constructed in remountable sections strong enough to travel without being packed, and air-conditioning was added.

The wing differs from the museum in that it exhibits only Ray Guns, whose form it replicates. Both are in the tradition of *architecture parlante*—the narrative architecture of the French Revolution—in which buildings are designed literally aping their functions, the most notorious example being Claude-Nicolas Ledoux's brothel shaped like male genitalia. The Mouse Museum's various displays, including plastic ice cream sodas, miniature bathrooms, gloves, rubber dog bones, false feet and a pattern for the rear quarter of "Airflow," belong in three categories: unaltered and altered bought or found objects; small models for sculpture; and leftover fragments from works in progress. William Rubin notes that just as object art depends on a visual context, pop art depends on a cultural context. For someone who had never seen comic strips, Oldenburg's rendition of such artifacts of 20th-century life would have little resonance. By making the Mouse and Ray Gun into freestanding, usable exhibition structures, he materializes the cultural context for his art.

Alternative Spaces and Two Museums That Look Like Them

Happenings by artists in lofts and other non-institutional settings proliferated in the 1960s, as did other new art forms. Video art, site-specific installations, minimal art and Arte Povera, earthworks and the deconstructed rooms of artists like Gordon Matta-Clark all defied conventional museum installation and, in many cases, museum politics. Artists in Europe were particularly active in their attempts to go beyond the museum's walls, as exemplified by the "Beyond the Limits" project (1971), in which specific works were commissioned for sites throughout the Netherlands by the Arnhem Park Sonsbeek, an outdoor museum. Many artists had difficulty finding galleries to represent them and at the same time rebelled against the censorship implied by corporate funding of museum exhibitions. The German Conceptual artist Hans Haacke spoke for his generation when he referred to the role of museums in the early 1970s as "managers of consciousness" because of their exclusion of certain work in accordance with sponsors' dictates.

Responding to the needs of this period, Brian O'Doherty, then director of visual arts at the National Endowment for the Arts and himself an artist, obtained a $30 million allocation for several programs, the strongest of which, "Spaces for Artists," came to be known as "alternative spaces." As O'Doherty describes it: "Artists needed to have somewhere to exhibit that they generated themselves." Thanks to federal and state funding, by the mid-1970s these nonprofit organizations, which the artists had a say in running, were a going concern nationwide. Among the first was Jeffrey Lew's loft at 112 Greene Street in New York (1971). He lived at the site, which was cut into and otherwise made part of the art exhibited in it; thus living and exhibition space were one and the same. The Los Angeles Institute of Contemporary Art (1972–73), P.S. 1 in Long Island City (1976), the Institute for Art and Urban Resources (1972) and the Clock Tower (1976) in Manhattan were among the alternative spaces that proliferated in the United States; many others followed in Europe. Located in a wide variety of existing buildings, these new initiatives flourished particularly in former industrial spaces like the large cast-iron buildings in which artists tended to live and work.

Temporary Contemporary (now ↑
Geffen Contemporary), Los
Angeles, by Frank O. Gehry &
Associates (1983). Interior.

Frank Gehry's 1983 renovation of two single-story sheds in Los Angeles for the Museum of Contemporary Art was significant. Typical of adapted spaces, the Temporary Contemporary (now the Geffen Contemporary) had a generosity of scale unavailable in most museum galleries, with structural elements providing a context for the art. Most important, the similarity of such places to the environment in which the art was created lent a connection with the artist's working conditions that was lacking in museums and conventional galleries. Gehry's sensitive remodeling set a precedent for subsequent alternative spaces like the Dia Art Foundation in New York (1987). Now even traditionally run museums like the Guggenheim in New York and the Bonnefanten in Maastricht, the Netherlands, have added converted commercial buildings to their facilities.

The success of these spaces has produced a new phenomenon: buildings for contemporary art with galleries designed to resemble renovated industrial architecture. Such is the case in Annette Gigon and Mike Guyer's 10,000-square-foot addition (1995) to the neoclassical Museum of Fine Arts in Winterthur, Switzerland, and Gwathmey Siegel's 12,000-square-foot Museum of Contemporary Art in North Miami (1996). Both of these relatively small, low-budget museums employ industrial materials—at Winterthur, in a particularly innovative manner. Gigon and Guyer used recyclable, semitransparent profiled glass to clad a load-bearing steel frame. On the ground level vertical glass panels are offset with spaces to provide light and air for the parking area they shield. The glass panels allow glimpses of the structure behind them while maintaining a light, ephemeral effect. Inside, the architects have created some variety within the nine shed-roofed galleries, three of which have large windows.

Addition to the Museum
of Fine Arts, Winterthur,
by Annette Gigon
and Mike Guyer (1995).

LEFT: Exterior. / RIGHT: Interior. ↑

Plan with original →
museum at left and
addition at right.

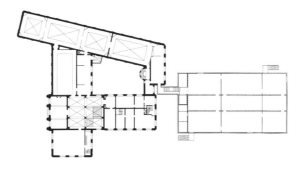

Gwathmey Siegel's $3.75 million museum is part of an urban renewal program for the city of North Miami. Its multicolored stucco exterior echoes other buildings in the area. More unusual are the interiors: a large main gallery, a separate art pavilion, an art storage and preparation area, offices and a gift shop. The 21-foot-high barrel-vaulted main gallery is open, with movable walls; its exposed trusses and ducts, long clerestory window on one side and concrete floors resemble a vast Soho loft. The smaller, butterfly-roofed art pavilion offers more formal, fixed spaces for exhibitions and installations that are limited in size. Grouped in relation to an outdoor court, the museum's different structures offer an interesting diversity of spatial options for a small museum.

Museum of Contemporary Art, North Miami, by Gwathmey Siegel (1996).

TOP: Exterior. →
BOTTOM: Main gallery.

Plan. ↓

THE CHINATI FOUNDATION / LA FUNDACIÓN CHINATI

Marfa, Texas

by **Donald Judd**

1972–94

116,500 square feet of exhibition space

cost undisclosed

The minimalist Donald Judd, who died in 1994 at the age of 65, loved living with art. He was one of many artists inhabiting Soho lofts in the late 1960s, but significantly he used the five-story cast-iron building he owned as a repository for artworks of his own as well as those by friends. Judd was disturbed by the museum's divorce of art from life; to him it meant "having culture without culture having any effect," which served "to make art fake." With his purchase in 1972 of a house in the small·town of Marfa, Texas, he began to realize what he considered to be the ideal museum.

No artist was more critical of museums than Judd. In his essays for *Arts* magazine, he wrote in a spare, brutally direct style about what he perceived to be a general mediocrity of culture, though architecture was of particular concern. Judd's exquisitely crafted wood and aluminum box sculptures are highly sensitive to placement, light and handling—even a faint fingerprint can mar a metal piece and scratches are irreparable. Not only had the artist personally suffered from insensitive installation of, and damage to, his work but, as witnessed by his statement that "everything which I've done has already disappeared," he was frustrated by the impermanence of museum exhibitions.

↑ Aerial view during renovation (early 1980s).

As is true of the work of other minimalists, or specific objects artists, the seamlessness of Judd's pieces necessarily establishes a special dialogue with the space they inhabit. The classic statement on the subject is the historian and critic Michael Fried's 1967 essay "Art and Objecthood," which also called three-dimensional art "a new genre of theater" that for him represented the negation of art:

> The better new work takes relationships out of the work
> and makes them a function of space, light, and the viewer's
> field of vision . . . One is more aware than before that he
> himself [i.e., the artist] is establishing relationships as
> he apprehends the object from various positions and under
> varying conditions of light and spatial context.

The depopulated southwestern region of Texas where Judd settled is over 200 miles from the nearest commercial airport. Highways 67 and 90 intersect at Marfa and stretch in endless straight lines across a plateau that is part of the vast Chihuahua Desert. In the distance mountains rim the horizon: the Davis range to the north and the Chinati peak to the southwest. The sparseness of this remote, grandiose landscape resembles the sparseness of Judd's work, and it is logical that the artist was attracted to it. In 1973 he purchased two airplane hangars next to the house he had bought the year before, and then three ranches some 20 to 60 miles from Marfa. In 1979 he added 32 buildings that were abandoned on 340 acres by the Army in 1946 after they had been used as Fort D. A.

Russell, an airport and military base, and, briefly, as a German prisoner-of-war camp. By the late 1980s, Judd had begun to buy up the entire town: the bank, the Safeway store, various warehouses and single-family residences. The New York–based Dia Art Foundation (with whom Judd severed his relationship in 1986 to create the Chinati Foundation/La Fundación Chinati) financed the Fort Russell purchase and the expenses of artists, notably Dan Flavin and John Chamberlain, who were to make permanent installations at Marfa. Executors of the Chinati Foundation and the Donald Judd estate plan to make all of the artist's holdings in the area—what had been private as well as what was open to the public—generally accessible.

Architectural drawings by Lauretta Vinciarelli (early 1980s). ↓

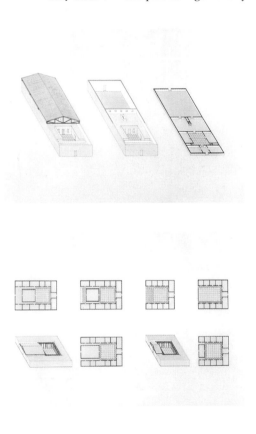

No new structures were built at Marfa, and yet the complex has received as much attention for its architecture as for its art. Judd's success in renovating a vast array of buildings—from small turn-of-the-century houses to enormous military sheds—lies in the artist's eye for proportion and a sensitivity to light as keen as that of Louis Kahn, the architect he admired most. (The most serious shortcoming of the Marfa structures is the absence of climate control: cross-ventilation is insufficient in hot weather, and the buildings can be uncomfortably cold in winter.) The process at Marfa was also helped by what Judd's companion at that time, the architect and artist Lauretta Vinciarelli, describes as their ongoing conversations about architecture and her participation in instructing workers on the site. Vinciarelli's sober, rectilinear vocabulary resonated in Judd, and he may have incorporated ideas contained in her theoretical drawings of the early 1980s at the time he was renovating Marfa's largest structures.

Like those of the other artists discussed here, Judd's museum was an extension of his art. In his 1985 essay "Symmetry" he stated:

> In one relief . . . the vertical rectangle is divided into
> quarters, each brown, by a recessed cross painted cadmium
> red light. Quartering is symmetrical and practical and in
> the last five years I've used it for gates, doors and windows.

Almost all the windows Judd designed are quartered—some pivoting on central supports to serve also as doors. First used in the 19th century, cross-mullioned windows were initially rejected by Modernists until Mies reintroduced them in buildings for the Illinois Institute of Technology campus in Chicago. Aldo Rossi favored them in his work; currently, Robert Venturi is among those who employ these strong, simple geometric forms that relate closely to vernacular architecture. Judd carried this formula even further at the warehouse he adapted in town for Chamberlain's sculptures; here, one of each window's quarters pivots to allow ventilation. Part of Judd's architectural symmetry involves the creation of axes: repeatedly, as in the Chamberlain building, large disparate spaces are cleared, then joined by a new axis that orders them. In the Chinati Foundation's so-called north artillery shed a dividing wall was opened to make a central axis; in the identical south shed only the peripheries of the same wall are opened.

← Artillery sheds, Marfa,
renovated by Donald Judd.
Exterior.

The whole Chinati complex, in a broad sense, was conceived as an enfilade of buildings in the manner of a traditional Beaux-Arts museum. The enfilade begins with Marfa's two most impressive structures, the 65-by-285-by-37-foot artillery sheds, built in 1938 and adapted by Judd for his piece *100 Untitled Works in Mill Aluminum* (48 are in one shed, 52 in the other), fabricated between 1982 and 1986. Most of Judd's renovations consisted of cleaning up structures to make open spaces for the art and blocking or adding windows or skylights. In the artillery sheds he did more. By opening their sides from floor to ceiling with continuous square windows, he made them transparent. The viewer can stand a fair distance from either building and see the sculpture within as if it were standing on the plain that stretches beyond. Judd's placement in the landscape of 15 groupings of concrete boxes measuring approximately eight feet square along a half

North artillery shed. ↑
Exterior.

North artillery shed. →
Interior with partial
view of Judd's
*100 Untitled Works
in Mill Aluminum.*

Barracks interior →
with Hyong-Keun
Yun installation.

mile parallel to the sheds continues the dynamic between interior and exterior. Inside, the region's crystalline light plays on the aluminum surfaces, making them seem alternatively like glass or water, sometimes appearing to dissolve them completely. The windows, quartered and framed with clear anodized extruded aluminum, relate to the grid of the existing concrete floor, beams and columns; the artworks are set in rows at equal intervals within this framework. No one who sees this work can question the importance Judd attached to installation. The interplay of space, light and viewer is essential to its full realization, and here the installation achieves a dimension that is rarely, if ever, perceptible in museums or galleries.

Michael Fried faulted minimalism for what he claimed was each object's lack of self-sufficiency or relationship between its parts, which necessitated the viewer's participation in a situation he disparagingly called theater. What one realizes at Marfa is that minimal art *is* theatrical—in the best sense of the word—something the critic Barbara Rose describes as the Duchampian art as an experience, not an object. Attesting to the dynamic theatrical quality of this art (which in less propitious surroundings could be dismissed as dull) is the fact that Chinati curator Rob Weiner's training is not in the fine arts but in drama.

Judd transformed the artillery sheds' flat roofs with corrugated-iron barrel vaults inspired by vernacular storage structures whose vaults stand on the ground (like the hangars in Le Corbusier's *Towards a New Architecture*). His choice of a curved roof was aesthetic, probably influenced by Kahn's Kimbell Art Museum (1972), and practical in that it was an efficient way of repairing the building's many leaks. He made the 18.5-foot-high vaults equal in height to the brick facades, thereby establishing yet another symmetry.

Eleven U-shaped barracks and related buildings continue the enfilade. The reduced scale (18.5 feet wide with 9-foot ceilings) and lower natural light level of these structures are better adapted to works on paper—such as the Carl Andre installation in a former mess hall—and small sculptures. The rough, wheat-colored plaster Judd chose for the interiors recalls the shade and texture of local adobe brick.

Coosje van Bruggen, who collaborated with Claes Oldenburg on *Last Cavalry Horse* (1991) for the Chinati Foundation, notes that Judd did not want to be the only artist at Marfa and felt that "artists need a dialogue away from pristine, institutional situations." What's more, the presence of work by others belies Ellsworth Kelly's rejection of a museum designed by an artist. Besides the Oldenburg outdoor sculpture, the installation of Russian artist Ilya Kabakov's

School #6 (1993) and the exhibition of work by John Chamberlain and additional artists attest to Judd's interest in providing a venue for different kinds of art. The realization of Dan Flavin's *Marfa Project* in six former barracks will substantially increase the exhibition area. Judd's own collection includes Old Master drawings, Modern paintings and artist's proofs, in addition to minimal art, all of which he intended to display.

Judd's intervention at the Arena, the other large Chinati Foundation structure, was much less than that for the artillery sheds. Here, he merely closed eight existing windows, carefully leaving crisp indentations on the interior to indicate their former presence, while opening pivoting wood-framed and quartered doors on three sides. An interesting element of the Arena, and of the two airplane hangars on the artist's private compound, is the continuous clerestory windows that sit atop the relatively high lateral walls. They are part of the original utilitarian structures, and their effect is similar to (but more effective than, because the space is larger) the more complex system of indirect natural light used by Herzog and de Meuron for their sophisticated Goetz Collection (see Chapter 1).

In 15 years, Judd had renovated and installed art and furniture in structures at the Chinati Foundation and in what he considered to be his private domain: the ranches and buildings in town. He treated the latter as his home, with a bed and bathroom and sometimes a kitchen in each so that he could live with the installations as he had at his residences in New York. Plans to add these formerly private areas to the 12 Chinati Foundation buildings currently open to the public raise the specter of a mausoleum-like display that would contradict Judd's belief in the interaction of life and art. One hopes that the foundation's program of artists' residencies and college internships will be active enough to prevent this.

What Judd did at Marfa has had significant repercussions. In the late 1980s the Massachusetts Museum of Contemporary Art (Mass MOCA) project to convert into a museum 28 mill buildings on a 13-acre site in North Adams was an elaboration of his ideas. Other massive adaptations of industrial complexes to incorporate the exhibition of art, like the Lingotto in Turin, Italy (see Chapter 6), also owe a debt to Marfa.

In a 1995 interview for *Art in America* Ilya Kabakov compared his first experience of Marfa to a visit to a Tibetan monastery: "the unbelievable combination of estrangement, similar to a holy place, and at the same time of unbelievable attention to the life of the works there." Certainly Marfa's remote location makes a trip to it into a pilgrimage of sorts. Eric Fischl stresses the importance of such pilgrimages: for him, journeying to see a great work of art is an affirmation of a culture. Once the traveler has arrived, the destination must fulfill some essential requirements: quiet conducive to contemplation, an environment that fosters a special feeling akin to a religious awakening and the revelation of something new. Marfa is capable of providing all of these. At the same time it retains a connection to the site and the animating presence of artists in residence that mitigates the isolation often associated with art in sacred spaces.

Frank Stella: Projects

Very different from Marfa's puritan Classicism are four baroque museum designs by Frank Stella —a pavilion for Groningen, the Netherlands, a complex in Dresden and two private museums— none of which, to date, has been realized. As with Judd, Stella's interest in museum structures stems from a profound dissatisfaction with contemporary architecture. He considers German Expressionism to be the high point of 20th-century architecture: Erich Mendelsohn, Otto Bartning, Hermann Finsterlin and Bruno Taut are his models. For him the extraordinary forms of these masters have been overwhelmed by buildings based on purely functional consideration. Stella sees today's glass and steel buildings as sad successors to the individual glass shapes created by Taut, for whom the expressive "will to form" had the implications of a new religion. In a 1994 lecture Stella voiced sentiments he shared with the British engineer Peter Rice, whose reputation was established by his work on breakthrough buildings such as the Sydney Opera House and the Centre Georges Pompidou in Paris:

> What we build is largely empty of feeling for the individuals
> who use it. Our buildings are cold. We have to find a way
> to warm them up without turning up the thermostat.

Stella and Rice met in Paris in 1988 while working together on a footbridge the artist designed for the Seine. As the only one of several consulting engineers who felt the design's aesthetics could be combined with practical engineering, Rice established an affinity with Stella. The two continued to collaborate until Rice's death from a brain tumor, in 1992.

William Rubin refers to Stella's involvement with architectonic concepts as early as the black pictures of 1958–60. At this time he in fact also explored architectural ideas, including an "ideal museum" with variable ceiling and walls suspended within a glass cage. While the subsequent shaped canvases (beginning in 1960) and other work increased architectonic tensions, Stella himself attributes the real turn in his thinking about architecture to his Moby Dick paintings of the late 1980s and early 1990s: large aluminum sculptural forms constructed out from the wall. One day, when viewing a piece in this series from the side, it occurred to the artist that it resembled "a building with a wave on top." Like the first members of the Bauhaus, Stella sees an interrelationship among painting, sculpture and architecture, and the dependence of all three on the pictorial. For him, the Moby Dick reliefs are both painting and sculpture: instead of shadows being painted, they are cast by one element in front of another. By the same token he emphasizes that "making architecture is the same thing as working on sculpture: the model becomes a sculpture." Stella thus reverses the Modernist form-follows-function credo, claiming that in a truly three-dimensional shape, space is created by a structure that is intrinsic to the form.

OLD MASTER PAVILION, GRONINGER MUSEUM

**Groningen,
The Netherlands**

by **Frank Stella**

1992

about 10,000 square feet

budget: about $3.5 million

Stella's first museum commission was for one of the four pavilions that constitute the Groninger in northern Holland (see Chapter 6). The artist's design combined forms from his Eccentric Polygons (1965) with waves that initially appeared in his Had Gadya prints (1982–84), after El Lissitzky. The result was an undulating roof consisting of two overlapping Chinese leaf patterns bent and twisted to generate curvilinear walls. Stella is a maker of exuberant forms that depend on complex layers of inspiration.

As planned with the help of Rice and Earl Childress, an artist with a degree in construction management, "the Leaves," the first project at Groningen, consisted of an armature, for which titanium, steel and wood were considered, with semitranslucent inflated Teflon (like the material used at Atelier Mimesis, see Chapter 3) for the roof spaces between. The two roof leaves were to be supported by columns that Stella wanted buried in partitions in which lighted vitrines would exhibit the art. While the ten-foot-high partitions would have been placed in relation to the free-flowing ceiling patterns, the vitrines were to be rectilinear, framing and giving a sense of scale to the Old Master paintings programmed for this wing.

Within a year Stella had made a paper model of the project that was then rendered in bronze. In this later version, referred to by the artist as "the Cage," the roof's structural veining extended to the walls; the floor was made to slope gently (like the Pantheon's); and the interior became column-free with temporary display partitions anchored to the metal floor members. Using the armature to support the pneumatic Teflon walls would have given the interiors abundant natural light and allowed the pavilion to glow like a lantern at night; industrial glass was to fill the spaces in the floor. (Certain structural problems—how the armature would meet the ground, for example—were not resolved until the idea was reused by Stella for another scheme, the Desert Museum.) Disagreement with the Dutch client, who preferred what Stella by then considered his inferior, first proposal (instead of "the Cage"), ended the artist's involvement with the Groninger Museum.

Stella's Groninger project is best evaluated in comparison with the design by the Coop Himmelblau office, then based in Vienna and Los Angeles, that replaced it (see Chapter 7). As exciting as the latter is for certain kinds of contemporary art, Stella's system of open, vitrine-like recessions in freestanding partitions would have better suited the size and style of the Old Master collection for which this gallery was intended. "The Leaves" would have been as distinctive as Coop Himmelblau's Deconstructivist pavilion, while the artist's installation would have framed the paintings and given them a sense of scale they lack in the space as built.

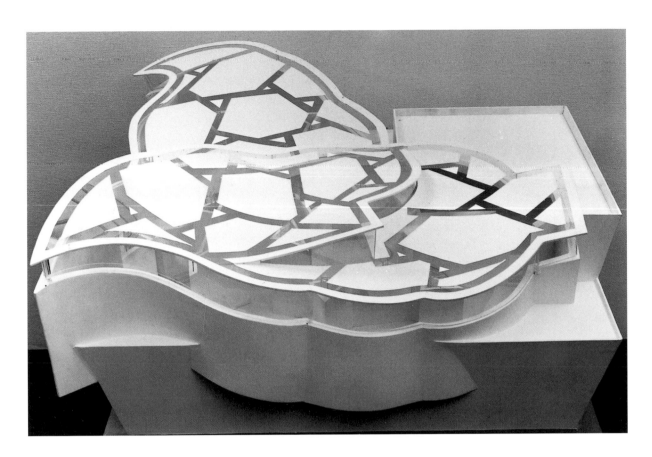

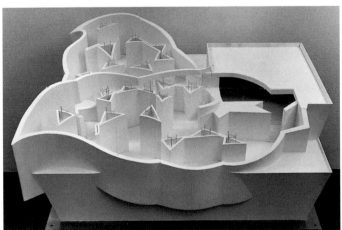

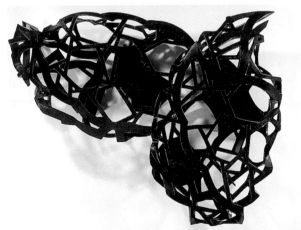

↑ "The Leaves." Unbuilt project for
the Groninger Museum.
TOP: **Paper model, exterior.**
BOTTOM LEFT: **Paper model, interior.**

→ BOTTOM RIGHT: "The Cage." Bronze model.

DESERT MUSEUM

Israel

by **Frank Stella**

1992

55,000 square feet

Shortly after his setback with the Groninger Museum, Stella embarked on another building design when the New York cosmetics heir, philanthropist and chairman of MoMA Ronald Lauder approached him with the idea of a museum in Israel. For Lauder's Desert Museum Stella would combine the cage he had developed for the Groninger with a ground plan based on one of his Sabra paintings (1967)—brightly colored, butterfly-shaped canvases that were part of the decidedly architectural Protractor series. Six 16-foot-high rectilinear and six gently curved galleries were laid out along the peripheries of the butterfly wings to be underground, as was an office mezzanine. Only "the Cage"—built in steel, wood or concrete—would rise above ground, anchored on two triangular forms housing stairs and elevators. The largely open-air cage served as a sculpture garden and contained a restaurant. Angled glazing below it covered the entrance and provided natural light for the mezzanine, where ramps—pulled away from the enclosing walls so that daylight could penetrate even farther—descended from the central office level to the galleries. The galleries also received natural light from continuous peripheral skylights diffused by an interior arch.

To a greater degree than the artist's first museum schemes, the Desert Museum was a collaborative effort. The highly visible cage and Sabra plan are pure Stella. Still, Childress attributes most of the underground design to Robert Kahn, an architect who met Stella at the American Academy in Rome and has worked with him on all his architectural projects. Kahn was in turn instructed by Lauder, who wanted the proportions of Larry Gagosian's Wooster Street Gallery in Soho to serve as a model for the museum's discrete spaces, which would each be dedicated to a single contemporary artist. Lauder eventually asked several architects to propose ideas for a museum in Israel; at present none has been implemented.

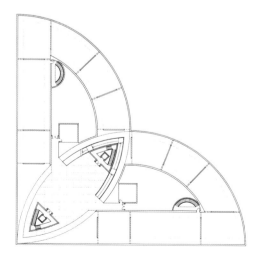

← Plan of underground galleries.

↑ Exterior with entry. Model.

← View from above showing
gallery skylights. Model.

↓ Transverse section.

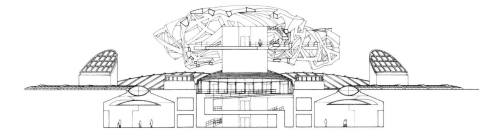

KUNSTHALLE COMPLEX, HERZOGIN GARDEN

Dresden, Germany

by **Frank Stella**

1992

54,000 square feet

22,000 square feet of exhibition space

budget: $16.5 million

At roughly the same time that he was working on the Groninger project, Stella was commissioned to develop a proposal for the city of Dresden. Real estate developers and passionate collectors of contemporary art, Rolf and Erika Hoffmann responded to the general optimism over Germany's reunification with a plan for informing East Germans of recent world art developments. The Hoffmanns offered to exhibit their own collection, together with works lent by an international array of equally idealistic private collectors, in a new Kunsthalle, whose financing and management the couple would guarantee. Rental revenues would fuel a tax-free foundation used to run the museum-quality exhibition program.

The Kunsthalle was to have been housed in two of five pavilions on a government-donated 270,000-square-foot lot near Dresden's few remaining historic buildings. Apartments for a curator and visiting artists, a restaurant, a bookstore, office space and a botanical garden were part of a multiuse complex incorporating art, as in other such enterprises in Italy and France (see Chapter 6). The Hoffmanns approached an artist rather than an architect partly to attract other collectors and partly to make the Kunsthalle, as they said, "symbolic of something new."

In line with a program of traditional restoration, city officials wanted a formal public park resembling the Renaissance Herzogin Garden, which had deteriorated even before Dresden's destruction in World War II. This would have entailed the re-creation of an orangerie, which had stood at one end of the garden, with the new Kunsthalle built to mirror it at the opposite end. Stella immediately rejected this idea in favor of a series of pavilions scattered through the park, which were inspired by Bruno Taut's visionary "Alpine Architecture" (1917), an organic landscape of low-rise buildings. (A small remnant of the orangerie was incorporated into a long, rectangular building.)

The site is separated only by a canal and a roadway from the Zwinger, part of an elaborate early-18th-century palace compound designed by Matthäus Daniel Pöppelmann for Augustus the Strong, the elector of Saxony and king of Poland. Familiar with Pöppelmann's design, which included flowing and spurting water, Stella eventually decided to use water to tie the pavilions and grounds together. To a series of sculptural forms he added that of an inexpensive rubberized Brazilian hat: lifting and twisting its spiral, it became the new two-part Orangerie. (Here the earlier process was reversed, and it was the architectural forms that inspired Stella's 1994 Imaginary Places, a series of paintings that wrapped around walls with one-to-two-foot bulges at their centers.) Taking his cue from another Pöppelmann palace, nearby at Pillnitz and, like the Zwinger, intended for festivities, the artist adopted celebratory colors for the exteriors (Pillnitz's chinoiserie had also suggested the Groninger's leaf pattern).

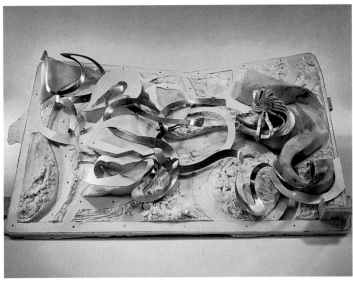

↑ Pavilions with Orangerie at right. Plaster model.

← Pavilions with modified Orangerie at right.
Plaster, Sintra, wood and aluminum model.

→ Final aluminum model.

Monsta, New Canaan,
by Philip Johnson (1995).

TOP: Exterior. ↑
BOTTOM: Interior.

Plan. →

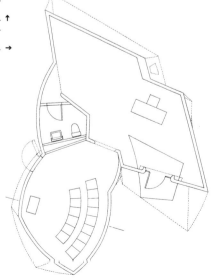

Philip Johnson's 1995 construction of one of Stella's Dresden pavilions (which the architect dubbed "the Monsta") as the gatehouse to his Connecticut property shows how that museum might have looked. The Dresden structure was to have been much larger—60 feet high as compared with Johnson's 21 feet, 18,300 square feet as compared with 900 square feet. Stella's baroque palette would also have differed from the black-and-barn-red color scheme chosen by Johnson, as would the lighting at Dresden via translucent roofs (similar to the Teflon exteriors he had proposed for the Netherlands). But the Monsta's strong, sensuous forms bear witness to Stella's design proficiency, even though the curvature of its walls might have been too acute for hanging art comfortably. Its complex *Caligari*-like interiors could, however, have been used with a system of partitions, like the one projected for the Groninger.

For Dresden, as he had for Groningen—and creating problems for both clients—Stella went backward from a more realistic plaster model that clearly indicated the buildings' different forms to an abstract metal cast that looked like a three-dimensional drawing. Stella concedes that when he presented his final, stainless-steel model, "we lost our audience." The German press had lauded the Hoffmanns' concept as remarkably enlightened: a "Wessie" real estate developer was willing to sacrifice commercial benefits for the good of the community, at no cost to the taxpayer. But favorable publicity was quickly overwhelmed by a storm of conflicting interests: music lovers who preferred an auditorium, preservationists who insisted on an exact replica of historic conditions and conservative officials critical of the design. Despite approval in 1992 by the Dresden City Council, which controls planning, the Free State of Saxony, to which most of the site belongs, subsequently rejected Stella's project.

MCI, PRIVATE MUSEUM FOR 20TH-CENTURY LATIN AMERICAN ART

Buenos Aires, Argentina

by Frank Stella

1997

45,200 square feet

about 22,500 square feet of exhibition space

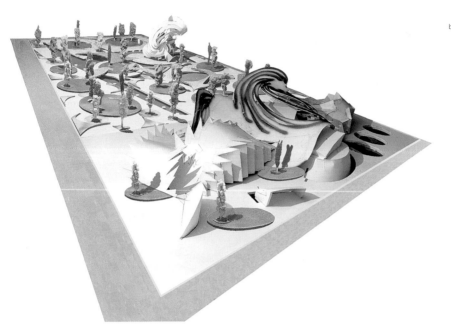

← Museum and sculpture
(at far end) in park. Model.

What Stella saw in the competition brief for a Buenos Aires park and museum to house the modern Latin American art of the Argentinian collector Eduardo Costantini was that the physical conditions seemed to replicate those of Dresden. The artist asserts that he "couldn't resist" the opportunity to improve his earlier design, for which, lacking a precise program, he had not specified interiors. He was also attracted by the challenge of redesigning the existing 75,000-square-foot park, which in the early 1970s the Brazilian landscape architect Roberto Burle Marx had laid out in rigid, geometrical forms, primarily as a children's playground.

Formally named MC I, this latest scheme of Stella's (the recipient of an honorable mention) is referred to by the artist as Dresden III, Dresden II being Philip Johnson's gatehouse. Indeed, several of the Dresden themes reappear here: water used as a unifying element in the landscape, the spiral inspired by a Brazilian hat and vivid exterior colors. But for the competition, Stella contained the meandering Dresden water in a T-shaped canal that, like the park generally, is more architectonic. At Dresden the spiral was used for two nearly freestanding pavilions in conjunction with a long structure that marked one end of the Herzogin Garden; for Buenos Aires the spiral is integrated with the single museum building it crowns, visually linking its two parts (one with galleries, a bookstore and a coffee shop; the other a 300-seat lecture auditorium and offices) and signaling the parkside entrance. (The store, shops and auditorium have their own entrances as well.) Echoing this swirling element at the far end of the site is a 50-foot-high sculpture. All construction was to be in reinforced concrete.

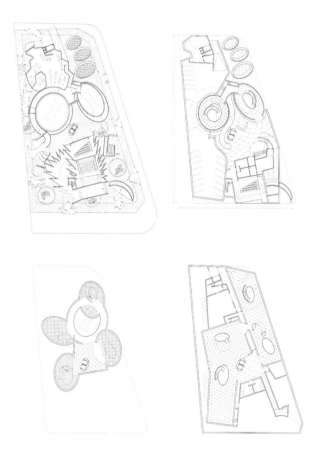

Marx's concept for the site, known as Peru Plaza, has not been successful. The plaza is isolated on one periphery by the broad Avenida Figueroa Alcorta, while factories and garages on the other periphery are a jarring note in the largely residential and cultural area. Offering no protection from the summer sun or winter winds, its concrete forms have little appeal. In order to make the area more inviting, Stella replaced stone pavements with lawns, punctuated by grassy mounds and trees, that are continuously accessible on all four sides. His proposal is a compromise between the formality of the existing park and a free-flowing picturesque landscape. Entry into the museum is from two sides, with views into one of the two soaring (26 and 30 feet high, respectively) ground-level exhibition spaces through a generous expanse of glazing. A ramp from the park connects with a system of ramps and stairways that leads down to three levels of exhibition spaces—oval on the first and third levels (the latter also includes a reflecting pool), rectilinear on the intermediary level—that Stella felt "could be used for anything." The artist envisaged painting installed in the oval galleries on freestanding panels or niches cut into the thick walls. Ceiling heights are different at each level (13 feet at the second, over 16 feet at the third), all of which receive some natural light. The gallery space throughout is assigned equally to temporary and permanent exhibitions.

↑ Plans.
CLOCKWISE: Ground level and three underground levels.

← Longitudinal section.

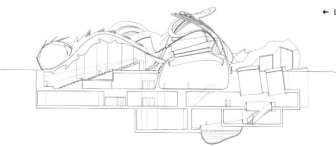

The two projects Stella initiated in 1992—for the Groninger Museum and the Dresden Kunsthalle—went through similar evolutions, eventually pairing geometrically shaped galleries with the initial sculptural spaces. While the Desert Museum's combination of rectilinear and curved underground galleries belongs to Stella's formal repertoire and relates to "the Cage" above ground, the more arbitrary, oval galleries for Buenos Aires are not fully integrated into the composition. Furthermore, "the Cage" enclosed an intrinsically sculptural exhibition space, whereas the equally exciting forms in Buenos Aires affect mainly the auditorium and only the two galleries at ground level. As many architects are—notably Frank Gehry—Stella is striving for a variety of spaces appropriate for the exhibition of different art forms. Stella and Gehry in fact sustain an ongoing dialogue, each one admitting influences from the other.

Stella repudiates today's large neutral exhibition spaces, which he feels lack the richness of 19th-century galleries. He asserts that "there are millions of square feet of warehouses available for contemporary art where it looks better than in a neutral box, so we need new forms." Only such forms, he claims, can compensate for what he calls the "grand parade" of many centuries that is typically shown in Beaux-Arts museums. One hopes he will have the opportunity to realize just such forms as he has conceptualized for Groningen and Dresden.

MUSEUM FOR JACKSON POLLOCK

**The Springs,
Long Island**

by **Peter Blake**

1949

unbuilt project

Jackson Pollock's museum was designed not by the artist but by the architect
and critic Peter Blake, though with the artist's approval. Pollock's paintings were
such an integral part of the architecture, however, that the museum appears to
be as much by him as by Blake. From the architect's first exposure to Pollock's
work on Long Island in 1948, he was struck by its relationship to the landscape
in which it was created. Indeed, some of the artist's earliest paintings after he
and his wife, Lee Krasner, came to live in the Springs in 1945 were inspired by
nearby Acabonack Creek, and his assertion "I am nature" has become legendary.
Shortly after settling at the Springs, Pollock moved the barn that would serve as
his studio to its present location at the edge of fields and salt marshes overlooking the inlets of the harbor and the bay.

When Pollock asked Blake to hang the second show he was to have in 1949
at the Betty Parsons Gallery, the young architect seized the opportunity to realize an idea he had had since his first visit to the artist's studio: a museum design
that would show Pollock's large paintings suspended within the Springs's landscape and adjusted to the outdoor scale by mirrors. Blake, who was then curator of the Department of Architecture and Design at MoMA, recalls looking at
the work with Pollock:

> It was a very sunny day and the sun was shining in on the
> paintings. I felt like I was standing in the Hall of Mirrors
> at Versailles. It was a dazzling, incredible sight.

The model Blake made was based on Mies van der Rohe's 1942 Museum for a
Small City project, a flat-roofed glazed pavilion (see Chapter 2). Using materials
he had at hand, Blake removed the exterior walls, leaving the floor (a piece of
plywood) and what was to be a frosted-glass roof (a two-by-four-foot sheet of
plastic) supported in the original model by I-shaped brass extrusions that

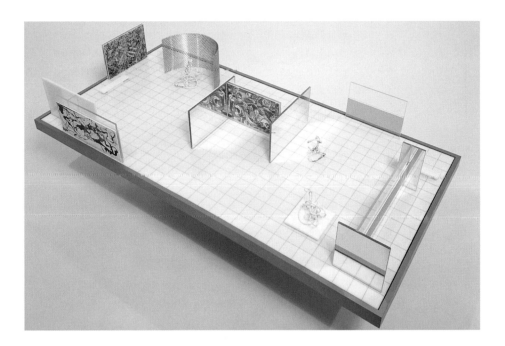

indicated columns. The intended 50 by 100-foot interior was divided by colored replicas of Pollock's paintings taken from a recent article in *Life*, some as long as 17 feet, and three paint-splashed wire-and-plaster sculptures made by the artist for the model. To simulate the landscape's broad scale, unframed paintings would be set at right angles to mirrored wall segments that reflected them to infinity. Blake eliminated the terrace and court at either side of Mies's museum as well as its interior garden and substituted a curved screen of perforated brass for the auditorium.

The two projects shared more than their open plans and transparency. Just as Mies had chosen Picasso's masterpiece *Guernica* for a presentation of interior partitions and freestanding objects in his museum, works from Pollock's "classic" period of 1947–50, which determined the model's replicas, became the masterpieces of their time. Mies's creation of columnless space for the museum's auditorium by hanging its roof from exposed spanning trusses prefigured his design for the Neue Nationalgalerie in Berlin (1967). Blake's use of Mies's exhibition of paintings as walls may have influenced Dorothy Miller's presentation of Pollock's *No. 30* at the center of a gallery in her 1952 "15 Americans" exhibition at MoMA.

Mies's museum was an abstract idea, submitted in response to a request from *Architectural Forum* for a church design to include in a "postwar buildings" issue. Despite the low mountains sketched in the background, there was no site for the building; it was a typical Modern design, conceived as an object that could be placed anywhere. In the absence of funding or space to build it, Blake's museum was also theoretical, but it was designed with a specific site in mind that would have provided a live example of the artistic process. In addition to proposing a simulation of the vast horizontal landscape by the paintings and their mirror reflections, Blake suggested that Pollock work on glass so that the countryside would be visible through the paint. The idea was not used for the model, but it was adopted soon thereafter by Hans Namuth for his renowned documentary film of the artist at work. The museum thus would have provided the means to view simultaneously what informed the painting and, through the glass acting like a tissue overlay, the painting's relationship to that inspiration. About his method of painting unstretched canvases on the floor, Pollock has been quoted as saying he worked "from the four sides" and could "literally be *in* the painting." Blake's museum would have placed the viewer *in* the natural habitat that inspired Pollock.

Of the few published discussions of the model at the time of its display, the most cogent is the January 1950 *Interiors* article by Arthur Drexler, who succeeded Blake the following year at MoMA:

> In its treatment of paintings as walls the design recalls an entirely different kind of pictorial art; that of the Renaissance fresco. The project suggests a reintegration of painting and architecture wherein painting *is* the architecture, but this time without message or content. Its sole purpose is to heighten our experience of space.

MUSEUM IN TODI, ITALY

by **Patrick Ireland**

in progress since 1978

1,760 square feet

In the small Umbrian hill town of Todi, the Conceptual artist Patrick Ireland has reinterpreted the architecture of the 18th-century house in which he vacations with his wife, the art historian Barbara Novak, so that here, as in Pollock's museum, painting *is* the architecture.

Ireland's ongoing dialogue with the work of Duchamp, with whom this chapter began, makes his own museum the appropriate conclusion. An episode in the dialogue was the evocative performance he staged for his name change in 1972 from Brian O'Doherty to Patrick Ireland: continuing to use O'Doherty for critical writing, he will sign his art and fiction "Ireland" until the British withdraw from Northern Ireland. Like Duchamp, O'Doherty achieved a double identity. His museum continues the autobiographical tradition of the Boîte-en-Valise; instead of being a complete replica it is a summary of the artist's career. Ireland has re-created key aspects of his work over thirty years, placing them so as to invite comparison and suggest process. He, too, protests conventional museum practices that allow Conceptual art to disappear (as many of Duchamp's objects have). He, too, restores art to a living context. As he says, "Modern architecture's sanitized, idealized, Platonic interiors aren't for people." At Todi he can "deliver the neutral space of the gallery and make it into a place."

↓ *Twenty-Five* Is, visible from entrance.

As do Pollock's, Ireland's paintings relate to Italian frescoes. His installations also bear an affinity to the architectural sculpture Merzbau, by means of which Kurt Schwitters gradually transformed his Hanover apartment from 1923 until he left Germany in 1937. Like Schwitters, Ireland has left the exterior intact while converting a domestic interior into an artwork.

The building lends itself well to its new function as a museum. The entrance door opens directly to a stair; the high risers signal that it will take some effort to visit this place, an effect similar to that produced by the elevated gallery thresholds at Giornico (see Chapter 3). At the top of the stairs is an ogham wall painting made up of 25 *I*s in an ancient Celtic alphabet based on a ritualistic language used by the Druids; this alphabet has been an ongoing factor in Ireland's painting since the late 1960s. This first floor is devoted mostly to works based on ogham, a serial language that constitutes the kind of nonhierarchical, noncentralized,

self-referential system frequently employed in Conceptual and postminimal art.

Past a five-foot-thick wall of great power and simplicity, the stairs rise to the airy living room where the house's primary work, *Trecento*, a rope installation and wall painting, takes its cue from local altarpieces with its triangular top, wings and predelle. Ireland describes it:

> The brown lines spring out from the painting and weave
> the space in front, talking to the room through points
> of attachment, and—as you move—opening, closing,
> and clipping slices of space until you find a point of view
> where a sudden framing calms everything into rational
> verticals, horizontals, and obliques—coaxing the painted
> wall outward into your eye.

Novak points out that as one moves within the rope pieces, their apparent order can quickly disperse, fracturing viewers' sense of place and even of their identity. Apparent from Ireland's name change is his preoccupation with identity. As the viewer ascends within the house, color intensifies so that on the top floor the visitor is surrounded by color and has, in a way, entered the works. This last ultramarine-and-turquoise level contains four semi-abstract windows depicting four times of the day: from different vantage points the viewer may travel through 24 hours. The resulting dialectic of interior and exterior is a theme begun by Ireland in his rope drawings in 1973.

In all the pieces, Ireland utilizes windows, doors and the other paraphernalia of residential architecture in expressing the ambiguities of his art. Additionally, the artist explains how the swells and scallops of the old walls play a part:

> The paintings hug the walls in an embrace that makes
> them part of the architecture. As I paint, I feel my paintings
> are rebuilding the house from the inside.

← TOP: **Top floor.**
Times of Day cycle.
BOTTOM: **First floor.**
Ogham cycle.

Together, these artist-designed museums address issues raised earlier and point toward the new directions described in the following chapters. In each one the intimate relationship between container and contained resolves matters of contextualism that have been discussed in reference to museum design for centuries.

Duchamp achieves contextualism and additionally forces the viewer into a tactile relationship with the contents of his Boîte. Oldenburg's Mouse Museum and Ray Gun Wing go even further in their creation of an environment unique to the displays. Judd's renovations at Marfa provide a model for adaptive reuse generally, and specifically his opening up of the artillery sheds shares with Blake's Pollock museum a freeing of objects from architecture. Asked recently to describe the ideal space for his work, the pop artist James Rosenquist envisioned "an appendage on the side of a skyscraper with a transparent Plexiglas floor and ceiling so that the surrounding walls are what you see, with no bottom or top . . . floating art in space." Judd's and Blake's transparent walls are the actualized version of Rosenquist's floors and ceilings.

The idea of making art part of the landscape was shared by several artists in the second half of the 20th century. Barnett Newman's widow, Annalee, recalls that in the early 1950s her husband discussed with Pollock what they considered a "democratic" way to exhibit art: huge paintings could stand outdoors like billboards, visible to everyone, and thus bypass the usual gallery and museum infrastructure. Newman and Pollock never solved the problem of exposing oil and canvas to the elements, but 40 years later graffiti artists like Jean-Michel Basquiat and Keith Haring realized the concept in their own way.

At the time of his involvement with the Dresden project, Stella urged architects to take into account artists' gestures, "gestures that seem casual and improbable but [that are] surprisingly effective in making art." New computer-designed and -constructed architecture, especially that by Frank Gehry, has indeed taken a giant step beyond Stella's own use of electronic images.

Ireland's adaptation of a residence for permanent installations of his work incorporates process, as does Judd's inclusion of living arrangements with many of his displays. The practice has been taken up by a number of public as well as private museums (see Chapters 1 and 2).

Finally, the theatricality inherent in these concepts is a major factor for future museums. Clearly, each artist is creating a stage set for art that plays a significant part in the viewer's perception of it. As will be seen, this is also the case with many new museums.

Chapter 5

Wings That Don't Fly (And Some That Do)

Just as an Empire, continuously expanding its borders,
ends up forgetting its center, and the center ends up no
longer knowing its limits, so too the Museum, extending
its collections to include the most eccentric areas of
human creativity, ends up forgetting, if not betraying,
that for which it was created. *Jean Clair*

No matter how problematic museum architecture may be, adding to it can
prove more so. Museum expansion is generally perceived as the direct result
of a need for additional space, but other, often extraneous considerations
can influence the decision to take on these consuming and costly projects.
Richard Oldenburg, director of MoMA from 1972 to 1994, notes that for one
thing, new people usually want new things, and physical expansion is a way
for trustees, or a director, to leave an indelible imprint.

That it tends to be easier to find funding for a new wing than for the restoration of an existing building encourages opting for the former, sexier project
(sometimes combined with restoration) rather than for the more prosaic one.
Trustees and museum staff, many with little or no experience as institutional
architecture clients, often make their selection of a designer on the basis of
questionable considerations. The candidate's personality or past work (usually residential) for a member of the selection committee are factors that can

influence a decision ideally dependent only on an objective assessment of talent and ability.

Writing in 1994 about museums, Paul Goldberger remarked:

> Many became caught up in a frenzy of growth that had something other than the democratization of art as its goal. Building museums became a badge of success for cities, and for people who had grown rich in the 1980's. New blood, often newly rich blood, joined old museum boards. Museums got bigger and more expensive to maintain, which in turn required them to find ways of keeping attendance high to pay mounting bills. Many seemed victims of their own success, caught in a spiral of expanding audiences, expanded facilities and the need for ever more money to support them.

The lack of architectural integrity that is characteristic of so many expansion projects is unexpected in institutions that stand for the highest standards of art preservation and connoisseurship. Repeatedly, museum trustees, directors and staffs have done things to their buildings that would be unthinkable if applied to their collections. The redundant enlargement projects undertaken between 1984 and 1987 by New York City's four major art museums—the Metropolitan Museum (whose Lila Acheson Wallace Wing, like the other museums' enlargements, was for 20th-century art), MoMA, the Guggenheim and, in its first, unrealized effort, the Whitney—as well as Paris's Louvre, all sacrificed architecture to expansion.

Wings That Don't Fly

THE METROPOLITAN MUSEUM OF ART

New York, New York

by **Kevin Roche John Dinkeloo and Associates**

1970–90

between $500 million and $600 million

The Metropolitan Museum of Art Master Plan (1970)
620,000 square feet

Robert Lehman Wing (1975)
25,000 square feet

Sackler Wing (1978)
33,000 square feet

American Wing and Charles Engelhard Court (1980)
175,000 square feet

Michael C. Rockefeller Wing (1982)
170,000 square feet

Lila Acheson Wallace Wing for 20th-Century Art (1987)
70,000 square feet

Henry R. Kravis Wing and Carroll and Milton Petrie European Sculpture Court (1990)
148,000 square feet

As the mother of all New York museums, the Metropolitan has set a poor example in dealing with its own architecture. The first initiative for a New York art museum was expressed in 1869 by the publisher George P. Putnam, who called for "a building spacious in its dimensions, and thoroughly fireproof." As it happens, practical concerns have repeatedly overshadowed a concern for architectural quality. What's more, the architects for the Metropolitan's nearly continuous construction, expansion and remodeling have often been chosen in ways and for reasons that were unlikely to produce great architecture: because they were board members (notably the mediocre Theodore Weston in 1880, more fortuitously Richard Morris Hunt in 1894) and in at least two cases (Hunt and, in 1970, Kevin Roche) without the usual board or committee approval. In one instance it was left to a Metropolitan president—Robert W. De Forest, the benefactor of the American Wing—to choose his own architect (Grosvenor Atterbury, in 1919). A seemingly unlimited willingness to satisfy donor demands has resulted in the museum's numerous unfortunate alterations.

In 1970 the Metropolitan's announcement of a new master plan, its fifth, by Kevin Roche and John Dinkeloo, was criticized for its size—doubling the museum's space—and its further encroachment on Central Park. At the time a number of art professionals, including the realist painter Fairfield Porter and the historians Linda Nochlin and Harry Bober, questioned the advisability of housing so many departments under one roof rather than allowing smaller museums to develop throughout the city. Probably the most prescient argument was that of the art and architectural historian Rudolf Wittkower, who remarked that the Metropolitan's size would make increasingly difficult its prime task of letting an individual work "speak for itself." As it turned out, the park land for which construction was planned lay within the tract originally leased to the museum by the city, and the Metropolitan proceeded to complete what now stands: a collection of 17 curatorial departments occupying a total area of over 17 acres. Philippe de Montebello, the Metropolitan's director since 1978, describes the new American Wing as "mazelike," with a "spatial complexity . . . [that] has defied the best mapmakers"—a description that can well apply to the whole complex. Little significant architecture survives, and with the latest five-wing addition the museum has lost all sense of place and procession. Equally disorienting is an unfortunate mixture of art and commerce created by the insertion of sales counters at critical points throughout the building.

The idea of a master plan was launched by Thomas Hoving shortly after he became director of the Metropolitan in 1967. Having scored a coup of sorts by obtaining the Temple of Dendur from the U.S. government (to which it had been donated by Egypt), he needed to make good the conditions of the gift: insurance of the monument's safety and its placement in "a setting appropriate to its archaeological character." As Hoving told the critic William Marlin:

> I had to find an architect! There was no time to have one
> of those committees traveling over the world, visiting
> museums, and interviewing their designers. What with
> Robert Lehman's collection coming to the museum, and
> with Egypt's already having committed Dendur to us,
> there was not time to spend six or eight months looking
> for the right architect. We had to get off the blocks fast
> and get a master plan underway.

As this statement makes abundantly clear, Hoving's desperate haste to secure various large gifts ruled out the thoughtful weighing of alternatives usually associated with a public institution's selection of an architect. The firm of Roche and Dinkeloo, with whom Hoving was unfamiliar, was engaged at the recommendation of the architect Arthur Rosenblatt, the director's deputy during his previous tenure as New York City Parks Commissioner (and who became vice

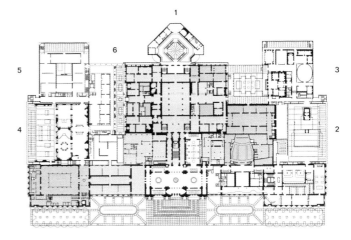

↑ Museum ground-floor plan with 1970 master plan unshaded.
Wings:
1. Robert Lehman
2. Sackler
3. American and Charles Engelhard Court
4. Michael C. Rockefeller
5. Lila Acheson Wallace
6. Henry R. Kravis and Carroll and Milton Petrie European Sculpture Court

TOP: Facade by Richard Morris Hunt (1902). ↑
BOTTOM: Facade with front steps by Roche and
Dinkeloo (1970) and exhibition banners.

Exterior by McKim, Mead and White (1913). →
At right, American Wing by Roche
and Dinkeloo (1980).

president for architecture and planning at the Metropolitan). The firm's fine reputation at the time, its highly praised Oakland Museum in California and Ford Foundation headquarters in New York, and its proven ability to remain within budget argued persuasively for its hiring. However, as with so many of the museum's previous comprehensive programs, by the time it was completed, 20 years later, the architects' monumental, geometric glass-and-steel aesthetic was hopelessly outdated. Furthermore, their design had been seriously skewed by changes made to accommodate new gifts.

In recognition of the museum's increased attendance, first on Roche and Dinkeloo's long list of tasks was the redesign of the front steps and Great Hall. While the new stairway, enlarged for lateral as well as frontal access, meets its intended function (although it has been plagued from the beginning by poor drainage), its scale and shape seriously compromise Richard Morris Hunt's elegant facade (1895–1902). The facade, with its three arches and flanking pairs of giant, freestanding columns, is a consummate example of Beaux-Arts composition. But the strong vertical emphasis of its colossal order—which survived even the addition of extensive wings by McKim, Mead and White (1911–1926)—was weakened when the new stairs made the facade appear to be part of a long horizontal background. Compounding the perception are the linear fountains (which become unsightly empty containers when they are inoperative, as they are much of the time). Banners advertising temporary exhibitions further detract from the facade by hiding its magnificent thermal windows.

In terms of preservation and overall effect, the renovation of Hunt's Great Hall is equally disappointing. Its former elegant gray has been repainted in several shades of rosy beige, isolating delicate moldings from the walls. The result is especially damaging in the north and south archways, where the contrast between dark walls and their lighter-colored stone framing contradicts their original monochromatic unity.

Of all the new wings, the triangular 25,000-square-foot Robert Lehman (1975), its $7.1 million cost paid for entirely by the donor's funds, was the first and most successful architecturally. Its clear organization of three gallery levels (two above grade) around a skylit, 82-foot-high court differs from that of wings designed as open space, within which displays are adjusted according to programmatic needs. The architects wisely left exposed the warm red-brick-

and-stone western facade (1880) by the museum's first architects, Calvert Vaux and Jacob Wrey Mould, which provides a nice transition to the modern addition. Fortunately, Roche and Dinkeloo's misguided project to replace the grand staircase with a wide corridor (flanked by escalators) from the Great Hall to the new wing was halted by preservationists.

The Lehman presents a truly great series of Old Master paintings worthy of the mini-museum that has been created for it. To secure such a collection any museum would understandably go a long way. But the Metropolitan's honoring of the donor's request to re-create seven rooms from his West 54th Street house is troubling. The Lehman interiors were designed in 1959 by a Paris decorator in imitation of 1905 rooms that were themselves an approximation of what the appropriate background for the paintings might be. As such, the museum's spaces ape a twice-fantasized reproduction and constitute a misleading use of historical replication. (At the Dallas Museum of Art, the re-creation of Wendy and Emery Reves's Villa La Pausa on the Côte d'Azur is an equally bizarre and contrived context for historical objects—in this case, decorative art.)

At the center of the museum's Central Park facade the Lehman's unfenestrated limestone walls are as uninviting as the museum's other limestone elevations; only the pavilion's lesser size and pyramidal skylight make it slightly less forbidding. Except for a few small, flat windows on the southern facade, the Lila Acheson Wallace Wing (1987) and the American Wing (1980) at the northwest are enclosed by the same solid masonry walls. The glass-and-steel facades of the other two new wings, the Sackler (1978) and the Michael C. Rockefeller (1982), as

well as those of the adjacent Charles Engelhard Court (1980) and the Carroll and Milton Petrie European Sculpture Court (1990), are designed in what the historian Helen Searing calls the "greenhouse aesthetic." From within, the formula works, but on the exterior the vast, sloping glass-and-metal walls of the wings (opaque during the day) look more like glazed airplane hangars than greenhouses. They are joined to older wings by unsightly concrete joints, and the juxtaposition of their cold materials with McKim, Mead and White's beautifully detailed limestone facades is as jarring an element here as I. M. Pei's glass-and-steel pyramid is at the Louvre.

In 1970, to appease protests about its incursion on the park, the Metropolitan promised to open its western side, and indeed both the Engelhard and Petrie courts have an array of doors that could do so. Alas, they have never been put into service. What a difference it would make to the museum's image and use if it could welcome visitors approaching on foot from the park—as well as Fifth Avenue—in a cross-circulation pattern common to the new European museums (see Chapters 6 and 7).

← Sackler Wing (1978). Temple of Dendur.

The Sackler Wing, with its famed Temple of Dendur, and the Michael C. Rockefeller Wing, housing Nelson Rockefeller's collection of tribal art, both suffer from design compromises unworthy of their treasures. Views to the park through the temple hall's glazed north wall provide a suitable backdrop of land and sky for the Egyptian artifact. Unfortunately, the hall's south wall— meant to be a glazed tilted surface in harmony with the opposite wall and through which mirrors were to reflect natural light and the changing sky-scape—was reconfigured by the museum to accommodate more programs. The result is a long blank wall with a heavy overhang that is deadening in its effect. Furthermore, placement of the diminutive temple (41 by 21 feet) and small gateway at the far end of their podium, to leave more space for social functions, accentuates the disparity of scale between the relatively small objects and the gigantic (165 by 200 by 72 feet) glass-and-steel cage in which they stand so forlornly.

By the same token, in the Rockefeller Wing the architects' intended second-level balcony was fully enclosed when plans for the installation of the Andre Meyer collection in the upper level elicited the former New York State governor's declaration that nobody else's gallery or collection was going to "look down on" *his* primitive art. If the upper part of this south-facing wall had been left open, the Andre Meyer Galleries (1980) would have had natural light and views to the park instead of being the closed boxes they are. Additionally, people moving on the balcony would have animated the peripheral space below, which, with far fewer visitors than the central portion of the Rockefeller Wing, is now lifeless.

As disturbing as many of these results are, they pale when compared to the design of the $26 million, 70,000-square-foot southwest wing (1987) named after *Reader's Digest* cofounder Lila Acheson Wallace. Originally allocated to European sculpture and decorative arts, and briefly to the ill-fated Annenberg School of Communications project for a fine arts center, this wing was not designated for Modern art in the new master plan. But in 1987 Montebello announced that "ninety-nine percent of all collectors—the rich, those who are interested and will support museums in the future—are collectors of contemporary art. We are not as an act of volition going to cut ourselves off from the supporters of the future." It was a shockingly opportunistic declaration for an institution with a record of indifference toward Modern art.

Given this shaky premise, the Lila Acheson Wallace Wing got the architecture it deserved. By the time he designed it, Roche had long since abandoned his 1970s late Modern vocabulary and was willing to work in almost any style, as witnessed by his neo-Gothic addition to the Jewish Museum (1992). Described by the critic Joseph Giovannini as "opaque in its organization, muddy in its details and leaden in spirit," the five-level addition of the Wallace Wing is a confusing jumble of undistinguished spaces.

Predicated by their relationship to the earlier Rockefeller Wing, ceiling heights vary from a relatively low 11 feet in the first rooms to 20 feet on the second level and 32 feet in the Blanche and A. L. Levine Court. None of these measurements works: the lower, track-encrusted ceilings are oppressive in dull galleries with no natural light, while the 20-foot walls on the second level are too high for the art they display. Even the largest works shown on them—Jackson Pollock's mural-size *Autumn Rhythm*, for example—are diminished by these overscaled planes (a recurring problem in new museums). In discussing the exhibition of large canvases typical of

Lila Acheson Wallace Wing (1987).

← Blanche and A. L. Levine Court.

↓ Second-floor gallery, with *Autumn Rhythm (Number 30)* by Jackson Pollock at center.

Abstract Expressionists like Pollock, MoMA's William Rubin cites Mark Rothko's statement, "I paint big to be intimate." Rubin points out that such paintings displace the wall itself and are best seen in relatively small spaces where they enjoy a breadth and intimacy that they lose on 20-foot-high walls: "When shown in overly large rooms, these paintings become like the easel pictures the artists wanted to avoid."

Height is not the only problem with the ceilings. In the top-floor galleries, wall partitions and light tracks intrude on skylights that should be uninterrupted. Capping the Levine Court, a heavy soffit effects an awkward transition between the glazed outer wall and the high ceiling, and detailing is crude. The court's generous dimensions (136 by 36 by 30 feet) should make the space a dramatic climax to the wing, but they don't. Instead, the gallery is constricted by its sloping glass wall, whose framing elements, like those in the Temple of Dendur Hall, cast distracting shadows throughout the interior.

The Metropolitan unquestionably maintains its status as a world-class museum, but where its architecture is concerned, it does not live up to that standard. Its recent renovations are the product of a curious design philosophy: in a laudable effort to provide more contextual settings for period collections, the museum has resorted to a reproduction style better suited to Disneyland. This is neither an accurate restoration of existing architecture nor a contemporary reinterpretation of historical sources; rather, it is the creation of something that looks old but isn't.

19th-Century European Painting and Sculpture Galleries, by David Harvey and Gary Tinterow.

The most egregious example of this kind of misrepresentation is the new 19th-Century European Painting and Sculpture Galleries. This area—formerly the Andre Meyer Galleries—was initially designed by Kevin Roche: its Modernist open space with movable wall panels, pedestals and freestanding casework lit by a gridded skylit ceiling was more appropriate to a transient exhibition than to the priceless collection of 19th-century art it contained. But the attempt to transform galleries that were inimical to their contents errs in the other direction: it replaces neutrality with pastiche. The Engelhard curator, Gary Tinterow, who with David Harvey, the Metropolitan's senior exhibition designer, undertook the renovation, describes the 1993 installation as an imagined reconstruction of a turn-of-the-century McKim, Mead and White gallery. In the absence of drawings or artifacts for such a design, Tinterow says "we re-created the past we wished we had had" (substituting painted wood and plaster-covered Sheetrock for limestone, plaster and marble). It is the kind of conjectural assemblage that produced the Getty Museum in Malibu, for which archaeologists worked from drawings and models of the Villa dei Papiri and other Roman villas to produce a building described by the writer Umberto Eco as what "it ought to have been." In both cases the result is kitsch inauthenticity, similar to that of the Lehman townhouse rooms. In the absence of an original Renoir the Metropolitan would not commission an imagined one; the Andre Meyer Galleries are the design equivalent of such an absurd substitution.

The light and views incorporated in Roche's original design would have been a far greater asset to the museum than this contrivance. They would have provided orientation that is now sadly lacking in the galleries' department-store-like assemblage of rooms; they would also have rendered the whole wing more intelligible, with the sloping glass curtain wall a visible reminder of the space's contemporary envelope. From the beginning the Metropolitan has made the mistake of attempting to unify new and old rather than leaving intact the legacies of each generation of architects. As a result, important designs have been lost and many areas of the museum feel placeless.

The Metropolitan's continuous growth did not end with the completion of the 1970 master plan: in the spring of 1997 that plan became Phase I of a newly conceived three-part expansion. In the $44 million second phase Kevin Roche will add 60,000 square feet to the air space above the grand staircase. The purpose of this expansion is to restore the Roman court, now occupied by the museum's restaurant, to its original function of exhibiting Greek and Roman art. The test will be whether the new addition can be connected with the existing structure in a rational way, and if it can justify construction over glazed roof areas that were meant to be unobstructed. The tentative third phase entails construction of a three-story building within the air space above what will be the restored Roman court.

THE MUSEUM OF MODERN ART, NEW YORK

New York, New York

by **Philip L. Goodwin and Edward Durell Stone**

1939

over 56,000 square feet

25,100 square feet of exhibition space

$2 million

Grace Rainey Rogers Memorial Annex (1951)
by Philip Johnson; Landes Gores, associate
17,850 square feet
$3.65 million

East and Garden Wings (1964)
by Philip Johnson Associates
63,000 square feet / 16,290 square feet of exhibition space
$5.5 million

Museum Tower Wing (1984)
by Cesar Pelli & Associates
164,000 square feet / 65,000 square feet of exhibition space
$55 million

Current Expansion Project:
"Toward the New Museum of Modern Art:
A Museum for the 21st Century"
580,000 square feet of which 280,000 is new space /
133,000 square feet of exhibition space of which 50,000 is new
$400 million capital campaign

One of the most unsettling aspects of MoMA's current plan to increase its size by almost 50 percent is the perception that the museum may eventually take over the whole block it now occupies (presumably with the exception of St. Thomas's Church). MoMA's ongoing expansions, coupled with the remarkably conservative design it most recently selected to implement the plans, remove it even further from the intention of its famed first director, Alfred Barr Jr. Barr wanted to "metabolically" discard older works as new art was acquired in what he called the "torpedo concept": to remain "modern," the collection would never span more than a 50-year period, a procedure of attrition that thc director likened to "a torpedo moving through time, its nose the ever advancing present, its tail the ever receding past." This emphasis on the cutting edge was abandoned in the early 1950s when it was perceived by Barr and the trustees as a deterrent to future donations. From then on the museum focused on building a permanent collection of Modern art—beginning with post-Impressionism, around 1880, through the 1970s. While MoMA now owns the most important such collection in the world, concentration on enlarging and showing it gradually changed the nature of the museum. What began in the 1930s as a revolutionary institution—with its innovative presentations of unfamiliar painting and sculpture and a new, interdisciplinary approach to art—by the 1960s had become primarily the repository and custodian of a permanent collection of accepted masterpieces that were presented with didactic authority. Descriptions of the museum after this change invoked religious imagery, as in Tom Wolfe's reaction to the 1964 expansion:

> It will reopen firmly established as a spiritual center, a sanctuary for what has become quite literally the new religion, the new Unitarianism, for intellectuals and socialites: Culture, and more particularly Art, with Picasso the great living saint and Matisse and Cézanne in the hagiology.

After another expansion 20 years later the *New Yorker* critic Calvin Tomkins declared that the "installations display the synoptic gospel of modern art according to MoMA . . . in which doubts seem to suggest a lack of faith."

In 1997 Rem Koolhaas, a participant in the museum's expansion charrette that year, asked:

> What can you challenge in a Temple?
> How do you cohabit with God(s)?

In a not uncommon progression the revolutionary turned establishment. Programming and presentation of art that was too good an investment to part with preempted experimentation. But times had also changed. By the late 1960s MoMA was no longer a pioneer in the exhibition of Modern and contemporary art, including photography and other media, which were by then widely available in America and Europe in art fairs, exhibition halls and galleries—in addition to museums. The museum had to settle for being the authoritative leader in the Modern field, which, as the century neared completion, appeared increasingly removed in time to a younger generation of curators more interested in the challenge of contemporary art. Along with a growing perception of the 1984 expansion as a museological failure, these concerns are behind the institution's present attempt to reinvent itself, for which it seems to position architecture as the guiding force.

MoMA's record in the architectural arena, however, is discouraging. While exhibitions like the seminal 1932 one on the International Style pioneered Modern architecture and design, and other exhibitions have demonstrated the importance of historic preservation and sensitive urban design, with its own building and its impact on the city, the museum has consistently fallen short of its stated ideals.

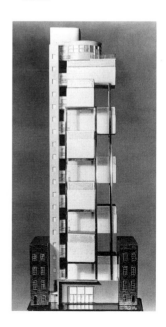

↓ William Lescaze and George Howe, unbuilt Scheme Number Four for the Museum of Modern Art (1930). Model.

MoMA's single daring design gesture remains unrealized. In 1930, the year after the museum's founding, while still at its first location in the Heckscher Building at 730 Fifth Avenue, the trustees approached the young partnership of George Howe, an Ecole des Beaux-Arts–trained architect, and William Lescaze, a Modernist, regarding schemes for a new building. It was a prescient move, as two years later Howe and Lescaze achieved wide recognition and praise for their groundbreaking Philadelphia Saving Fund Society building. Among the several proposals they made to the museum, Scheme Number Four was particularly interesting: nine gallery boxes stacked at right angles to one another (five short galleries extending east to west, four long ones north to south) included glazed chambers that mixed natural and artificial light; the ceilings anticipated ingenious Swiss museum designs such as current ones by Peter Zumthor and Gigon and Guyer (see Chapters 2 and 3). Structurally, the way each gallery box rested on a framework of beams carried on columns rather than on the gallery below was also forward-looking. This and several other of Howe and Lescaze's schemes were more innovative than anything MoMA has ever built.

← LEFT: **View of museum by Philip L. Goodwin and Edward Durell Stone** (1939).
RIGHT: **Ground-floor plan.**

↓ **Galleries** (1939).

Rather than implement one of these proposals, in 1932 the museum moved into a townhouse at 11 West 53rd Street leased from John D. Rockefeller Jr. When interest in a new building revived in 1935, the trustees turned to one of their own, the ultra-conservative architect Philip L. Goodwin, ignoring Barr's entreaties for assistance from an established European Modernist like J. J. P. Oud, Walter Gropius or Mies van der Rohe. Instead, Goodwin was allowed to choose his own collaborator, the young American Edward Durell Stone, thus pairing, as in the case of Howe and Lescaze, a Modernist with a Beaux-Arts romanticist. But as Howe's biographer, the architect Robert A. M. Stern, observes, Goodwin's designs were generally less interesting than Howe's, and Stone's work was more moderne than Modern. Thus, MoMA's new 56,000-square-foot structure—completed in 1939—was a hybrid of Beaux-Arts, Art Deco and Modernism that a later trustee, Philip Johnson, described as "a watered [down] version of an International Style building." As an early, though cautious, example of the new architecture, however, the taut, boxy six-story structure appeared revolutionary, and the loftlike, columned spaces, in which three floors of galleries were created at will by movable panels instead of fixed walls, certainly provided a fresh way of exhibiting art.

Within eight years of the building's inauguration, Goodwin was asked to design an additional wing whose funding was supposed to come from a $3.6 million capital campaign. It was the first, and in this case unsuccessful, effort in what was to be the museum's pattern of associating what it called "an exciting building project" with fund-raising.

In 1951 a seven-story wing for offices, classrooms and a gallery was added on the site of a townhouse west of the museum. Called the Grace Rainey Rogers Memorial Annex, it was designed by Johnson, the director of the Department of Architecture (Design was added definitively in 1949) from 1932 to 1934 and again from 1946 to 1954, who, together with the historian Henry-Russell Hitchcock, had curated the museum's International Style exhibition. An admirer and proponent of Mies van der Rohe's, Johnson simply applied the European Modernist's glass-and-steel vocabulary to the addition's facade. As New York's introduction to a style that subsequently swept the world in the form of skyscrapers like Mies's Seagram Building (1958), on which Johnson collaborated, the addition was well received and established him as the museum's architect of choice for the next two decades.

↓ At west of 1939 building, Grace Rainey Rogers Memorial Annex by Philip Johnson (1951).

That Johnson's facade was a novelty in the United States detracted from the fact that it destroyed part of the contextual contrast that was so important to the original building. When framed by dark brownstones and ornate Beaux-Arts townhouses, Goodwin and Stone's flat white facade, with its great rectangle of translucent glass, was considerably more effective than when viewed as just another modern planar surface.

Like Goodwin before him, Johnson was asked to design an expansion, again associated with an effort to raise money. In 1959 MoMA trustee Nelson Rockefeller, whose passion for construction was routinely referred to as his "edifice complex," spearheaded a $25 million Thirtieth-Anniversary Campaign. The plans for an eight-story wing included 31,000 square feet of galleries east of the museum's garden on West 54th Street. Johnson's projected sidewalk arcade and unfenestrated, travertine-clad facades, broken into narrow bays articulated by pilasters, were in the same quickly dated neoclassical mode that he would be using for other buildings, notably the Amon Carter Museum of Western Art in Fort Worth, Texas, and the New York State Theater at Lincoln Center. The trustees were prepared to see this inappropriate structure, proposed as the museum's new entrance, upstage the older building, to which it was to be linked by a five-story, Miesian steel-and-glass connector and a windowless brick stair tower. Fortunately, height and other concerns halted the project.

Within a year Johnson's scheme was relaunched in a reduced format: a 37,680-square-foot wing on the site of two newly purchased brownstones east of the museum on West 53rd Street and a smaller garden wing. (In 1953 Johnson's widely acclaimed Abby Aldrich Rockefeller Sculpture Garden had replaced the original flat and curvilinear design with what he conceived as a series of rectilinear outdoor rooms.) To accommodate the enlarged institution, Johnson centered what had been the lobby's corner entrance, so as to lead visitors from the street to the garden on axis, and replaced the original wavy canopy with a rectangular one. But the ambitions of the 1959 plan were not abandoned, and in the early 1970s, before the Museum Tower plan was in place, a proposal was launched that might have been used to justify an enlarged garden wing. Observing that at the time the Guggenheim Museum was used mainly for changing exhibitions, MoMA's Rubin suggested a merger of the two institutions that would allow the Guggenheim to exhibit its rarely seen permanent collection and coincidentally let MoMA fill in the missing links in its holdings. Rubin argued that together the two collections would present a nearly complete history of Modern art. Off-the-record discussions between Richard Oldenburg (who became director of MoMA in 1972), Rubin and Thomas Messer, then director of the Guggenheim, were inconclusive.

Johnson used the same Miesian idiom for the East Wing facade as he had for the Rogers Annex (but with the addition of curved fillets at the corners of the steel frames). Bracketed on both sides by steel-and-glass wings, the original facade was now completely overpowered. Furthermore, Johnson's transformation of the intimate lobby into a wide marble concourse began the move from the museum's distinctive townhouse scale toward a large, impersonal institution.

The East Wing's three floors of galleries (each 50 by 100 feet) and the garden gallery gave MoMA its first large free-span exhibition spaces. With slightly higher ceilings than in the old rooms (which varied from 12 to 14 feet), the biggest East Wing gallery was described by Rubin as "a single space of exquisite proportion, with light at both ends." Intended for large-scale contemporary art, this generous, daylit gallery is arguably the museum's most accomplished space (with the exception of the sculpture garden)—and one of the few galleries with a sense of identity. But the process that had compromised other aspects of the building soon destroyed its merits.

The austerity of MoMA's 1939 galleries had been tempered: the main galleries had enjoyed daylight thanks to the translucent Thermolux

↓ Large East Wing gallery (1964).

that replaced clear glass in the facade, and the third-floor galleries were skylit. Windows provided occasional views to the exterior. Walls here and there were darkened to relieve the monotony of pervasively white interiors; curtains separated and softened some spaces. This was never architecture to make the heart leap, yet gradually even its distinguishing features were eliminated. To obtain more wall space, curators permanently covered the Thermolux, despite the provision of adjustable cement asbestos panels that were easily fitted into the glazing bars. Although the Thermolux was retained behind the stairway a little longer than elsewhere, here too light was eventually blocked, thereby eliminating the stair's dramatic silhouette. The third-floor skylights were plastered over, curtains and color banished. In like manner the windows in Johnson's gallery were almost always covered, and the excessive use of partitions to maximize hanging space created what Rubin calls "rabbit-warren-like" rooms.

From the time it reopened after the 1964 expansion, MoMA's finances worsened: with only one exception the museum ran an annual deficit of $1 million, and its stock market portfolio dwindled from $27.1 million in 1969 to $16 million in 1975. (It nevertheless acquired in 1966 the former Whitney Museum building—now called the North Wing—on West 54th Street.) Within four years of the East Wing addition, MoMA lawyer Richard H. Koch came up with a new expansion plan to be coupled with a novel approach to fund-raising. While financially brilliant and still successful, this scheme further impoverished the museum's architecture and contradicted standards it had championed since its founding.

Koch proposed that the museum sell its air rights and participate in the development of a revenue-producing high-rise condominium made possible by the sale. To carry out this scheme, he brought in a planner and a lawyer who had served in the city's design and planning agencies, Richard S. Weinstein and Donald H. Elliott. As Mayor Lindsay's director of the Office of Lower Manhattan Development, Weinstein had implemented incentive zoning to animate particular neighborhoods. One product of this strategy was the South Street Seaport Historic District, which would become a model for MoMA's air-rights transfer. Elliott created legislation for a non-profit state agency, the Trust for Cultural Resources, which allowed the purchase of air or property rights from cultural institutions and provided the means for the profitable real estate development of that property.

Basically, Elliott's complex plan was threefold: the $7 million sale of air rights to allow construction of a $23 million condominium tower whose height was announced variously as between 40 and 55 floors, a $17 million gallery expansion and a $75 million capital campaign to finance the project and boost the endowment. An intricate tax-exemption scheme on income from the tower (starting at $350,000 and rising in time to several million) permitted the trust to receive most of the monies the condominium would normally have paid in taxes to the city. The scheme eventually solved MoMA's financial problems, but its announcement in 1976 outraged the architectural community, whose members had a hard time accepting the implied desecration of the city's historic balance between low mid-block zoning and high-rise avenues. That such a breach of the respected norm should come from this former advocate of quality design and planning made it particularly shocking. The *New York Times* architecture critic Ada Louise Huxtable called the project a "dubious undertaking" and the tower "bad news."

As well as criticizing the tower's impact on zoning, Huxtable questioned the condemnation powers—for revenue-producing rather than public-use purposes—given to the museum by the trust legislation. These were aimed at ensuring MoMA's ability to take over the adjacent quarters of the Museum of Contemporary Crafts as well as two historical, but not landmarked, townhouses. The two museums came to an amicable agreement in 1978, and the condemnation rights were not exercised; the houses, however, were demolished.

Cesar Pelli, then a promising young architect whose Pacific Design Center in Los Angeles had opened in 1971 to general acclaim, was chosen in 1977 to execute the project. He was tapped for his proven ability to deliver on time and on budget—something the trustees were uncertain whether Philip Johnson could do. (Johnson, who had been working with his partner, John Burgee, since 1969 on expansion studies that included the tower, was so enraged at this decision that he revoked the promised bequest to the museum of his Glass House.) By the time of Pelli's selection, Weinstein had located the exact site the Museum Tower would occupy, determined its size and come up with the idea of a glass enclosure in the museum's garden to house escalators. "It wasn't an opportunity for strong architectural statement," Weinstein said, "because by the time you solved all the problems, there were very few choices you could make"—a condition intrinsic to most expansion projects. The tower's columns, elevator and stairwell core limited the sequence of spaces and the heights of the new galleries, as they will in the museum's current expansion. Pelli's restructuring of circulation with a greenhouse-like enclosure of escalators and open corridors in the so-called Garden Hall reduced the garden area significantly, intruded on its privacy and completely changed the museum's character.

↑ At east of 1939 building, wing by Philip Johnson (1964). At west, Museum Tower by Cesar Pelli (1984).

Escalators in museums are almost always problematic. It is not without reason that a grand stairway was an essential part of the great 19th-century museum prototype: it conveyed a sense of ceremony, procession and anticipation that is still valid in today's automated world. Frank Gehry's combination of stairs and a ramp (the modern equivalent of stairs) in the Bilbao Guggenheim's monumental atrium (see Chapter 7) and Richard Meier's gracefully curved stair in the entrance rotunda of the J. Paul Getty Museum (see Chapter 6)—not to mention the dazzling ramps of his other museums—prepare the visitor for looking at art in a way that escalators do not. The activity required by stairs contrasts favorably with the passivity with which people are moved—like inanimate objects—by noisy escalators. Questionable in the first place as a solution for MoMA's circulation, Pelli's segmental escalators do not create the excitement of continuous movement as do, for example, those at the Centre Pompidou (see Chapter 6). (An exception to the rule, the Pompidou's exterior escalators are a success because of their link to the urban experience.)

In the hall's sharp daylight the shoddy detailing that characterizes this expansion is painfully noticeable (at a cost of $55 million, Pelli claims it was "the cheapest of any major museum ever built"). The original marble staircase was eliminated between the ground and first floors, rendering its preservation between the second and third levels meaningless, even more so since it was no longer backlit. The new underground galleries for contemporary art are oppressive; the restaurant that replaced the large Garden Wing gallery unwelcoming.

The entrance lobby's various incarnations illustrate the museum's changing image. Most of Goodwin and Stone's ground floor was occupied by a large gallery; as if reluctant to take anything away from space for art, the architects squeezed a small ticket-and-information desk into the narrowest possible entrance lobby. In all its corporate sleekness, Johnson's 1964 substitution of circulation space for galleries at least retained the presence of art, with a clear view from the entrance to the sculpture garden and two small exhibition rooms. But in 1984 the escalator and a large central information desk blocked sightlines to the sculpture garden and left only a pair of short walls to hang pictures on. Art was progressively moved farther away from MoMA's entrance hall in favor of circulation spaces more akin to a shopping mall than to an art museum. Indeed, when approached from Fifth Avenue, the bookstore entrance upstages that of the museum.

One of many problems with the 1984 expansion was the uninterrupted linearity of the galleries. By extending MoMA's rectangular footprint under the Museum Tower, the sequence of exhibition rooms became longer and, because of the tower's core, more rigid. Compared with the exciting museums going up worldwide, the Pelli building aged poorly. Within ten years of its completion MoMA's endowment had risen to over $220 million, its annual revenues ($16 million before the expansion) to $58 million. But unhappiness with the building had also increased, and in 1996 the museum announced its purchase of the

← TOP: **Lobby by Goodwin and Stone (1939).**
CENTER: **Lobby by Philip Johnson (1964).**
BOTTOM: **Lobby and Garden Hall by Cesar Pelli (1984).**

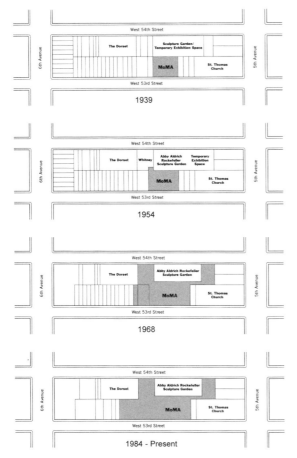

Dorset Hotel on West 54th Street and two adjacent townhouses. There are rumors that MoMA is negotiating for other properties on West 54th Street as well: linked with the current project to add over 200,000 square feet to the museum's 380,000 is a $400 million funding campaign, $250 million of which is allocated to acquisition, demolition and construction. A second tower development in order to meet these goals has not been ruled out.

For the first time in its history, MoMA—whose Department of Architecture and Design has vigorously sponsored design competitions for low-cost furniture and for posters, textiles and architecture—in March 1997 opened the selection of its own architect to the competitive process. However, rather than a clear-cut competition, the selection committee opted for an initial charrette (a process whereby schemes are developed according to strict rules and within a tight time frame) in which ten firms were invited to participate in November 1996. These architects were chosen at the end of a lengthy process that included trustee visits to new museums in Japan, Europe and the United States and a private conference of artists, architects, museum directors and a handful of trustees at the Rockefeller estate at Pocantico Hills. In view of what the present MoMA director Glenn Lowry calls a need "not for more space, but a fundamentally different space," it was surprising to see a list of architects who, for the most part, work in the same Modernist style that MoMA has espoused from the beginning: Wiel Arets and Rem Koolhaas from the Netherlands; Herzog and de Meuron, Switzerland; Toyo Ito and Yoshio Taniguchi, Japan; Dominique Perrault, France; and four New York–based firms—Steven Holl, Bernard Tschumi, Rafael Viñoly and Tod Williams Billie Tsien.

In the absence of a clearly defined mission for the museum, the candidates were expected to help develop a program. This strategy can be successful for new buildings, as in some instances at the Getty Center, but it is trickier for a project handicapped from the outset by an existing building and by a zoning code that is one of the most restrictive in Manhattan. In the late 1970s, when MoMA was preparing for the Pelli expansion, a change in location was considered. The trustees preferred to remain at the old site, despite its strictures. The West 53rd/54th Street location imposes even greater restraints on the design of the current expansion—ironically as a result of the museum's own high-rise development. Reacting to the Museum Tower and to other similarly overscaled midtown structures, the city revised its zoning for this area, creating a preservation district to prevent what it regards as a loss of air and light equal to that for which New York's seminal 1916 zoning code was enacted. The FAR (floor-to-area ratio) for West 54th Street, which is lower than that applied to the rest of midtown, combines with the structure of the tower's core and the site's awkward L-shape to further complicate construction. It is what Philip Johnson calls "an insoluble problem on an insoluble site."

Without a specific assignment, and instructed to conceptualize the new museum rather than actually to design it, the charrette results were disappointing. As the only proposal to embrace rather than ignore the disruptive tower, Rem Koolhaas's rejected scheme dealt the most skillfully with the complexities of the site. However, the Dutch architect's irreverent approach to the institution

← **Museum Tower Wing by Cesar Pelli (1984). Gallery.**

← **Site plans of MoMA from 1939 to 1998.**

↓ **Site plan of current expansion project.**

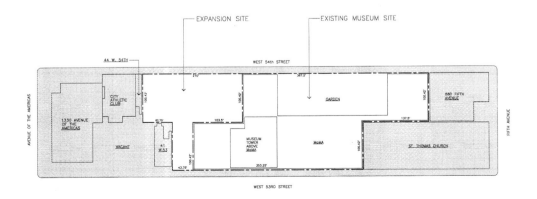

ruled him out in favor of the more respectful proposals of the three finalists—Herzog and de Meuron (see Chapter 1), Yoshio Taniguchi and Bernard Tschumi. Of Herzog and de Meuron's two charrette proposals, one placed galleries around the garden and dressed up the existing building with glass facades; the more radical scheme removed the garden to the roof of their addition and introduced behind the existing West 53rd Street entrance two square courtyards reminiscent of the Kunsthalle in their native Basel. Taniguchi and Tschumi both left the garden in place but moved the entry to West 54th Street. Taniguchi then segregated the activities, putting commercial—the restaurant and store—on 53rd Street, cultural on 54th Street. Tschumi was the only participant in the charrette to concentrate on the interior rather than the exterior, positioning what he called "core" galleries (permanent collection) in central instead of peripheral spaces, which he left to "satellite" galleries (temporary exhibitions) to make the museum a "hotbed of experimentation."

MoMA's selection in December 1997 of the most restrained of the three competition schemes belies its repeatedly stated intention to treat architecture as the signal for change. In presenting Taniguchi's winning entry, Lowry remarked that the architect had used the same vocabulary in his Toyota Municipal Museum of Art in Toyota City, Japan (1995), as that of the original MoMA. The architect's proposal is indeed so beholden to Bauhaus Modernism that it could well be a product of the 1940s.

The merits of Taniguchi's proposal lie in its reallocation of space rather than in formal invention. The scheme breaks down a large and unwieldy program (whose excessive scale ensures a corporate, rather than a cultural, identity for the museum) into three quasi-separate structures; it restores to its original size the sculpture garden (including the south terrace) from which, as in the schemes of the other two finalists, Pelli's escalators have been removed. And it exposes the base of the tower, giving it a dignity it lacked when embedded in the museum's mass. The new Dorset Wing on West 54th Street at the western part of the area allocated for construction (a strip was kept in reserve) contains the painting and sculpture galleries; the Goodwin-Stone building houses departmental galleries, the auditoriums, some offices,

Winning entry for ↑
MoMA expansion by
Yoshio Taniguchi
(1997). Model, West
54th Street facade.

the design/book store and café. Another new 54th Street wing at the garden's east is designated for education and research, staff offices and an entrance for group visits.

MoMA's main entrance is moved to the Dorset Wing on West 54th Street, where three setbacks faced in aluminum panels allow skylights for the galleries. Both new West 54th Street facades are clad in black slate—in deference perhaps to Eero Saarinen's black granite CBS headquarters on West 53rd Street at Sixth Avenue—each with a single window. The principal entranceway leads to a large skylit and amply fenestrated atrium providing vertical circulation, daylight to the adjoining galleries and views of the garden (its sculpture is the only art visible at this level). Taniguchi addresses the museum's program by foregrounding the permanent collection's contemporary art in second-floor galleries that offer the building's highest and balconied exhibition spaces; above them will be smaller galleries for the Modern collection and, at the top, skylit spaces for temporary shows. The 1939 off-axis West 53rd Street entrance and curvilinear canopy will be restored to provide access to the film theaters. A public passageway with views of the garden connects West 53rd and 54th Streets.

While the two other finalists suggested new images for MoMA—Herzog and de Meuron's by means of a slim, asymmetrically faceted office tower and new imprinted glazed facades, Tschumi's by means of an enormous electronic billboard and a gallery cantilevered over the existing north wing—the museum preferred Taniguchi's reinforcement of what was already there. His re-creation of the streamlined West 53rd Street entrance; his exact restoration of the Goodwin-Stone facade (recalled in his new West 54th Street facades) and of Philip Johnson's 1964 facade; his extension of the Bauhaus stairway to connect the department levels; and most significantly, his strictly rectilinear white galleries all look to the past, not the future.

Taniguchi's elegant building will upgrade the quality of MoMA's current plant and reinstate important earlier design elements such as skylights and views to the exterior. However, as neat as its plan seems to be, the scheme ignores the museum's wish for more interplay between departments, which remain as separate as ever. With all its shortcomings, the Goodwin-Stone building introduced a way of showing Modern art for which the new scheme offers no equivalent. Those invited to take part in the charrette were told that "throughout its history, the Museum of Modern Art has used architecture as a vehicle of self-expression and regeneration, articulating and re-articulating its evolving understanding of modern art in built form." As with MoMA's past expansions, this translates into more of the same: a sacred sanctuary for MoMA's gospel of art.

THE SOLOMON R. GUGGENHEIM MUSEUM ADDITION AND RESTORATION

New York, New York

by **Gwathmey Siegel &
Associates**

1992

23,240 square feet

12,500 square feet of exhibition space

and renovation of existing building

$57.9 million

Like MoMA and the Metropolitan, the Guggenheim and the Whitney were both willing to sacrifice the architecture of their original buildings for more space. But there was a big difference. Whereas the Metropolitan had undergone so many changes that it no longer had any particular architectural identity, and MoMA was never perceived as a masterpiece, the Frank Lloyd Wright and Marcel Breuer buildings were still relatively intact and regarded as modern icons. Both projects raised important questions about the public's attitude toward museum expansion in terms of aesthetics and civic obligation: the Guggenheim's announcement in 1985 of a plan to add a wing designed by Gwathmey Siegel provoked as much controversy as the original building had: soon after excavation at Fifth Avenue and East 89th Street began in 1956, 21 artists, including Willem de Kooning and Franz Kline, signed a formal objection to its curvilinear galleries, adding their protest to that of the general populace. From the moment it opened over three years later, however, many critics and the public loved the Guggenheim—called "the most beautiful building in America" by Emily Genauer in the *New York Herald*.

Thus in 1985, since the dispute concerned the city's only public building by America's best-known architect, New Yorkers generally, and in particular Upper East Side neighborhood groups, joined the architectural community in opposing the addition. Gwathmey Siegel proposed an 11-story tower whose top half, covered in green tiles, was to be cantilevered over the smaller of Wright's two rotundas—originally called the Monitor—adding a square box to the round building in a configuration that was likened to a toilet tank and bowl. The project's offensiveness was heightened by what appeared to be the museum's rush to beat the clock against landmarking, for which the building would be eligible when it turned 30. Given the special nature of Wright's building, this ill-conceived design shows the same indifference to architectural and urban quality as do other "wings that don't fly."

The Guggenheim Museum was produced by three remarkable individuals: Solomon R. Guggenheim, a wealthy businessman courageous enough to become one of the first American collectors of abstract art; Baroness Hilla Rebay, an Alsatian-born painter whose passion for this art approximated religious fervor; and Frank Lloyd Wright, whose design philosophy corresponded exactly with what Guggenheim and Rebay had in mind. Sadly, the product of this extraordinary collaboration never materialized as it was first conceived.

Shortly after meeting Guggenheim, Rebay sparked his interest in such avant-garde artists as Wassily Kandinsky, Piet Mondrian, Albert Gleizes, Fernand Léger, László Moholy-Nagy, Robert Delaunay and Rudolf Bauer, all of whom Guggenheim began collecting instead of traditional art. In 1936 Rebay organized a series of traveling exhibitions with Guggenheim's holdings, the last of which, in 1939, inaugurated a temporary Museum of Non-Objective Painting on East 54th Street near MoMA. Unlike MoMA, with its changing exhibitions and growing collection, the Guggenheim was to be a permanent memorial to its founder, exhibiting only those paintings which he had acquired. Rebay referred to these abstract easel paintings as non-objective: "order creating order and sensitive (and corrective even) to space." In his description of the museum's creation, the architectural historian Neil Levine quotes Rebay's description of the paintings as "organic creations . . . prophets of spiritual life" that announce "the religion of the future." Essential to her concept of how to experience the work was, in Levine's words, "the substitution of passive reception for active engagement." To ensure this experience, in 1943 Rebay contacted Frank Lloyd Wright.

Wright's experiments with spiral shapes over many years, beginning with his 1924–25 project on Sugar Loaf Mountain in Maryland—the Gordon Strong automobile objective and planetarium, a tourist attraction with accompanying parking facilities—were climaxed by his thinking, starting in 1944, about the Guggenheim Museum. His decision to use the spiral for the Guggenheim may have been influenced by the square spiral of Le Corbusier's Musée Mondial part of the unbuilt Mundaneum project for a cultural center in Geneva (1929): its design furthered Wright's continuing effort to break down the box of conventional architecture and create the fluid sense of a space-time continuum by eliminating walls and horizontal floors. His organic philosophy of architecture perfectly complemented Rebay's vision of abstract art. Rebay deliberately rejected European Modernists like Mies and Le Corbusier, whose museum projects were characterized by flexibility and, in the case of Le Corbusier, potential expansion— just what she and Guggenheim did *not* want. Their collaboration with Wright produced what the architect called a "Modern Gallery": it provided a new relationship between viewer and viewed, with multiple vistas of the art instead of the conventional single, frontal one and a complex integration of the paintings with their setting. Like several other forward-looking architects, notably El Lissitzky and Frederick Kiesler (and a number of artists throughout the century), Wright wanted to create an environment for abstract art that would be different from the static presentation of existing museums. The way in which he did this at the Guggenheim has had a profound influence on the museum as environmental art (see Chapter 7). Unlike the painters who opposed Wright's design in 1957, the artists whose work was to be exhibited in the museum welcomed it. Among these were Kandinsky and Gleizes, who called the spiral a universal form, "the alpha and omega of all form . . . and the very essence of God."

With Solomon R. Guggenheim's death in 1949 and his succession at the foundation by his nephew Harry, Wright's intentions were seriously compromised. The new president quickly dismissed Rebay in favor of James Johnson Sweeney (who had been director of painting at MoMA), and the two men promptly redefined the museum's purpose and program, no longer limiting it to non-objective art or restricting it to the original collection. Levine points out that with this reversal of the institution's charter concept, "very little about the building still made sense." To make matters worse, Sweeney subscribed to precisely the orthodox "rectilinear frame of reference" for exhibiting art that Wright was striving to eliminate. Working with Josep Lluís Sert, a Corbusian Modernist whose aesthetic was incompatible with Wright's, Sweeney devised a system of presenting the paintings vertically by means of rods projecting from stark white walls (Wright had specified a cream color) and substituting artificial for natural light—all of which was totally at odds with Wright's concept.

As late as 1958, the year before he died, Wright drew perspectives of sample exhibits in a last-ditch attempt to make Sweeney understand what he was trying to do. They showed two, or at most three, paintings per bay, with some single, larger works occupying a whole bay or displayed on freestanding easel-like partitions. Paintings were placed against the slanted walls so that their slight upward tilt exposed them to daylight from the clerestory—a continuous skylight circling the top of the ramp wall—in conditions similar to those of a working artist. Wright also indicated the placement of hassocks throughout the gallery. Sweeney ignored these suggestions, and the architect's wish to "make the picture more natural to the sweep, natural to its environment" was never carried out as he envisioned it. This failure to use the building as intended explains many criticisms of the Guggenheim.

On top of the handicaps of misuse and a change in program, Wright's building has been subject to damaging renovations as well as an addition that preceded the Gwathmey Siegel wing. In 1965 the Justin K. Thannhauser bequest was installed on the second-level bridge between the rotunda and the monitor. The exhibition of art—and representational art at that—in what had been designed as a library created the kind of static display the architect had sought to avoid. Moreover, for greater access to the bridge William Wesley Peters of Wright's successor firm, Taliesin Associated Architects, interrupted the spiral's continuous flow by cutting an arch from the main ramp to this space. Peters also designed a four-story annex (1968) for storage and conservation that was crammed into the northeast corner of the site and stood on foundations capable of supporting ten floors.

In 1974 came what the critic Martin Filler later called "the most ill-considered and defacing alteration" to that point: the glassing in of the curved driveway beneath the bridge between the two spirals to make room for a bookstore and tea room. Filler observes that this seemingly small modification caused tremendous damage to Wright's composition by filling in the void "that gave negative emphasis to the sculptural and propulsive nature of Wright's bipolar arrangement of rotunda and monitor." With the exception of Richard Meier's deferential Aye Simon Reading Room (1978), slipped into a leftover space off the main ramp, the various Guggenheim renovations have mutilated a great work of art, just as surely as slashing the *Mona Lisa* or chipping *The Thinker* would. The damage is modest, though, when compared with the results of the most recent addition that replaces the annex.

← Exterior of museum by Frank Lloyd Wright (1959).

Shortly after the announcement of the controversial "toilet tank" project, a meeting of the architects, Guggenheim president Steven Swid and representatives of various protest groups (including the author) took place at the Swids' Gwathmey Siegel–designed apartment. In justification of the new wing, the architects referred to Wright's own unexecuted 1952 design for a 15-story studio-residence to be erected next to the museum. However, a number of those familiar with the studio project, including Taliesin West archivist Bruce Pfeiffer, pointed out that the studio slab was to be placed not on the cramped museum site but on the site of the adjacent apartment building—which was no longer available since the museum had sold it to finance the 1968 annex.

In response to Charles Gwathmey and Robert Siegel's presentation, Edgar Kaufmann Jr., the distinguished Wright scholar and heir to one of Wright's greatest creations, Fallingwater, inquired if the architects might consider using as a model for their own design the unobtrusive studio slab that they had introduced to justify an addition. (Kaufmann later specified that this suggestion was not an endorsement of the addition but merely an attempt to make the best of it.) The idea resulted in Gwathmey Siegel's second scheme: the museum's 28,935-square-foot program was reduced to 23,240 square feet, and the green-tiled cantilever was replaced by a more neutral beige limestone slab 14 feet narrower and 29 feet lower than the first. Even so, many shared the critic William Marlin's sentiment that any addition to Wright's building was "just plain wrong." In 1986 the debate came before New York City's Board of Standards and Appeals, to which the museum had applied for a

zoning variance in order to begin construction. Opponents presented a feasibility study for underground space and proposed off-site locations as alternatives to the addition. The museum's director, Thomas Messer, dismissed each suggestion on the grounds of cost and technical difficulty. The board went along with the museum, and the addition, which began construction in 1990, was completed in 1992.

Ironically, Thomas Krens, who succeeded Messer as director in 1988, adopted the very alternatives to the new wing that were rejected by his predecessor, including the excavation of a 10,000-square-foot area below the museum and the leasing of two off-site locations: a warehouse for technical support and storage and what is now the Soho Guggenheim. The latter, a downtown high-ceilinged loft space renovated by Arata Isozaki, has three times the area of the new wing and is ideally suited to overscaled works too big for Wright's building. But the museum continues to squeeze large pieces—those in the Ellsworth Kelly exhibition (1996–97), for example—into the old rotunda (which the museum had argued was ill-adapted for such work), while often showing smaller paintings from its permanent collection in Soho.

The Guggenheim is a building that should never have been altered. The problem is not so much with the design of the alteration as with the decision to alter it at all. The only positive outcome of the enterprise was the simultaneous restoration of Wright's building, accomplished with sensitivity by Gwathmey Siegel. Elements of the original design that had never been seen, like the continuous clerestory, were revealed for the first time. Other welcome changes were made: storage was cleared from the ramp's top spiral so that it could be used, as intended, for exhibition; the skylight's glazing was improved; the restaurant was relocated to East 88th Street; and the auditorium was restored. With so many corrections made, one wonders why Wright's important driveway opening was left enclosed and why the rotunda interior was repainted white instead of cream. The use of the monitor office areas for exhibition is also questionable, as their large windows and small proportions are not ideal for viewing art. (Could Wright's ghost be taking revenge by filling the galleries with mega-dustballs and perpetrating ongoing problems with humidity condensation?)

Wright claimed of the Guggenheim that:

> When the first atomic bomb lands on New York it will
> not be destroyed. It may be blown a few miles up into the air,
> *but when it comes down it will bounce!*

To suggest a self-sufficient coil ready to spring, the building must be seen in the round, but in its abutment of the large rotunda, the new wing's west facade rudely interrupts the spiral's swirl into space. In a 1957 interview for the *New York Times* with Aline B. Saarinen, the newspaper's art critic, and wife of the architect Eero Saarinen, Wright described his design as "a consistent, organic whole . . . When you go into it . . . you will feel it as a curving wave that never breaks." Opening the large ramp's walls for access to the monitor and the new wing do,

↓ Rotunda interior by Frank Lloyd Wright (1959).

indeed, break the "curving wave" and allow space to leak from the rotunda's intended self-containment. The four new rectilinear galleries also contradict Wright's stated goal to eliminate "to and from, back and forth." Visitors to them must now retrace their steps to the rotunda.

In 1958, the year before the museum's completion, Wright proudly announced:

> For the first time a building has been designed
> which destroys everything square, rectilinear. It
> destroys the rectilinear frame of reference.

Those to whom this incomparable treasure was entrusted have destroyed his concept.

There are broader implications of the Guggenheim addition that are troubling as well. In granting the variance that made the new wing possible, the Board of Standards and Appeals introduced two precedents that appear to be without legal basis. First, the "unique physical condition" required for a variance is met by the Guggenheim's mere presence on a zoning lot (if this explanation is taken to its logical conclusion, any built lot is therefore entitled to a variance). Second, the museum was allowed to define its needs so narrowly that the board, in truth, allowed it to write its own special permit. The new wing is a sliver, a type of building outlawed before the variance was granted, and the curators' description of the program as "the continuous and sequential exhibition of [the permanent] collection" is not the way the addition has ultimately been used. Such capricious flaunting of protective controls on behalf of illegal "spot" zoning presents a real danger for the city. As Ada Louise Huxtable pointed out at the time, "Art may be sacred, and the Guggenheim hallowed ground, but light and air are the same on Fifth Avenue or Avenue A."

THE WHITNEY MUSEUM OF AMERICAN ART

New York, New York

unbuilt project by

Michael Graves

1985

144,000 square feet

30,000 square feet of exhibition space

$37.5 million

built expansion by

Richard Gluckman Architects

1998

9,000 square feet of exhibition space

$14 million

Like the Guggenheim expansion, the Whitney Museum's plan for a Michael Graves addition to its 1966 building by Marcel Breuer was proposed just a few years shy of the original's 30-year eligibility for landmark status. But there was a different emphasis: at the Guggenheim, the building itself was the main issue; at the Whitney, the building was the symbol of a fight to protect the neighborhood from the enlarged scale and the increased traffic that would ensue (a loading dock was planned for the residential side street). For all its importance as a prime example of Modern Brutalism, the Whitney never engaged the public's affection as the Guggenheim did, and it was the size and impact of the project, as much as potential damage to the original building, that riled supporters of the Upper East Side Historic District. The Whitney's need to demolish five 19th-century brownstones to implement the expansion gave its opponents the means to fight it.

Even though Graves used only two-thirds of the "as of right" volume permitted, his design appeared enormous, incorporating as it did a program that called for more than doubled exhibition space, offices, commercial facilities along Madison Avenue, a 250-seat theater, a library expansion, archives, a study center for works on paper and a restaurant on top of the building. The proposal placed a squarish structure that echoed Breuer's box next to it and joined them by a prominent cylindrical hinge —two five-story elements that were to be crowned by an additional five-story columned setback resembling a Greek temple on a high podium. Like other architects of his genera-

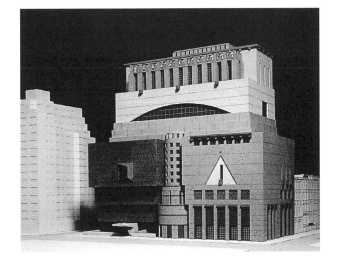

↑ Unbuilt project by Michael Graves (1985). Model.

tion, in the 1970s Graves had switched from Modernism to a neoclassical post-modernism that was still unfamiliar to many who were critical of his ironic reinterpretation of traditional detail. In 1980 the design of his Portland Building in Oregon had stirred considerable controversy, and he applied the same bold historicizing vocabulary to the Whitney addition. Whatever the design's undeniable merits, there is no doubt that it cannibalized the Breuer building, reducing it to a subsidiary element in a totally new statement. Not only did the symmetry and neoclassical ornamentation of Graves's facade negate Breuer's asymmetry and rugged Brutalism, but important aspects of the interior were transformed. Graves's enclosed galleries did not relate well to Breuer's open spaces, and the hinge deprived the original stairway of its defining views to the exterior.

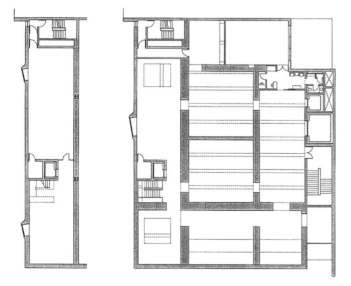

The Whitney opted for an architect whose style was the polar opposite of the original building's. While this kind of contrast can work for a wing that reads as an independent structure, as in the case of Louis Kahn's Yale University Art Gallery (1953), it is less likely to do so in a closer relationship—though museums have shown a perverse tendency toward such odd pairings.

Graves went back to the drawing board twice, attempting to overcome the Landmarks Preservation Commission's objections with a reduced program. When the commission made it clear that it didn't want *any* major addition to the Breuer building at the price of demolishing the brownstones, the Whitney gave up.

Ten years later the museum announced its intention to move its offices, research library and lecture and conference room into two townhouses nearby on East 74th Street, freeing the fifth floor for exhibition purposes. This slightly enlarged floor increased gallery space by a third. Richard Gluckman, the architect of the Warhol Museum (see Chapter 3), has designed what has been described as an "almost imperceptible" expansion (including a link to the townhouses) that leaves the original architecture basically intact.

At the time of the Graves controversy Flora Biddle, then president of the Whitney, expressed surprise at the community's negative reaction. Her statement that "We thought we were making a great gift to the city" reveals a general assumption on the part of museums that the public wants bigger facilities and is indifferent to changes made to existing institutions. This is clearly not so.

↑ Richard Gluckman expansion (1998).
TOP: Two-story library atrium.
BOTTOM: Plans. Fourth-floor mezzanine and fifth floor.

LE GRAND LOUVRE

Pyramid →
by I. M. Pei
& Partners
(1989).

Paris, France

in progress

825,000 additional square feet

384,270 square feet of exhibition space

approximately $1.38 billion

Phase I:

by **I. M. Pei & Partners**

1989

the Pyramid, Cour Napoléon and

underground expansion

550,000 square feet

Phase II:

by **Pei Cobb Freed & Partners**

1993

275,000 square feet of new space

within the Richelieu Wing

232,000 additional square feet of

exhibition space

The controversy surrounding I. M. Pei's proposal for a pyramid entrance to the Louvre dramatically illustrated the public's strong feelings about altering an institution. Few landmarks in France are more present in the nation's collective consciousness or more intimately associated with the heart of Paris than the Louvre, and the proposal in 1984 to reconfigure access to it via a glass pyramid elicited reactions that went so far as to call for a national referendum to decide its fate.

The pyramid was only the tip of the iceberg in the Grand Louvre project, one of seven Grands Travaux, the major public building projects in Paris inaugurated by François Mitterrand shortly after his election to the presidency in 1981. Even though the Grands Travaux constituted the largest construction program since Baron Georges Eugène Haussmann's wide boulevards changed the face of Paris under Napoleon III, it must have been a thorn in Mitterrand's side to know that with a whopping eight million visitors annually, his predecessor's Centre Pompidou had become the city's most popular attraction. By comparison, the Louvre's yearly attendance of under three million was miserable, as was its outdated technology and near lack of even basic amenities, such as toilets.

At the core of Mitterrand's plan to transform the old Louvre into a new and improved Grand Louvre was the addition of 275,000 square feet in the Richelieu Wing, built in the mid-1850s and, with the exception of one state apartment, occupied since 1871 by the Ministry of Finance. Turning this large portion of the building over to the museum meant that for the first time all parts of the former

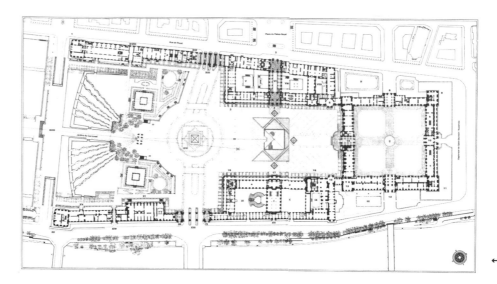

← Ground-floor plan.

palace would be devoted to art. In the creation of new galleries, the enormous U-shaped structure of two and a half million square feet, with the expected increase in traffic, needed some rethinking.

The critic Charles Jencks compares Pei's response to the French president's personal invitation to renovate the Louvre with that of Le Corbusier, who, when asked to design a fountain for Paris, produced a scheme for a new city. Indeed, announcement of Pei's 71-foot-high glass-and-steel pyramid atop a 50-foot excavation for the Cour Napoléon's huge new centralized entrance prompted the question of why the Louvre's several existing entranceways were not retained. Considering the decision in 1978 to place the Louvre's holdings from 1848 on in the new Musée d'Orsay, why was this move toward decentralization not continued by separating the seven remaining departments into distinct, more manageable museums within the building? The scholar Antoine Schnapper was one of many informed Parisians who argued for these alternatives, plus cleaning and a general upgrading of facilities. But the French government, like the private funders of American museums, is more likely to chose expensive new museum construction than less costly renovation and maintenance. Furthermore, Mitterrand's backing ensured that the pyramid, with everything that went with it, would win out: a reconfiguration of circulation; the addition of new galleries for the permanent collection and for temporary exhibitions; an auditorium, massive support services and amenities, commercial space and sizable underground parking facilities.

Of all the innovations the pyramid provoked the most comment. Its structure resembles the glazed space frames that have long been a feature of Pei's vocabulary, notably at his East Building (1978), the freestanding addition to the National Gallery of Art in Washington, D.C. But in Washington the frame crowns the dramatic central space of a masonry building whose cladding discreetly harmonizes with the pink limestone of the existing museum next door. In Paris the

glass-and-metal walls of the pyramid clash with the historic Paris limestone facades fronting them. And whereas the East Building's massing of two unequal triangles solves the problem of aligning the old and new structures, the pyramid in no way creates a dialogue with the Louvre but stands like a foreign object within its central courtyard. The triangular reflecting pools, fountains and mini-pyramids at three of its sides do not make it more contextual.

In his early presentations of the project, Pei insisted on the pyramid's "transparency," but it is anything but transparent. French building codes for this kind of structure mandate thicker glass and supporting members than are required in the United States, and despite the clarity of its custom-made Saint-Gobain glazing, the pyramid appears opaque when seen in daylight. Furthermore, the slant of a pyramid is fundamentally inimical to a portal; Pei's incision at the base in order to create the vertical plane needed for an entranceway demonstrates why.

Inside the pyramid a platform overlooks a vast, skylit reception hall, from which escalators descend at the right and a dramatic spiral stair encircles a piston elevator at the left. This square assembly area is turned 45 degrees so that the corners point toward the museum's three main wings; escalators provide access to each one. The fourth corner leads to the Louvre stores, other commercial areas and parking facilities. For all the perfection with which the hall is executed—lush honey-colored Burgundy stone (matte for walls, polished for floors) and finely patterned white concrete columns and coffered ceilings—this is not a museumlike space. If the introduction of escalators to MoMA's lobby made it into a mall, at the Louvre it has created an airport. The airport aesthetic continues in the Richelieu Wing, where lengthy escalators are enclosed by towering masonry walls. Even the views afforded by the walls' giant oculi do not dispel the alien character of this circulation area, which upstages the wing's three beautifully preserved historic stairways.

In the Richelieu Wing the architects Michel Macary and René Provost, following Pei's concept, have excavated two large open-air courtyards—the Cour Marly and the Cour Puget—to the level of the underground concourse so that they connect. Sinking the ground floor makes a lower, and consequently a distorted, view of the surrounding building. Additionally, raked terraces inserted for the display of sculpture, in stone ambiguously close to the original, seem more appropriate to a 1930s monument than to the Louvre. The arched skylights of both courtyards do, however, produce an excellent quality of light for the exhibition spaces within.

Besides the pyramid there are two other ways to reach the Cour Napoléon. The first of these—reserved for groups, members and those headed for the auditorium and restaurant—is by escalator in the Richelieu passageway, which leads from the rue de Rivoli. Previously the private domain of the Ministry of Finance, the route was opened by Pei to pedestrian traffic, creating an important additional access to the pyramid. Like Pei's rationalization of the Louvre's labyrinthine circulation paths, his establishing this passageway is an improvement, which he made all the more attractive by glazing its walls so that the museum's sculpture courts are visible at either side.

The second, westernmost access to the Cour Napoléon connects with the parking areas and is an even more dramatic example than the main entrance of the negative impact that a museum's intermediary spaces can have. New parking facilities to relieve the congestion caused by tour buses were a major feature of the Grand Louvre master plan, but the cost of these facilities was overlooked in the final estimates. Upon discovering its mistake, the government came up with the idea of turning over an adjacent 190,000-square-foot underground space to a commercial shopping mall whose occupants, in return for setting up shop in this privileged

location, would subsidize the parking. As did MoMA's real estate dealings, the Louvre's commercial enterprise produced regrettable results.

The underground area (planned and designed by I. M. Pei/Pei Cobb Freed & Partners and executed by others), euphemistically called les Galeries du Carrousel as if to give the shops equal billing with the art, is distinct from the Louvre's own museum-related stores (by I. M. Pei & Partners with Michel Macary), which are in the same style and have the same ceiling height as the Cour Napoléon. Late medieval fortifications were discovered during excavation of the garage and mall and were integrated into the new architecture: these defensive walls are handsome and important archaeological artifacts. But oppressed by low ceilings and juxtaposed with the shiny metal facing and glass of the mall's shops and restaurants, the second of the two walls looks fake; because there is no clear demarcation between mall and wall, the latter appears to be a prop for the former's glitzy clutter of clothes and cosmetic boutiques.

The Louvre's current renovation of existing galleries and its building of new exhibition spaces have produced mixed results. Like the Metropolitan Museum, the Louvre has undergone numerous interventions. Built originally in the 1190s as a fortress for Philippe Auguste, by 1549 it had been made into a rectangular palace. It became a museum officially in 1793 with the transformation of the palace (including former stables) into the Muséum Central des Arts. For historic spaces such as the museum's first exhibition area, the Grande Galerie (built from 1595 to the 1660s), only climate control has been added and lighting improved, mercifully leaving the original intact. The massive reorganization of art incorporated into the Grand Louvre project led to the renovation of some galleries in the spirit of earlier spaces for the same art: thus the bright red walls, sober gray door frames and wood floors in the Sully Wing's rooms for

19th-century French paintings recall the Mollien Gallery for large-scale art of this period. The rebuilding by Pei, Macary and Jean-Michel Wilmotte of the Richelieu Wing's interiors, which were previously occupied by cramped government offices, has achieved some pleasing rooms. Particularly successful is the top floor's alternation of large, skylit interior spaces and small exterior spaces—each of the latter generously fenestrated—devoted to Northern painting. Generally, designs reminiscent of historical models are more successful than the starker, modern rooms. For example, the galleries where the Nicolas Poussins now hang sadly lack the context of the paintings' former installation in the Grande Galerie. Many of these spare modern rooms also suffer from being topped by heavy-looking skylights consisting of a central cross set within nested squares.

The problems of the Grand Louvre's galleries are, however, less troubling than the disjunction between these galleries and the museum's circulation areas. In museums such as the Centre Pompidou and both Wright's and Gehry's Guggenheim museums, a similar handling of light and proportion in gallery and non-gallery spaces makes them equal, integral parts of the same structure. Conversely, the vast reception atrium of Pei's East Building is an awe-inspiring tour de force, but it is unrelated to the relatively small-scale, artificially lit galleries to which it leads: a different aesthetic is at work in the two areas, as if they belonged to two distinct buildings. At the Louvre the disparity between galleries and the spaces in between is even more consequential, because it effectively obscures what had previously been one of the museum's greatest assets: its role as a palace in which art had been lived with as well as seen.

The advantage of a real-life context for art has been argued by artists and critics since the Louvre opened. In this respect its aura of a royal residence was infinitely preferable to the decontextualized, artificial setting of most purpose-built museums. Even in their neglected state the Louvre's entrances prepared the visitor for a regal experience, exciting in its historical resonance and in its anticipation of soon-to-be-revealed treasures. Now this experience is effectively denied by the underground entrance—circulation spaces designed for crowd control rather than as part of a cultural event—and the integration of a retail operation. You don't enter a palace through its basement or via a shopping mall.

Usually more successful than attempts to integrate a new wing with an existing museum is the creation of a quasi-separate structure. Louis Kahn at Yale, James Stirling in Stuttgart, Venturi, Scott Brown and Associates in London and Rafael Moneo in Houston exemplify this approach: in each case the wing reads as a new museum, an innovative statement that leaves the original building intact.

Wings That Fly

YALE UNIVERSITY ART GALLERY

New Haven, Connecticut

by **Louis I. Kahn**

1953

83,870 square feet

45,110 square feet of exhibition space

$1.5 million

Had it not been for World War II and a combination of circumstances that ensued, Yale University would have had Philip Goodwin's 1941 variation of MoMA for its art gallery instead of Louis Kahn's masterpiece of structural and aesthetic innovation. A new university president, reductions in the budget and changes in the program led to Goodwin's withdrawal from the project in 1950, clearing the way for the selection of Kahn. The building was his first major commission, his first museum and his first structure in the reinforced concrete that was to characterize his work: it launched a career that profoundly marked American architecture in the second half of the century.

Yale's art museum was an undistinguished neo-Romanesque-Gothic building by Egerton Swartwout (1928). Without emulating it, Kahn was respectful of it—subtly echoing its masonry on the Chapel Street entrance facade, reserving modern steel-and-glass elevations for the courtyard facades—and at the same time creating a strong statement of his own. In response to a cost-conscious program that called for galleries and drafting rooms to be interchangeable, the architect proposed a simple loft structure with five floors of undifferentiated open space around a central utilities and circulation core. Buckminster Fuller was lecturing at Yale at the time, and his tetrahedral space frame influenced Kahn's structural system for floor slabs, which allowed the wide spans needed for maximum flexibility in the galleries and drafting rooms. Building codes forced Kahn to change his three-dimensional space frame to a joist construction; although altered technically, the ceiling retained its dramatic effect. In addition, the architect's insertion of heat and air-condi-

↑ Exterior with entry.

tioning ducts and electrical cables within the hollow pyramids was a first step toward his later division of servant and served spaces.

The historian Vincent Scully was one of the first to acclaim Kahn's art gallery and the power of its interior:

> Much of this vitality resides in the tetrahedral slab. It makes a spreading canopy over the gallery areas. Its triangles are insistent. Their surfaces have also been left rough and untreated as they came from the forms. They, too, have that plastic sculptural quality which is reminiscent of Le Corbusier's concrete at the Unité d'habitation at Marseilles and which was certainly inspired by Le Corbusier's work.

To display art the so-called pogo stick panel was developed with synthetic rubber-tipped feet and spring-mounted projections at the top that could be pressed into the tetrahedrons' flanges. Here, too, Kahn's intended openness and articulation were ignored when these panels were eventually discarded for permanent partitions that hid most of the columns and concrete block walls and enclosed the open stairway. Fortunately, the original has been largely restored.

The strong sculptural presence of the tetrahedral ceiling distinguishes the galleries from neutral loft spaces associated with modern museums like MoMA. Similarly, the toplit, angular stair set within a circle is worthy of a Baroque palazzo, and on the exterior, floor levels are expressed in projecting string courses that run along the unfenestrated masonry entrance wall. These departures from a strictly Modernist approach opened the way for new attitudes and designs that were to revitalize architecture. The historian and architect David De Long remarks how structures roughly contemporaneous with the Yale Art Gallery—Philip Johnson's Glass House, Gordon Bunshaft's Lever House (for Skidmore, Owings & Merrill), Le Corbusier's Unités—were all closed chapters, with architects looking for alternatives to them. With few constraints from existing conditions, Kahn was able to design a new building that, while remaining modern, provided this alternative.

← Interior.

STAATSGALERIE NEW BUILDING AND CHAMBER THEATER

Stuttgart, Germany

by **James Stirling, Michael Wilford and Associates**

1983

164,690 square feet

67,920 square feet of exhibition space

$48.6 million

← Exterior with entry.

The Staatsgalerie in Stuttgart is a masterpiece of the mature style of English architect James Stirling. Like Kahn's Yale Art Gallery, it is a wing that reads as an independent building, making a new statement while remaining in harmony with the 19th-century museum it enlarges. And again like Kahn's building, the Stuttgart museum presents an alternative to Modernism.

Stirling playfully used aspects of the original 1842 design to create a thoroughly 20th-century structure. The old gallery is a U-shaped building preceded by a semicircular drive; the new wing is also U-shaped, with a circular court replacing the curved driveway. Stirling rejected prior interpretations of the entranceway for an experiential progression across terraces and sloping ramps: the visitor can either enter the museum's tall entrance lobby, with its undulating glazed facade held within a bright green metal framework, or follow a ramp along the periphery of the courtyard's drum and emerge in the street on the other side. Like those for the two prior Modern art museum competitions in which Stirling participated in the 1970s (in Düsseldorf and Cologne), the Stuttgart scheme weaves the building into a historical urban fabric by means of a pedestrian path.

Stirling wanted to make his addition monumental enough to convey the museum's traditional meaning but egalitarian enough to be the "place of popular entertainment" that museums have become. To do this, he twists a number of conventional elements to suit his purpose. For example, the sobriety of the museum's two-tone travertine banding is relieved by thick, bright-pink-and-blue parapet handrails. And open joints in the cladding reveal the metalwork frame to which thin masonry blocks are attached, blocks that in one area appear to have fallen off the wall behind them (in reality leaving vents for the air intake funnels).

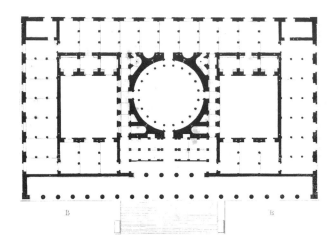

Altes Museum, Berlin, ↑
by Karl Friedrich Schinkel
(1830). Ground-floor plan.

Inside the building, neoclassic allusions include Ledoux, Erik Gunnar Asplund's Stockholm City Library (1928) and, most prominently, Karl Friedrich Schinkel's Altes Museum in Berlin (1830), with its central circulation rotunda and enfilades of galleries. Schinkel's use of the fanciful rotunda, or circular space, as a focal passageway and of sober rectilinear rooms for art display has been repeated in many subsequent museum designs. At Stuttgart, however, as noted by the architectural historian Francesco Dal Co, the traditional association of circle and square with truth and stability is overturned, and the circle conveys a "precarious" and "fragile" image. While Stirling's rotunda serves the same orientation purpose as Schinkel's, it is no longer firmly anchored within the building but is enveloped by an isolated "evasive" wall. Stirling specified that "the central pantheon, instead of being the culminating room is but a void, a room-like non-space. Instead of having a dome, it is open to the sky."

The architect continued to overturn convention by replacing the usual polished stone in corridors with strident green rubber flooring. The free-flowing ground-floor plan includes a large mushroom-columned temporary exhibition gallery and a lecture theater. On the second level enfilades of 15 square and rectangular rooms are connected by pedimented portals inspired by ancient Greece. As in the typical 19th-century museum gallery, ceilings are coved with skylights that differ from their predecessors in the bright green of their metal armature and in allowing glimpses of the roof structure through their misted glass. Many galleries are, additionally, flooded with daylight from large windows that provide access to an upper terrace. In the multiple paths they offer, these enfilades are also atypical: galleries can be bypassed and the route interrupted at a number of points.

The spaces on the second level are clearly different from their classical models, but not as different as one might expect from the promise of Stirling's innovative overall plan and entranceway. Nevertheless, avoiding an impoverished recourse to historical reproduction, Stirling has reinvented neoclassicism to make a building of its time appropriate to the art of any time.

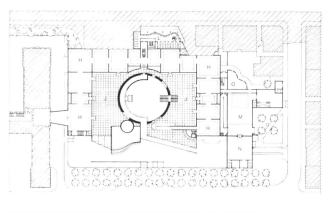

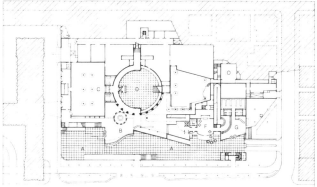

← Plans.
TOP: **First floor.**
BOTTOM: **Ground floor.**

↓ Gallery.

SAINSBURY WING, LONDON NATIONAL GALLERY

London, England

by **Venturi, Scott Brown and Associates**

1991

170,170 square feet

45,000 square feet of exhibition space

cost undisclosed

Louis Kahn's Yale Art Gallery suggested new directions for Modernism; Venturi, who worked with Kahn in the 1950s, and taught with him, set forth a theory of such alternatives in his influential book *Complexity and Contradiction in Architecture* (1966). Venturi's argument for a richer architectural vocabulary cites a range of contextual and historical allusions that inform his work. Exemplifying it is the Sainsbury Wing in London, which resembles the Kahn and Stirling additions in that it is a freestanding building.

William Wilkins's design for the National Gallery (1837) was criticized on aesthetic and functional grounds; upon its completion, objectors to the building went so far as to propose its immediate replacement. Over the years several renovations and additions at the back of the structure corrected some of the problems, and by 1958, when the government acquired the adjacent Hampton site (where the Sainsbury Wing is now located), the National Gallery's once-maligned facade had become a fixture at the north side of Trafalgar Square. Indeed, respect for the Wilkins building was such that projects to extend it, in order to house the National Gallery's extraordinary collection of early Renaissance paintings and various support services, opened up almost three decades of renewed controversy. (Notable was the debate ignited by the Prince of Wales in 1984 when he compared one proposal to "a monstrous carbuncle on the face of a much-loved and elegant friend.")

To circumvent the necessity of financing the museum extension by making it part of a revenue-producing office tower, the three Sainsbury brothers, heirs to a supermarket fortune, pledged the cost of a building for the sole use of the National Gallery. One result of the project's tumultuous history was the clear message that the new wing should complement rather than contrast with what it was supplementing; to find an architect equal to the task, the search committee embarked on an arduous consultation process comparable to the Getty Center's (see Chapter 6). Venturi, Scott Brown and Associates was selected from a final list of six contenders for a design that is highly contextual and referential yet, like other successful additions, makes a statement of its own.

As in the case of Kahn's Yale Art Gallery, the Sainsbury Wing's masonry facade defers to its predecessor, reserving its modern, glazed wall for the more discreet east side, which faces the original museum. Using the same Portland stone and the same roof height as the Wilkins building, the architects adapted Classical elements of the old facade to the extension. Their Corinthian pilasters are clustered in new rhythms, however, with only one column echoing those of Wilkins's three porches—a reference to Lord Nelson's Column in Trafalgar Square. Windows are blind and cornices greatly simplified. The most startling of the exterior innovations is the replacement of the original's solids with three

← Exterior with
entry; at right,
William Wilkins's
1837 building.

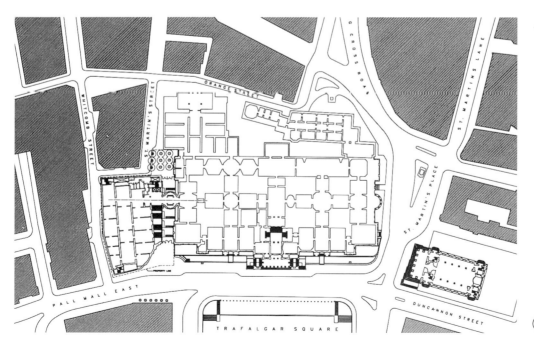

← Site plan showing
Sainsbury Wing
at lower left and
Wilkins building
at center.

entrance voids, skewed on a diagonal to face the square. The historian Stanislaus von Moos points out that the way in which the Sainsbury's contours follow the irregular site makes it a "soft" extension of the original: "as the speech balloons in comic strips or a Lichtenstein painting correspond with the heads (or the people) whose thoughts they visualize in typographic abstraction."

Inside the extension a low-ceilinged entrance hall is flanked by a grand granite stairway—inspired in part by Bernini's monumental Scala Regia at the Vatican—that rises between the glazed outer wall and the interior stone wall. Here again is an echoing of the National Gallery, in this case the great stairway designed in 1884 by Sir John Taylor. At its top are 16 top-floor permanent galleries, arranged in three parallel rows on the same level as Wilkins's main rooms. Connected to them by an octagonal bridge, the enfilade formed by the last rooms in each row of the new wing aligns with the central enfilade of the old rooms.

In designing the galleries, Venturi, Scott Brown and Associates looked to the palaces in which paintings were displayed in rectangular rooms defined by traditional walls, floors, ceilings, doors and windows. The architects have used a similar approach for other museums, but the Sainsbury specifically suggests the early-Renaissance architecture for which the paintings were made. Columns and archways are typical of this architectural style, as is the contrast of light-colored walls with darker details: at the Sainsbury, *pietra serena* frames archways, doors and oak floors. The ceiling lunettes, coves and lanterns of Sir John Soane's Dulwich College Picture Gallery (1814) were also an influence, though the adaptation of these elements is not completely successful. Inflation of the columns' entasis and of Doric capitals creates a rubbery effect and the exaggerated scale of the ceiling details makes them appear heavy. There is a similar discordance between the monumentality of the grand stairway and the apparently arbitrary Victorian-style metal arches that crown it. Notwithstanding these reservations, Venturi, Scott Brown and Associates has enriched one of London's historic squares with an original statement, and their allusive vocabulary provides a welcome context for the collection.

↑ Dulwich College Picture Gallery, London, by Sir John Soane (1814). Interior.

← Enfilades.
LEFT: Looking west from first room on gallery level.
RIGHT: Central range of galleries.

AUDREY JONES BECK BUILDING, MUSEUM OF FINE ARTS

Houston, Texas
by Rafael Moneo
with Kendall-Heaton
Associates
1999
197,500 square feet
57,020 square feet of exhibition space
approximately $63 million

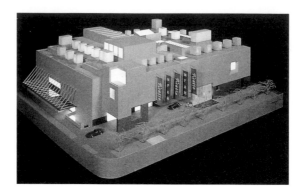

Sir John Soane's remarkably effective skylight design at Dulwich College has inspired an array of museums. It is therefore not surprising to see architects whose work is as different as that of Venturi, Scott Brown and Rafael Moneo sharing this source, in both cases for a freestanding museum wing. The Spanish architect and teacher, who headed Harvard's Architecture Department in the Graduate School of Design from 1985 to 1990, cites historical references from the late-Renaissance Venetian master Vincenzo Scamozzi to the 1930s Rationalist Giuseppe Terragni. But Moneo adapts these styles to a sober Modern vocabulary that is unrelated to the Venturis' ironic neoclassicism, and his siting of the Audrey Jones Beck Building of the Houston Museum of Fine Arts predictably contradicts the suggestions made by Venturi, Scott Brown and Associates in the firm's 1990 master plan for the cultural area near the Menil Collection.

The Beck Building, which will house the museum's permanent collection of art from antiquity to the 1930s and provide space for temporary exhibitions, is the last in a series of additions to the original museum, designed (1924) and extended (1926) by William Ward Watkin. The best known of these, by Mies van der Rohe, was finished in 1958 as part of his master plan for the museum; in 1974 the Brown Pavilion by the Houston architect S. I. Morris provided the second phase of that overall plan. A major feature of the Mies addition was its 180-degree shift of the museum's entranceway from the south to the north, Bissonet Avenue side. The Venturi office wanted to reinforce this northern orientation with an arcade linking Mies's entrance to a Bissonet Avenue entrance for the expansion across the street and eventually to the Fannin Service Building in the next, eastern block. Moneo rejected this pedestrian-oriented scheme for a western entrance that favors the predominantly vehicular traffic and attenuates what he considers to be the existing museum's excessive frontality. An underground passageway will extend from the Mies addition to the Beck Building and beyond to a garage in the Fannin Building.

As for his earlier Museum of Roman Art at Mérida, Spain (1986), the Davis Museum and Cultural Center at Wellesley College (1993) and the Museum of Modern Art and Architecture in Stockholm (1997), Moneo's almost entirely unfenestrated masonry facades for the Beck Building will be austere. The cladding of Indiana limestone is the same that Mies used, but the strict linearity of Moneo's rectangular box contrasts with the semicircle of the original museum and the later wings. Only in its echo of Houston's distant downtown skyline does the roof's mini-village of clustered lanterns acknowledge the building's locale. The neutral container belies a variety of interior spaces

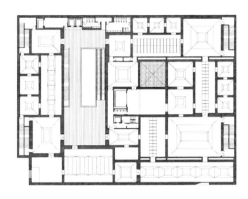

that expand the Stockholm Museum's more tentative diversity and may prove to be Moneo's most accomplished museum design since Mérida. The apparent discrepancy between what the architect describes as "a regular, outwardly closed structure" and a complex interior is a recurrent theme in Moneo's work that he calls "compactness": it involves the traditional enclosure of the biggest volume in the smallest surface but with an unconventional mosaic plan that brings to mind the diverse architecture of walled Muslim cities.

↑ Second-floor plan.

← Model.

↓ Longitudinal section.

A 24-foot-high portico with angled panels and sculpted lettering by the New York designer Massimo Vignelli opens into a skylit entrance lobby reminiscent of the Thyssen-Bornemisza Museum in Madrid (which is housed in the Villahermosa, a 19th-century palace whose 1992 renovation by Moneo preserves the original's elegance). As in the Madrid museum, the soaring, light-filled lobby is positioned off-center and has a discreet lateral stairway. The stair is supplemented by escalators that lead to both the mezzanine level and the main exhibition spaces at the top, some of which rise to over 37 feet. Moneo has planned the greatest diversity of spaces possible while remaining within Euclidian geometry. The rooms will be of various shapes and sizes; circulation between the galleries will be random. Every ceiling will be different, with alternating shed and lantern skylights; a generously proportioned light shaft that penetrates the building's full height will diffuse daylight to the lower galleries. In breaking down the new wing's com-

ponents into relatively small spaces, Moneo avoids the problem inherent to his Modern idiom when applied to oversized galleries. The Beck Building's individual rooms—the antithesis of Mies's undifferentiated, open space (to be devoted to art from 1930 to the present)—should be more sympathetic to the historical collections they will present. Moneo has deferred to his predecessor in his choice of material and siting but makes a design statement that acknowledges the need to relate art and architecture.

Does the success of these freestanding wings imply that when it comes to expansion, museums should think in terms of independent new institutions rather than the enlargement of existing facilities? Richard Koshalek, director of the Museum of Contemporary Art in Los Angeles, asserts that museums have a life span of approximately 30 years, after which their holdings should become a historical collection and a new institution founded:

> A museum is like a living organism which thrives on a particular set of circumstances and is justified by them—and only by them. An authentic museum senses its natural, "organic" size and capabilities. It comes into existence because a unique confluence of artistic, social, political, and economic forces creates an opportune moment which a few clear-eyed individuals seize and channel into its necessary containment—an institution for and of its time . . . If the institution fails to recognize this period of greatest self-understanding—the true fulfillment of its purpose—or tries desperately to "re-create" itself in new guises despite the fact that circumstances have vastly changed—it will quickly and irrevocably lose its authenticity and vitality.

The art historian Yve-Alain Bois attributes a similar sentiment to Dominique Bozo, who at the time of his death in 1993 was president of the Centre Pompidou. Regarding the Pompidou's perennial problem of growth, Bozo stated that Modern art was defined only up until 1980, after which "the honest solution would be [to admit] that this is a period that is closed." He conceded, however, that "we can't do this because we don't want to be antiquarian curators and we need the public."

A more radical proposition is Wolf Prix's "Disappearing Museum," which would consist of a small core in which administrative offices, storage and exhibition space were located. If larger exhibition spaces were needed for contemporary art, they could be rented in local stores, shopping centers, schools or empty lots, the choice made jointly by the museum and the artist whose work would be displayed. Like Koshalek, Prix gives the museum a limited life span, with parts of the collection being periodically disseminated, thereby realizing his intention "to integrate art with the city."

This option was adopted in at least one case when Rudi Fuchs, as director of The Hague's Gemeentemuseum, deaccessioned part of its decorative arts collection. Now director of Amsterdam's Stedelijk Museum, Fuchs has reduced the size of that museum's intended expansion, because, in his words, if you are "too big you can't have a real relationship to the avant-garde." He points out that by keeping the Stedelijk relatively small, he has a flexibility that larger institutions like the Tate and MoMA have lost: "I can make an exhibition . . . of a young artist that I see tomorrow in two weeks." Thomas Krens presents yet another alternative with his global concept that calls for museums to be scattered worldwide and loosely related to a guiding institution in New York (see Chapter 7).

Wings that don't fly often result from a museum's attempt to stretch the limitations of its "opportune moment." This was the case with the Metropolitan Museum's new interest in contemporary art, which applies the historical concept of an encyclopedic collection to an era in which its validity is doubtful. It was also true of the Guggenheim's decision to use its Frank Lloyd Wright building for art that hadn't figured in its original program. MoMA's current expansion is based on the questionable assumption that the same standards of excellence that successfully defined its collection of Modern art can be applied to a postmodern scene that defies such criteria. MoMA was notoriously late to recognize the importance of Abstract Expressionism, acquiring its first Jackson Pollock several years after the American master was generally recognized as a major force in 20th-century art. Is it the memory of this misjudgment that now drives the museum's preoccupation with new art forms, for which it intends to completely redesign and enormously expand its current structure?

Just as the first Whitney expansion plan ignored the fact that the museum's relatively small size was an important asset, the Grand Louvre project dismissed that institution's defining characteristic as a royal residence. The French socialist government's fixation on creating a democratically centralized entrance ignored practical considerations as well. Waiting lines outside and bottlenecks inside the pyramid attest to the failure of a single entrance and have resulted in the decision to reopen one of the Louvre's original portals, in the Pavillon de Flore.

What impact the expanded Louvre will have on its management remains to be seen. Many fear that as in the case of Versailles, its direction, traditionally by a scholar, will be taken over by a financial manager whose priorities could change the nature of the institution still further.

One of MoMA's first exhibitions after its unsuccessful 1984 expansion was "Primitivism in 20th-Century Art: Affinity of the Tribal and the Modern." In 1987, on inaugurating its 20th-century wing, the Metropolitan showed "Van Gogh in Saint-Rémy and in Auvers." Both exhibitions were scholarly and aesthetic achievements of the highest order, compared with which the quality of the museums' additions in the same periods was woefully deficient. Until architecture is identified as an integral part of the art experience, and treated with the same seriousness, museum expansion and museums in general will continue to offer a flawed agenda.

Chapter 6

The Museum as Entertainment

I don't want to be
educated; I want
to be drowned in
beauty.

*Diana Vreeland on the
Metropolitan Museum of
Art's Costume Institute*

Man plays only when
he is in the full
sense of the word a
man and he is only
wholly human when
he is playing.

Friedrich Schiller

The public museum, which began with an educational impulse and later came to represent a new secular religion, is now widely perceived as a vehicle for entertainment. Recent decades have seen an immense increase in museum attendance, partly due to mass tourism, and crowded institutions have required adjustments in design to preserve their intrinsic qualities: the Grand Louvre failed in its attempt, the Centre Pompidou was more successful. Pontus Hulten, the Centre Pompidou's first director, thinks of museums as erotic —places that are "not about explaining but dreaming, excitement." The notion of pleasure rather than pedagogy is the sense in which "entertainment" is used here—in reference primarily to the art experience but also to the commercial amenities that are now an important part of most museums. To think of art in terms of entertainment is simply a return to the astonishment and delight associated with the first private Renaissance museums: a sensuous, thought-provoking discovery quite different from the dutiful didacticism of most large contemporary institutions, where visitors often spend more time reading about the art than looking at it. The museum's much-criticized shops and restaurants have the capacity, when handled in an appropriate manner, to serve this experience—just as jugglers, acrobats and other popular entertainers enlivened medieval religious festivals.

Already in the early 1920s El Lissitzky called for a new approach to the exhibition of painting and sculpture that would have an underlying sense of fun. The historian Yve-Alain Bois compares Lissitzky's attitude toward museums with Bertolt Brecht's toward theater: "If it's odd enough, interesting, strange or funny it will make the beholder want to know, to think." This was the philosophy furthered by Marcel Duchamp in his Boîte-en-Valise (see Chapter 4) and that generally informed his art.

In a 1967 interview with the critic Annette Michelson, Öyvind Fahlström, a Swedish painter who worked with cartoon images, pictured the ideal art exhibition as "a pleasure-house." He was convinced that museums would eventually involve theaters, discos, meditation grottoes, versions of Luna Park, gardens, restaurants, hotels, swimming pools and the sale of art replicas. Fahlström's concept was prophetic. His "pleasure-house" has become today's museum model.

A 1990 article in the journal *Museum News* describes how Disneyland offers challenges to the way museum decision makers take stock of display techniques and audiences:

> Theme parks . . . propose a new vision for education and exhibition, one based not on a literal or historical vision but on archetypes and community consensus history. They speak a new language: multisensory, entertainment-based, three-dimensional, symbolic.

The theme park derives in turn from the tradition of International Exhibitions and World's Fairs; the ramp of New York's Guggenheim has been likened to that of Norman Bel Geddes's General Motors Pavilion at the 1939 New York World's Fair: "the archetype of a series of architectural performances equal to the content of a thematic/architectural park." Thomas Krens defines the art museum as "a theme park with four attractions: good architecture, a good permanent collection, prime and secondary temporary exhibitions, and amenities such as shops and restaurants." Krens's frequent references to "the museum industry" have prompted the scholar Rosalind Krauss to suggest that the much-publicized leveraging of the Guggenheim collection brings the museum into the realm of other industrialized areas of leisure—like Disneyland. And in a recent lecture MoMA director Glenn Lowry pictured the future of his venerable institution as a scene from the Marx Brothers' *A Night at the Opera*: "a loud, cacophonous environment in which fun is had by all."

In a world where television has led in making every aspect of our lives into a form of entertainment, the museum has followed suit. Entertainment can be a welcome alternative to the museum/mausoleum, but when mishandled it quickly degenerates into crass commercialism that diminishes the art. The department-store atmosphere of the lobby of San Francisco's Museum of Modern Art taints its galleries, just as the Grand Louvre's shopping mall robs the approach to that institution of its grandeur. To be entertaining in a dignified manner is as difficult to achieve for a museum as is lively neutral space (which, more often than not, is a contradiction in terms).

Astronomical attendance figures belie the hard economic fact that American museums run an average 22 percent annual deficit: revenue-producing attractions are therefore essential to their survival. In Europe, also, reduction of long-standing government support for cultural institutions has initiated alternative methods of financing them. Few museums have the luxury of the Menil Collection in banning commercial activities altogether, and in fact such activities are tolerable when they do not invade spaces reserved for culture.

The English architect Colin St. John Wilson defines culture as raising the necessary to the level of the celebratory. To achieve this, one might look to the model of a carefully planned town as opposed to the uncontrolled sprawl of the American strip. In this chapter three museums—the now historic Centre Pompidou in Paris, the Groninger in the Netherlands and the Getty in Los Angeles—and the Lingotto exhibition spaces in Turin, conform to this ideal. Each in its distinct way signals art as entertainment while it offers other, clearly separate, attractions. Consequently, art becomes part of a lived experience as it maintains its own aura.

THE CENTRE NATIONAL D'ART ET DE CULTURE GEORGES POMPIDOU

Paris, France

by **Renzo Piano**
and Richard Rogers

1977

1,000,000 square feet

183,000 square feet of exhibition space

$100 million

Its theme park analogy notwithstanding, Wright's Guggenheim was conceived as sacred space and has been called "a light-flooded cathedral with a roadway to heaven winding 'round its walls." There is no such ambivalence at Paris's Centre Georges Pompidou, the building that inaugurated the museum as entertainment. The 1971 international competition for this mixed-use cultural center (to which 681 proposals were submitted) was won by Renzo Piano and Richard Rogers (since 1991 Lord Rogers), an Italian and an English architect, who associated specifically for this project, which was to mark the beginning of their individual meteoric careers. At a time when French museums were dusty old places with little popular appeal, Piano and Rogers ensured excitement from the beginning by replacing the competition program's description of "a cultural center for Paris" with "a live center of information and entertainment." Rogers actually talked of a "more ludic" definition of culture: "a cross between an informational Times Square and the British Museum."

The architects' intention was to create a new kind of public forum, a nonmonumental building of such infinite flexibility that it would be in constant process. The structure's interdisciplinary organization was supposed to democratize the arts: it was hoped that visitors headed for one facility would wander naturally into others. In the words of Pontus Hulten, the Pompidou's first director:

> Museums are no longer places to preserve works that
> have lost their social, religious, and public functions,
> but places where artists meet the public and the public
> becomes creative.

Entertainment was built into the Pompidou's architectural antecedents. The immediate precursor of its design is the high-tech work of the British Archigram group of the 1960s and Cedric Price's Fun Palace of 1961. But its sources stretch further back in time to Jean Prouvé's mobile elements supported by steel girders and glass in his 1939 Maison du Peuple at Clichy (Prouvé headed the Pompidou competition jury) and the girders of the great 19th-century engineer-architects. The Pompidou derives ultimately from the greenhouse architecture of London's Crystal Palace (1851). That structure was created for the Great Exhibition by Joseph Paxton and designed to entertain as well as educate the masses that flocked to it, a concept the French quickly adopted in the second half of the 19th century for International Exhibitions that have been described as "loud, aggressive and tempestuous, defying the inherent passivity of the visitor."

The Pompidou was in part meant to function as the linchpin of a massive urban renewal project. During the last two decades this role has become increasingly frequent in Europe for museums that, in this respect, are equal players with performing arts centers in the United States. Because major renewal projects normally spearhead gentrification, dislodging low-income populations, they cause tremendous social and economic upheaval and tend to be highly controversial. This was true of the plan for the historic Marais neighborhood in the first arrondissement where the Centre Pompidou is located.

As early as 1918 part of the Marais had been designated an *îlot insalubre*—an unhealthful area. But plans to renovate the district were repeatedly stymied by the problem of what to do with its beloved Halles, the produce market. When in 1969 the market was moved to the suburbs, and its elegant 19th-century glass-and-metal pavilions were destroyed, adverse reaction to the construction of a massive commercial program in their place led to the compromise of an underground mall and a park, with the planned Centre Pompidou situated at the adjacent Plateau Beaubourg. As the first large Modernist building to go up within the city's center, the Pompidou appeared aggressively alien to many. Piano and Rogers scored positively, however, by leaving more than half the site open for a public square on which the area's rich street life could continue. Their concept of a lively outdoor plaza, whose animation would be reflected in the facade's moving escalators, proved successful, and the vitality of this space is one of the Centre's greatest accomplishments. The brightly colored erector-set behemoth was too massive, however, and its siting beside the square too prominent, to escape being monumental, despite the architects' stated wishes. But the Pompidou's multitude of differently scaled elements in fact relates to Paris's ornate 19th-century Beaux-Arts architecture, and placement of the IRCAM (Institute de Recherche et de Coordination Acoustique-Musique) facility underground opened new views of the late-Gothic church of St. Merri to the south.

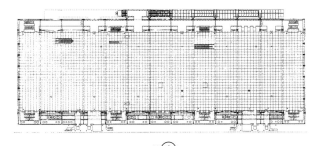

N◀

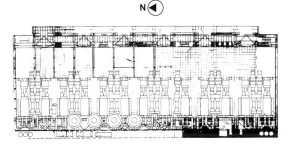

The building has four levels underground and five levels above ground on the north-south axis along the rue du Renard. In addition to containing the Museum of Modern Art and space for temporary exhibitions, the Pompidou includes a library, IRCAM, an industrial design center, the Cinémathèque Française auditorium, a restaurant and a bar. To Parisians the most important component was the city's first open-access public library—the sole institution designated to occupy the Beaubourg site until France's president Georges Pompidou, upon his election in 1969, decided to incorporate other cultural activities into the complex. Now over 20 years old, the Pompidou has been abundantly discussed; the

↑ Entry facade.

← Plans.
TOP: Original exhibition
space (1977).
BOTTOM: Exhibition
space renovated
by Gae Aulenti (1984).

following is therefore limited to recalling the client's changes in the design and program before and after the building's completion; to outlining future plans; and to emphasizing the museum's decisive importance as entertainment.

Shortly after Piano and Rogers won the competition, fire regulations obliged them to reduce the structure's height from 200 to 140 feet: the length of a Paris fire ladder. This reduction determined the lower, 23-foot ceiling height, which has been criticized as insufficient for floor spans equivalent to two football fields laid end to end (with beams and ducts taking up the top 10 feet). With Valéry Giscard d'Estaing's succession to the French presidency in 1974, after Pompidou's death, a program of whittling down government expenditures produced other changes in the design phase of the project. One of the reasons for pushing all the building's mechanical systems to the exterior in the colored ducts and tubes was to achieve a maximum internal flexibility, of which adjustable pneumatic floors were to have been a part. The elimination of these floors also meant suppressing a system of adjustable mezzanines that would have made possible a dramatic series of high spaces. As a result, only one permanent, double-height gallery was created in the museum (in addition to the forum entrance hall).

Huge video screens planned for the plaza facade to deliver the building's media role were also jettisoned for political as well as economic reasons. Technical considerations obliged reconfiguration of the exterior escalators from a V-shape to a snaking horizontal. Finally, blockage of the windows on the eastern, rue du Renard facade seriously compromised the building's intended transparency. After a political demonstration on the plaza caused minor damage to the building, the government invoked security as a reason to reduce four entrances—one at each side of the Pompidou—to a single public access on the square. Without the multiple entranceways intended by the architects to extend the city's activities within, the hoped-for pedestrian cross-circulation was ruled out. The plan to open the basements of houses adjoining the sunken plaza directly onto it was abandoned, as were projected underground links from nearby streets and from the Halles area. The idea of requisitioning surrounding houses for artists' studios and other functions related to the Pompidou was also postponed.

More important to the fate of the art within the building was the ongoing debate about what the collection should consist of. An initial plan to house the permanent collection of the Musée National d'Art Moderne, then located in the 1937 Palais de Tokyo on the Chaillot hill, was set aside after the competition, because heirs of the many artist-donors to the museum opposed the move. Consequently, instead of a museum, the architects were asked for a *Kunsthalle*. Only belated acceptance of the relocation by representatives of the Brancusi estate turned the tide in favor of the museum moving to the Pompidou. As Rogers explains: "This uncertainty led to a lack of clarity and direction during the first three years and ruled out any possibility of a tailor-made design for the museum." By the time Pontus Hulten was in place as director, the basic design concepts had been established.

Aspects of the building that have been criticized in terms of the permanent installations lend themselves well to the different requirements of changing exhibitions: the *Kunsthalle* function addressed by the architects. The vast, uninterrupted spaces allow multiple options for temporary installations for which the exposed colored ceiling ducts and beams provide a visual framework. And while the Pompidou's interdisciplinarity has not succeeded in luring visitors from one facility to another, the shows themselves often call on the Centre's varied resources. Presented with painting, sculpture, stage sets, photography, architectural models, historical newspapers, periodicals and video, viewers are able to create for themselves an overall background for the art. This interactive, multimedia approach, for which the Pompidou's exhibition spaces were intended, is an effective means of providing a context often missing in museums.

↑ Permanent collection gallery by Piano and Rogers (1977).

Notwithstanding the immediate success of its temporary exhibitions, there was continuing dissatisfaction with the installation of the permanent collection. In 1981 Dominique Bozo, the founding director of the Picasso Museum, replaced Hulten at the Pompidou on condition that the collection's fourth-floor galleries be renovated—a task for which he commissioned Gae Aulenti. The Italian architect was completing her postmodern interior renovation of a former Paris railroad station, the turn-of-the-century Gare d'Orsay, into the Musée d'Orsay for 19th-century art. This design was the opposite of the Pompidou's: whereas the latter bespoke mobility and a random, nonsequential approach, Orsay represented permanence (what could be more permanent than ancient Egypt rendered in stone?) and controlled linearity.

To solve the problem of overhead beams deemed intrusive (and to which there was much objection), Aulenti placed six-foot-wide cross corridors under each of the twelve largest transverse beams and crowned the walls with pedimented glass ceilings. The corridors, which run into a broad interior street almost spanning the length of the building, left the loftiest areas for rooms of various sizes and shapes; their 15-foot-high walls are topped by inward-tilting panels that partially mask the ceiling ducts and uniformly deflect light. Aulenti also used the structure's ability to adjust exterior space to create three sculpture terraces. Welcomed by critics of the original installations (large, temporary panels usually placed in clusters), her pristine white rooms are antithetical to a building conceived as an industrial structure, and many consider them a betrayal. The sculptor Kiki Smith is among those who enjoy exhibiting in the Pompidou's original spaces, which she compares to a vast convention center. Others, however, like Eric Fischl, feel Aulenti improved the Pompidou ("I'd

never seen a work that looked good there"). As with the New York Guggenheim (see Chapter 5), the Pompidou's change in art program had a negative impact on the effectiveness of its exhibition spaces.

Whatever the Pompidou's problems, they have not deterred the eight million visitors who flock to it annually, making it Paris's number one tourist attraction. In this too the Pompidou resembles the Guggenheim: criticized as an exhibition space, it is beloved by the public. However, the Pompidou's attendance of five times the highest projections has taken its toll, and the building's twentieth anniversary marked the beginning of a two-year, $45 million renovation. This includes a reorganized circulation to and from the library and museum, whose respective spaces will be in part redistributed; a new reception area; the removal of administration offices (freeing 85,000 square feet); creation in the basement of spaces for performance, films and lectures; and the possible implementation of the four public entranceways originally planned.

Nineteen percent of the Pompidou's visitors come for the views alone, a phenomenon that delights Rogers, who for this reason likens it to the piazza di Spagna in Rome. Detractors point out the relatively small proportion of Pompidou patrons who frequent the museum itself, but almost two million people visit it annually—more than at New York's MoMA—and attendance at two-to-three-month exhibitions has been high, frequently around 200,000 and occasionally over 700,000, as for "Matisse" (1993) and "Féminin/Masculin, Le Sexe de l'Art" (1995). Even if viewers of the permanent collection are fewer than hoped for, the flow through the Pompidou has surpassed all expectations. Not only has this building succeeded in terms of general attendance and the number of those who come to exhibitions in it, but it also has brought an enormous potential audience to the museum's threshold in an atmosphere of fun and expectation that has radically changed public perception of the institution.

THE LINGOTTO EXHIBITION SPACES

Turin, Italy

by **Renzo Piano Building Workshop**

1983–96 for the first two of three phases

7,500 square-foot gallery

75,000 square feet of temporary exhibition space

$400 million (total)

Since the Centre Pompidou, Renzo Piano has received greater attention for the smaller, more classical museums for specific collections that he has designed than for the large, loftlike exhibition spaces that have paralleled them (see Chapters 1 and 3). An example of the latter is his renovation of Fiat's Lingotto factory in Turin, in which he is still involved. The original factory represented the true machine-age environment that the Pompidou merely simulated; Le Corbusier included no fewer than three illustrations of it in his *Towards a New Architecture*.

Chris Dercon, director of Rotterdam's Boymans–van Beuningen Museum, regards exhibition spaces like those of Lingotto as "the best example of new museum architecture yet to come." Greatly expanding the Pompidou's concept of a cultural complex, the Lingotto mixed-use facility accommodates conference rooms, stores, offices, a hotel and restaurants in addition to a music auditorium and art viewing spaces. Piano's 100,000-square-foot Museum of Contemporary Art in Lyons is part of a similar complex: the Cité Internationale de Lyon combines the renovated 1918 International Trade Fair buildings with new structures. Dercon feels these mixed-use developments demystify art by making it part of a more inclusive experience. They also offer possibilities for alternative or radically different uses of museum spaces.

Targeting Switzerland and France as well as Lombardy, of which Milan is the capital, Lingotto belongs to a new breed of regional rather than city-oriented projects, increasingly common in light of the EEC's breakdown of national boundaries. Besides Lingotto's 7,500-square-foot gallery, more than 75,000 square feet of its massive exhibition hall is periodically devoted to the display of art.

In the same way that pop art—to wit, Claes Oldenburg's "store" (see Chapter 4)—would work if exhibited at Lingotto, Jeff Koons's postmodern, oversized paintings and sculptures of everyday objects would play well in spaces inserted within commercial facilities. With ironic humor, Koons cites the commercial art gallery as the optimum exhibition space "because of a sense of tension, playing on desire." In other words, the work is for sale. In its resemblance to a large art fair, the Lingotto exhibition area is much like the commercial setting Koons describes.

The 3,000,000-square-foot Lingotto Fiat factory was completed in 1921 by the engineer Giacomo Matté Trucco in response to Fiat founder Giovanni Agnelli's wish to emulate Detroit's assembly-line production. It consists of two parallel five-story manufacturing buildings, each longer than an ocean liner, joined by five shorter, transverse service buildings, with courtyards between them. Cars were tested on the roof's famous racked track, reached via helicoidal ramps at the slabs' north and south ends. Beyond the southern ramp was the vast one-story press shop. The factory ceased to function in 1982, and given its landmark status, Fiat was faced with the problem of what to do with it. From proposals by 20 architects the people of Turin voted in favor of Piano's scheme for a mixed-use center to serve technological innovation, commerce and culture. Conservation measures such as window replacement and the use of sophisticated materials for interiors have modified the buildings' original toughness, but by and large the spirit has been preserved.

Here, as in Lyons, Piano has tried to create what he calls "a city within a city." The architect transformed the courtyard side of one long factory building into the Portico, an outdoor shopping street that is arcaded like those of 18th- and 19th-century Turin. It is reached by stairs and a glass-enclosed funicular that immediately sets a festive tone. Between up-market boutiques and entrances to the offices above them is a small gallery that includes fine and decorative art of different periods in its noncommercial exhibits.

The press shop was in large part gutted and rebuilt as a hall for trade fairs to serve in conjunction with a gallery in the southern end of the old factory. The hall, with a broad free-span central nave, is used in the manner of a *Kunsthalle* for an annual art fair and for museum-quality art exhibitions as well as for trade fairs. Both the gallery's and hall's renovated spaces are structured by a 20-foot grid of columns typical of the supports in industrial buildings (Soho art galleries were a model for the Lingotto renovation). The two most important exhibitions that have taken place here—"Russian and Soviet Art 1870–1930" (1989) and "American Art 1930–1970" (1992)—benefited from thoughtful installation designs by the Renzo Piano Building Workshop that, respectively, masked and utilized the building's structure. Like the Centre Pompidou's loft spaces, these big open areas require a specific setting to be made for each show.

In 1994 the handsome Giovanni Agnelli Auditorium was inaugurated. Housed in a new underground structure, it can function as a

TOP: **Portico gallery.** ↑
BOTTOM: **Lingotto Fiat factory, Turin, by Giacomo Matté Trucco (1921).**

↑ Exhibition space with "Russian and Soviet Art 1870–1930" (1989).

← Exhibition space with "American Art 1930–1970" (1992).

2,000-seat concert hall or, by lowering the ceiling, as a smaller conference hall.

Thanks to their clear delineation within the complex, cultural facilities like the gallery, temporary exhibition areas and auditorium are not cheapened by the proximity of commercial amenities. On the contrary, commerce unrelated to the arts is less intrusive at Lingotto than are the ubiquitous sales desks that hawk art-related merchandise inside museums (the Metropolitan is a prime example).

A contrast to Lingotto is offered by a similar renovation in Prague, which fails without the enlivening factor of commercial activities. The Czech Republic's National Gallery (1995) now occupies the Veletržní Palace, a former trade fair hall that was built at about the same time as Lingotto. But in Prague, reservation of the large industrial structure for art alone leaves unoccupied areas that contribute to the museum's moribund atmosphere.

Lingotto, for all its design sophistication, is not without its problems. Piano originally emphasized the need to tie the new complex into its suburban neighborhood by means of paths and roadways and a series of green areas that would extend into the buildings. This has not happened. Even the $400 million spent to date (approximately $280 million from Fiat, $118 million from other private sources and the city) has not been enough to pay for these important interventions. Consequently, the complex has no local roots, nor is it integrated with the city, from which it is a 20-minute car ride away. Its current 2.5 million annual visitors are half of what the organizers had hoped for, and only the careful coordination of events—concerts, a trade fair, a series of conferences and art exhibitions—attracts enough people to justify the effort. Equally troubling is the elimination, for lack of funding, of the educational and research facilities that were to occupy a third of the Lingotto space, so that a student population, which would have animated the buildings, is excluded. Completion of all phases of the project—including the establishment of linkage with its surroundings and the creation of a railroad station—may improve attendance.

Dercon predicts that museums will become one of a few "safe havens"—places where people will feel comfortable within an increasingly threatening urban environment. Already, in this sense, the Lingotto mini-city is not unlike a secure, controlled and entertaining theme park.

THE GRONINGER MUSEUM

Groningen, the Netherlands

by **Alessandro Mendini**
with **Francesco Mendini,**
Michele de Lucchi,
Philippe Starck and
Coop Himmelblau
1994

86,650 square feet
47,360 square feet of exhibition space
$13 million

When the 100-year-old Groninger Museum received financing for a new building from the local Dutch gas company in celebration of the latter's twenty-fifth anniversary, the museum's director, Frans Haks, decided to implement a daring concept. He was determined that the architecture would be so different from that of conventional museums that it would make visitors drop all preconceptions about art and allow them to reach fresh conclusions about what they saw. He looked to Disneyland, where separate pavilions, each one different from the next, plunge the visitor into distinct experiences. Haks points out that "the Groninger is not like the Met, where you have to pass through one department to get to another: each of our entrances leads directly to what you want to see." In an effort to make every aspect of one's visit pleasurable, a Delft tile piece by Belgian artist Wim Delvoye adorns the underside of the museum's entrance drawbridge so that waiting in line becomes an art-viewing experience. Even the guards' dress was designed to avoid what Haks describes as "the military look of most museum guards, who make you feel like a criminal."

To realize his plan, Haks went to Alessandro Mendini, the founder, with Ettore Sottsass, of the Memphis Group, known for its irreverent postmodern style. Having led a team of six architects and designers in the creation of the Casa della Felicità (1988), a house near Lago Maggiore in the form of a mini-village with a different author for each component, Mendini was the ideal coordinator for the individually designed pavilions of the Groninger.

Mendini has long inveighed against what he calls the "cultural terrorism" of official art, preferring architecture inspired by memory and fantasy rather than that beholden to function. Specifically he rejects traditional hierarchies such as valuing painting above decorative art, the separation of different disciplines and historical classifications of time and place. As an alternative, he proposed the "room of miracles" approach based on the 17th-century *Wunderkammer* (see Chapter 1). Mendini's interest in making possible the interaction between architecture, objects and the viewer found a kindred spirit in Haks, whose "self-museumizing" system requires the visitor to "playfully experience" an object and its history instead of passively observing it. Added to this is Mendini's concept of the museum not as neutral but as intimate, "a poetic moment in the life of the city."

A search committee for a suitable site headed by Josef Paul Kleihues (whose Chicago Museum of Contemporary Art opened in 1996) and Rem Koolhaas (see Chapter 7)—each an architect and planner—favored incorporating the museum into a new plan for developing the inner city. In collaboration with the architect Georgio Grassi they developed the concept of locating the museum in the Canal Link on an artificial island that would act as a bridge between the old center and the railroad station in a newer, marginal part of the city. The same idea had been proposed in 1928 by H. P. Berlage, the architect of the Amsterdam Stock Exchange, but the scheme's impressive origins did not help sell it to a resistant public in the 1980s. Initial designs for the island were criticized for, among other things, blocking views of the historic cityscape. Public opinion was finally swayed by separating the pavilions sufficiently to allow views through them and by Mendini's proposal to add a tall tower as a boundary marker between the old and new cities.

Museum für Moderne Kunst, ↑
Frankfurt, by
Hans Hollein (1991).
TOP: Isometric site plan.
BOTTOM: Entrance.

Joined by bridges to either side of the canal, the Groninger's central island has in effect become a gateway to the city through which 1.8 million people are expected to pass each year. This insertion of the museum into the community's circulation patterns resembles Piano and Rogers's original plan for the Pompidou, which has been adopted by several new museums (see Chapters 5 and 7). Even when there is no walk-through from one side of the building to the other, museums are now increasingly placed in critical urban locations where they serve a number of functions, such as signaling the transition between different neighborhoods. In this the Groninger resembles Hans Hollein's Museum für Moderne Kunst in Frankfurt (1991). Located between the medieval town center and the business district, Hollein's triangular building conforms to the site's pie shape. At the base of the triangle its entrance opens at one corner (like Kahn's Center for British Art in Hew Haven), beside which a café-portico has established a new focal point for the neighborhood.

Looking at the Groninger from the canal's southwest bank the visitor sees stacked pavilions on three small islets connected by corridor/bridges; with one exception the exteriors reflect the contents. The rectangular central islet is the work of Alessandro and Francesco Mendini: its distinguishing feature is the 200-foot-high storage tower, clad in gold plastic laminate to suggest a treasury from which continually changing displays are created. An entrance hall, café and shop are at ground level; below are an auditorium, library, seminar rooms and two galleries.

On the islet to the west of this central mass Michele de Lucchi's rectilinear archaeology and history pavilion, covered with local red brick, serves as a base for Philippe Starck's circular decorative arts pavilion, sheathed in aluminum sheeting embossed with vase-shaped reliefs. On the islet to the east is the Mendini team's rectilinear pavilion for contemporary art and temporary exhibitions, its colorful laminate an enlarged detail from a painting by the French

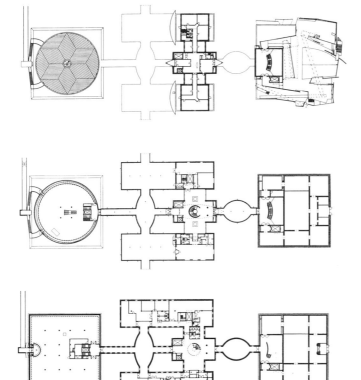

↑ Exterior.

← Plans.
TOP: Upper level.
CENTER: Middle level.
BOTTOM: Lower level.

↓ Central islet by
Alessandro and
Francesco Mendini.

pointillist Paul Signac. The Mendinis' pavilion, in turn, supports what appears to be a random pile of rust-colored steel plates, many splattered with black, alternating with tempered glass. This explosive design by Coop Himmelblau replaced one proposed by Frank Stella (see Chapters 4 and 7).

Within the entrance lobby of the central islet, a multicolored mosaic, spiral stairway leading *down* is the first in a series of surprises. At this, and at the lower level, generously fenestrated bridges connect the central islet with the eastern and western ones. To the west the dramatically darkened historical galleries are divided into spotlit aedicules in a gamut of reds related to the exterior; they present periods from prehistoric to modern. Ascending to the decorative arts pavilion above, visitors emerge from the archaeology department's nocturnal atmosphere into Starck's dazzlingly bright, surrealistic setting. Here, walls are replaced by what the architect calls "fog banks or clouds"—diaphanous white curtains hanging the full height of each gallery on either side of continuous neon ceiling tubes. To convey the circumstances of its discovery at the bottom of the South China Sea, the jewel of the collection, 8,000 Oriental ceramics, is shown reimmersed in a sunken aquarium.

Compared with these pavilions, the Mendinis' two levels of galleries at the east—one each for contemporary and changing exhibitions—are fairly conventional. They consist of rectilinear rooms in short enfilades with a large central space at each level. Their only distinctive features are the brilliant wall colors (developed by the artist Peter Struycken) and splayed door jambs, both inspired by Copenhagen's Thorvaldsenianum (see Chapter 3). More interesting are the Mendinis' transitional spaces. Vertical circulation in the two lateral islets is as unusual as the colorful main entrance stairway. At the west a narrow stairwell is clad in the bright blue, green and yellow tiles frequently found in bathrooms (a contrast to the regal gold mosaics covering the walls of one corridor); at the east, a curvilinear staircase spirals upward like a large white sculpture within a triple-height, sky-blue area where art is displayed. The bridges between the islets are the only areas, apart from the Coop Himmelblau galleries, with natural light and views to the exterior. In their oval galleries often startling juxtapositions of fine and decorative arts indeed make the rooms of miracles Alessandro Mendini envisioned.

The individual character of each Groninger pavilion allows for settings uniquely suited to the displays. In each case the architecture relates directly to, and enhances, the art objects and artifacts, just as Haks and Mendini intended. The installations are sufficiently offbeat to create the hoped-for sense of surprise and discovery; the pavilions have traded architectural form for a colorful, eye-catching conglomeration that calls to mind a trayful of the cleverly designed household utensils for which Mendini is famous. Given that its collections are of secondary importance, the Groninger could easily be overlooked were it not for the exoticism of its architecture.

↑ Triple-height circulation hall
by Alessandro Mendini.

← TOP: Contemporary art gallery
by Alessandro Mendini.
BOTTOM: Decorative arts pavilion
by Philippe Starck.

THE J. PAUL GETTY MUSEUM

**J. Paul Getty Center,
Los Angeles,
California**

by **Richard Meier & Partners**

landscape architects

**Olin Partnership/
Fong & Associates,
Emmet L. Wemple
& Associates and
Office of Dan Kiley**

1997

360,000 square feet

155,000 square feet of exhibition space

total cost of center approximately

$1 billion

There is no overlooking Richard Meier's Getty Center, dominating, as it does, a hilltop above a freeway in the Brentwood section of Los Angeles. Its series of structures (65 feet high for the museum, 45 feet elsewhere) overwhelms its site, but visibility was the point of this new campus, built to augment the late John Paul Getty's secluded museum in Malibu.

For the exhibition of his antiquities, paintings and period furniture, the expatriate oil billionaire reproduced a first-century A.D. villa at Herculaneum above the Pacific in Malibu; it was inaugurated in 1974. That museum's loose archaeological reconstruction and quirky collection are the foundations of today's Getty Center. Development of the small villa museum (now being renovated by Rudolfo Machado and Jorge Silvetti to improve its historical accuracy and add contemporary buildings) into a vast, multi-program institution was the brainchild of then Getty president Harold Williams, a former chairman of the Federal Securities and Exchange Commission. To signal the change, in 1982 the Getty Museum became the Getty Trust, which within a few years employed over 600 people in various Los Angeles locations with no particular identity. Just as current museums seek recognition through high-profile architecture, Williams sought to legitimize this newcomer to the academic world of cultural studies and humanities centers by consolidating its dispersed programs in a setting commensurate with its ambitions. To this end, in 1982 the Getty Trust purchased a 110-acre site in the Santa Monica foothills.

In 1984 a selection committee chose Richard Meier to design the complex from an initial list of 80 candidates. Upon receiving the commission, Meier's statement that he would "try and bring a little bit of order into that chaos" of southern California corresponded perfectly with the Getty's conservative mandate to revitalize the fragmented present by reconstructing the history of Western high culture. In a repeat of William Randolph Hearst's attempt to dignify his palatial San Simeon by means of a European style, the Getty looked to Modernism to rid the trust of its robber baron associations in favor of a more serious and permanent image. The museum is one of six units housing the trust's different departments—conservation, art education, electronic art information, grants and a research institute that can accommodate 180 scholars; the program includes offices for the Getty Trust, a 450-seat auditorium, a restaurant and outdoor cafés. Meier has created a modern-day Xanadu replete with luxuriant gardens, cascades, fountains and pools. John Walsh, the museum's director, remarks that the Getty is the reverse of the villa in a valley: the new complex, a "modern building on a ridge," expands the Roman allusions of the parent institution to truly imperial proportions.

← East front.
LEFT TO RIGHT: Museum,
conservation institute,
education and grant
programs, auditorium.

Kurt Forster, who was director of the research institute when it was being designed, has compared Meier's scattering of these separate units along two facing north-south ridges with the way in which the different components of Hadrian's Villa at Tivoli embrace that rolling landscape. The villa's sprawl is an urban paradigm (as cited by the scholars Colin Rowe and Fred Koetter), and Meier's reinterpretation of the Roman precedent has indeed produced a mini-city—but it is as protected and controlled as Disneyland.

From the beginning, the Getty was a difficult client. Its invitation to Meier to formulate the program for each structure made the architect dependent on the changing demands of a dozen staff members and 40 key users. The resulting difficulties were compounded by cost-cutting measures and a fast-track construction method that entailed concurrent design and construction. While breaking the program into separate entities was a valid response to the site, accommodating the activities of nearly 1,000 employees is just too much program for the 24 acres on which the Getty was authorized to build. Furthermore, the decade that has elapsed between approval of the master plan and its completion has dated the design; the museum and the research institute alone escape a type of bland uniformity usually associated with a corporate headquarters. Nevertheless, the complex's structures, controlled by Meier's usual grids, relate to each other at a more human scale than one would suspect from their intimidating, fortresslike appearance from afar.

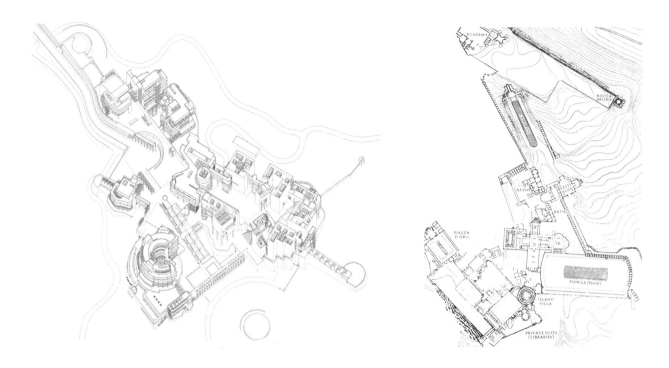

LEFT: Axonometric drawing. ↑
RIGHT: Hadrian's Villa, Tivoli
(between A.D. 118 and 134).
Plan.

Tram station looking →
toward the center.

Of the complex's six buildings only the museum is open to the public, and its five pavilions are designed as much for the enjoyment of southern California's temperate climate and the site's spectacular mountain, city and ocean vistas as for their contents. An anticipated 1.5 million visitors a year are expected to spend at least half a day at the Getty, which, like the Centre Pompidou, should attract a large percentage of its audience for the views alone.

The Pompidou analogy ends there: whereas the Paris landmark was an innovative, trend-setting achievement intended to democratize culture, the Getty is an ultraconservative statement at home with its well-manicured suburban neighbors and removed from the messy urban realities of across-town Los Angeles. However, the Getty's location effectively opens to the public an area that would not otherwise be available. Every four minutes throughout the day a tram leaves from the 1,200-car garage, transporting visitors on the scenic, uphill trip to a museum that is, in effect, the most rarefied version of the theme park formula yet devised.

Beginning with the selection of a site on a seismic fault that has required costly stabilization (and additional work after the 1994 Northridge earthquake), many of the Getty's decisions appear perverse. Among the first was restricting Meier from using his emblematic sleek, white building materials—a gesture comparable to forbidding Le Corbusier the use of concrete. The ban was due to community opposition to the prominence and glare of white stucco and enamel —but the selection committee was surprisingly acquiescent. Uppermost in their minds was that the complex be unique: their visit to Meier's porcelain-tile-clad High Museum in Atlanta raised concerns about maintenance and led to the feeling that the Getty should be unlike anything the architect had ever done. Faced with this charge, Meier took two years to settle on the travertine he describes as "what all of Rome is made of" (and, incidentally, a large part of the United States). The Getty's beige exteriors juxtapose open-jointed rugged blocks with smooth porcelain-enameled tile; the rough-cleft method devised by Meier to break the travertine into two-inch-thick panels creates rich textures and reveals beautiful fossil patterns. Like the center itself, the stone gains from close viewing; at a distance it reads as huge uniform surfaces. Meier insists that as merely one of over a hundred conditions imposed by the city, the limitation on his choice of materials was a challenge rather than a restraint:

> I struggled, flying back and forth to Los Angeles, mesmerized
> by views of the Grand Canyon: how would I find a stone
> that had the roughness and power of the Grand Canyon—
> or the dignity of it?

Italian umbrella pines that continue the Roman theme shade the tram-arrival plaza, where a monumental marble stairway consisting of steps at either side of giant central blocks leads directly to the museum. The stairway is bordered by rushing water that greets the public with its refreshing sound.

Walsh's acknowledgment of what he terms the "immaturity" of the Getty collections and their disparity—painting, sculpture and drawings, illuminated manuscripts, photography and decorative arts—prompted his suggestion that they be presented individually but in a connected way. The precedent he cited was the Louisiana Museum near Copenhagen. Walsh notes that Meier's first models reflected the program exactly: the introduction of the museum pavilion plan to southern California is one of the Getty Center's few innovations.

The pavilion arrangement is ideal for museums in temperate climates. In India, for example, several of Charles Correa's museums have a succession of indoor and outdoor spaces. Correa attributes the inspiration for his pavilions to Asian religious architecture—certainly in the Hindu temples of southern India the pilgrimage through the sacred, open-to-the-sky areas that lie between these temples' shrines is as important as the shrines themselves. The analogy—more apt than Meier's comparison of his museum to a cathedral—brings together sacred and profane in the pavilion, a structure that has served both religious architecture and the theme park.

Reminiscent of the High Museum's atrium, the sun-drenched entrance rotunda of the Getty Center Museum is easily transformed into a captivating indoor-outdoor space by enormous sliding doors that make up most of its south-facing side. A bookshop is at one side and two elegant, maple-paneled orientation theaters are at the other (with a lecture hall below). Like the many tube-rail stairways throughout the complex, the one that spirals up within the rotunda is masterful. The airy lobby provides access to the five two-story pavilions (or clusters, as Meier calls them) grouped around a garden courtyard of noble proportions, in which a 100-foot-long fountain is fed by arching water jets inspired by Granada's Alhambra Palace.

Plans. ↓
TOP: **Upper level.**
BOTTOM: **Ground level.**

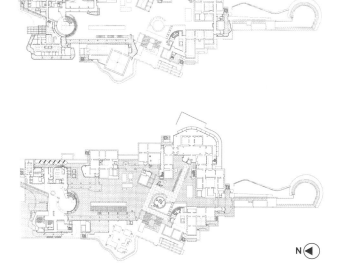

N ◀

↑ Northeast quadrant.
LEFT TO RIGHT:
Auditorium, information
and trust building,
conservation and
education institutes.

← Museum entrance
rotunda.

 Upper corridor. ↑

Painting gallery. →

Covered outdoor walkways at ground level and enclosed glazed passageways above connect the four clusters for the permanent collection. In them painting and sculpture from the medieval period to the 19th century occupy the upper level's 20 skylit galleries, while objects requiring more controlled light (including 20th-century photographs) are shown in the 29 ground-level galleries. On the exterior, transitional spaces are expressed by enameled metal cladding and glass, the permanent gallery spaces by stone. From the entrance rotunda, a clockwise route through the first four pavilions presents the collections in roughly chronological order, though a random path may also be taken. The fifth pavilion, rotated in relation to the others and joined only with the entrance rotunda, offers 7,200 square feet of more contemporary, irregularly shaped temporary exhibition space. Its lower level has been left open for a café terrace: placed between the supporting columns, it enjoys prime views.

Each of the permanent collection's clusters is organized around a skylit, double-height central space in an arrangement inspired by that of New York's Frick Collection. Views of the sky from these travertine-clad atriums reinforce the museum's relationship with the exterior. Walsh's admiration for what he calls the original Getty villa's "intervals of relaxation," found on its balconies and in its gardens, carries over here in the openness of the museum's upper corridors to the views and in the cappuccino carts and inviting seating of its outdoor terraces.

The central atriums direct movement around the relatively short peripheral lengths of each pavilion; only three rooms in one of the clusters, devoted to Rembrandt, are in a formal enfilade. Off-center doorways further syncopate the rhythm of the circuit. Most of the rooms are cubes or double cubes—all are 27 feet wide with various lengths; ceilings range from 20 to 30 feet at their center, while perimeter wall height is limited to 15 feet. Sir John Soane's Dulwich Picture Gallery provided the model for the lantern skylights that crown the sloped-soffit ceilings. (Meier has, however, simplified the model, compared with Venturi, Scott Brown and Associates' adaptation of the same source at the Sainsbury in London; see Chapter 5.) Above a small changing exhibition gallery two enormous inverted-V skylights hover like giant wings; elsewhere skylights are supplemented by clerestory windows. In every case automated exterior louvers diffuse natural light. Daylight levels vary, and there are even glimpses of the sky, but what is gained by the presence of these natural phenomena is lost by the computerized correction of color discrepancies that attempts to match evening light to daylight.

Paintings are suspended from wires tinted to match the color of the walls. These 15-foot hanging walls are delineated by a molding at the top and by Bavarian oak baseboards; the same oak was used for door jambs and floors. For acoustical reasons handmade rugs partially cover the floors in half the galleries. Handsome upholstered walnut settees designed by Meier add to the rooms' intimacy. Rather than his usual white cubes, Meier has deployed a variety of proportions, details and ceiling treatments that gives each gallery its own character.

Meier's willingness and ability to bend the stringent rules of his Modern vocabulary did not satisfy the Getty, whose trustees came to yet another perverse decision. In 1994, with construction underway, the New York–based French architect Thierry Despont—who had been engaged initially to develop interiors for the decorative arts collection, which consisted mainly of 18th-century French furniture—was asked to "decorate" the art galleries as well. Despont's traditional interiors are sumptuous, but they belong to a design aesthetic totally at odds with Meier's. In the 14 decorative arts galleries Despont's faux-marbre wainscoting, plastic moldings, extensive dentilated cornices and assertive classical columns are what Corbusian Modernism, including Meier's, has tried for almost a century to replace. In some of the fine arts galleries, the addition of fabric wall coverings, whose colors and textures are meant to complement the painting and sculpture, is also unnecessary in view of Meier's agreement to tint the plaster in each room to the same effect. Neatly illustrating the two architects' different approaches is the atrium between the fine and decorative arts rooms, where Despont continues the aesthetic of the latter with classical symmetry and period-inspired stone door jambs, while Meier introduces the art galleries with the asymmetry and plain jambs of his Modern vocabulary.

Period rooms like those of the decorative arts collection were considered outmoded already in the 1920s when Alexander Dorner, then director of the Landesmuseum in Hanover, Germany, replaced them with what he called "atmosphere rooms" in which proportion, light and color subtly suggested past eras. Since Carlo Scarpa, Louis Kahn and others in the 1950s, many architects have used a Modern idiom to create contextual museum settings— just as Meier wanted to. But Despont's decorative arts galleries—and the painting galleries with his wall fabrics added—are so different in style from Meier's Modern lobbies and circulation areas that they themselves appear to be exquisite artifacts on exhibit within the museum. Despite significant accessions to the initial collection, which now includes works from the early Renaissance to 1900, the Getty's paintings are secondary—the quality and range of works in the Norton Simon Museum in nearby Pasadena far out-shining it. In fact, the excesses of the new Getty Museum galleries underscore the shortcomings of the collection.

The Getty's addition of a garden installation by the Conceptual artist Robert Irwin has created an equally bizarre mixture of sensibilities. This decision was doubly perverse: in contradicting the architect's aesthetic and in commission-ing $8 million worth of landscaping from a man who knew nothing about plants. With the help of the landscape architect Dan Kiley, who was succeeded by Laurie Olin, Meier had planned his typical exterior application of a grid sys-tem similar to the one governing the building plans. For the main outdoor pub-lic space—the ravine lying between the museum and the research institute—this concept was to be implemented with partly planted, partly paved small-scaled areas divided by a watercourse. In 1992, to offset such formal landscap-ing, which the Getty felt contrasted too starkly with the site's natural chaparral, Irwin's organic artwork was commissioned. Its Cor-Ten steel plates delineate a huge amphitheater for lush flowering plants and a floating maze of azaleas embellished by a waterfall. The effect is as foreign to Meier's outdoor environ-ment as Despont's decoration is to the interiors.

Having committed itself initially to a classic Modern architect, the Getty Trust gradually allowed its commitment to erode. By imposing Despont, Meier's Modernism was overshadowed by academic historicism. By bringing in Irwin, Meier's orthogonal landscaping was confused by an intervention equally at odds with it. The client in fact outflanked its architect both to the right and to the left, seriously compromising his intentions.

The wish to attract visitors to the museum, what the *Los Angeles Times* calls the "must visit . . . as important as the Louvre or the National Gallery," and at the same time provide a reclusive setting for intellectual and eleemosynary pur-suits, had, even before the Getty Center's opening, conveyed mixed signals, as have many of the trust's other decisions. That so early in its history an institu-tion should reject the possibility of change and growth with such a finalized plant is puzzling, as is the trust's indecisiveness as an architectural client.

From the beginning Walsh had specified the need to relate the new museum to the one in Malibu, with its proven popular appeal. Indeed, Despont's historic re-creations conform to the precedent of a fake container for real contents. The Roman villa imitation in Malibu, replete with air-conditioning and a garage, is likened by the writer Umberto Eco to the kitsch, imitation-Renaissance Hearst castle at San Simeon: it is one of California's many "examples of the conjunction of archaeology and falsification." In this respect the villa, and now the new museum derived from it, continues the regional tradition of entertainment fan-tasy pioneered by the Hollywood film industry.

William Marlin's description of the Centre Pompidou as "a source of enter-tainment as much as of enlightenment, of relaxation as much as revelation" applies to most museums today. With the exception of a few institutions that continue to treat art solemnly as a secular religion (the Bregenz Kunsthaus, Chapter 2, is an example), museum architecture has opened up to the surrounding world, acknowledging realities that had previously been excluded from mausoleum-like structures.

The Groninger's integration with the urban fabric plugs it into the community's circulation patterns: isolation in a park or monumental aloofness within a city belongs to the past. As for the hilltop Getty Center, offsetting a location that is uncomfortably like that of an acropolis, a context has been created for the museum that Forster insists will provide "a more intensely urban experience than you can get in most of L.A."

The Pompidou inaugurated a series of museum functions that go well beyond the preservation and exhibition of art: museums now play an important role in weaving together disparate neighborhoods; they are a status symbol and perform a social function much as the 19th-century opera house did. Separate access to museum auditoriums and restaurants (where nondescript cafeteria fare has been replaced with gourmet food) has become common, giving them a life independent of the galleries. And the popularization of art has brought it to unexpected locales.

Multiuse facilities like Lingotto and the Cité Internationale de Lyon integrate art with a much broader range of activities than the strictly cultural departments of the Pompidou. Culture sells (the three-month Cézanne exhibition in 1996 at Philadelphia's Museum of Art brought the city 122.6 million tourist dollars), a fact that is being taken into account by an increasing variety of commercial oper-ations. If museums are adopting the lessons taught by theme parks, Disney is in turn using culture to lure tourists, with plans to add quality music, dance and art to its parks' attractions.

And Las Vegas is not far behind. In a near literal interpretation of Fahlström's "pleasure-house," for his new $1.5 billion, 3,000-room Bellagio Hotel on the Strip, casino mogul Steve Wynn will include a permanent exhibition of some two dozen Impressionist and post-Impressionist paintings. Imitating the historic juxtaposi-tion of spaces for art and for greenery (as in the 19th-century Donner pavilion, Chapter 1), the gallery will adjoin a botanical garden. And like so many other col-lectors who present their art to the public, Wynn wants to avoid the feeling of a museum. Together with Jon Jerde, a California architect known for his theme streets, he intends the gallery, with its velvet-covered walls, to evoke "the private salon of a great collector." To those who criticize the use of art as a draw for gam-blers, one could respond that, on the contrary, Wynn is legitimizing Las Vegas's new image as a family entertainment mecca in the same way that Meier has legit-imized the Getty Trust's image as a serious intellectual institution. In effect, Wynn seems to be taking one step further the "combination of fine art and crude art" urged by Robert Venturi, Denise Scott Brown and Steven Izenour in their now classic 1972 book *Learning from Las Vegas*.

Chapter 7

The Museum as Environmental Art

When a museum and its contents come together as an integrated esthetic whole, something special happens. The art is enlarged and exalted, and the viewer's rewards and responses are increased. Creating that synthesis of art and setting is the challenge that still faces architects and directors. It is the secret of a great museum.

Ada Louise Huxtable

↑ Guggenheim Museum, New York City, by Frank Lloyd Wright (1959). Rotunda interior.

From the time of the first purpose-built public museums, people have fought over whether the architecture should be an active or a passive container, a background or a foreground for the museum's contents. Introduction of new muscum typologies in the 20th century has escalated discussion from a whisper in the 1930s and early 1940s, with the gridded open space of buildings such as MoMA and Mies's, to full voice in 1959, with the directed flow of Frank Lloyd Wright's Guggenheim. It is currently a pitched battle, equal in intensity to Renaissance conflicts between the proponents of Classic versus Gothic facades.

If the open spaces of MoMA and of museums by Mies represent Modernism's paradigm, Wright's spiral is its antithesis. In progress since 1944, Wright's design was finalized by 1956. It went far beyond a new interaction between container and contained that Italian architects, notably Carlo Scarpa and Franco Albini, began to implement in the mid-1950s. At the Guggenheim Wright respected the classical museum typology of a central dome and grand stair (transformed by him into a ramp) and at the same time revolutionized the relationship between art, architecture and the viewer. Like Le Corbusier in his Musée Mondial project, Wright emphasized movement as opposed to geometry. The Guggenheim's curvature freed paintings of rectilinear framing architecture; the ramps and rotunda allowed viewers to observe each other as well as the exhibits from an unprecedented number of perspectives. Long before the Pompidou, it gave people an importance equal to that of the art for which it established a whole new environment (see Chapter 5).

The influence of the Guggenheim has been phenomenal, but there are other important 20th-century precedents for present attitudes toward museum design. In 1959, the year Wright's museum was inaugurated in New York, Le Corbusier's National Museum of Western Art opened in Tokyo. Compared with the Guggenheim, this austere building has received little attention. While its galleries are problematic, the museum's central hall provides another alternative to what the critic Joseph Giovannini calls "the missionary position" for viewing art. Within the hall's square space, two semienclosed balconies that can be used for exhibition overhang ground-level display areas; a ramp allows changing views of both. A prominent triangular skylight with cruciform beams forecasts today's sculptural gallery ceilings.

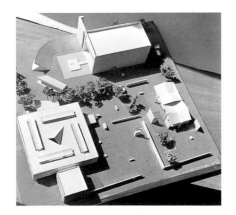

Yet another aspect of Le Corbusier's work relates to current museum architecture. From 1925 on, the Swiss-French architect designed a number of small, radically experimental exhibition pavilions for national or international fairs, some of which were built. After World War II, he incorporated equally daring pavilions into three projects for cultural complexes: two in India and one for the Tokyo museum complex. None of these museum-related pavilions was built, and to visualize their scope one must look to the exhibition building—the Centre Le Corbusier —designed by Le Corbusier and executed in

↑ National Museum of Western Art, Tokyo, by Le Corbusier (1959). Central hall.

← Cultural complex project for Tokyo, by Le Corbusier. Model with National Museum of Western Art and library at left and exhibition pavilion at right.

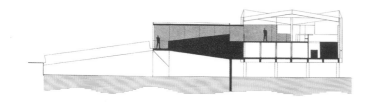

1967 by Heidi Weber in Zurich as a private gallery. Supported by peripheral rectangular posts, the umbrella-like steel roof is independent of the glass-and-steel building, with colored enamel facade panels inserted beneath it. Like the earlier pavilions, the complex form and unusual structure of the one in Zurich are in marked contrast to Le Corbusier's austere museums in his cultural centers and must certainly have contributed to the broadening range of museum design; the inflected ceiling of Rem Koolhaas's Kunsthal, for example, is reminiscent of the pavilions'. By the same token, the forms of Frank Stella's projects for Dresden and Buenos Aires (see Chapter 4) bear an affinity to Le Corbusier's Philips Pavilion for the Brussels World Fair (1958), a building that also attracts Frank Gehry.

Rejected at the time of its inauguration by a number of artists and critics, the Guggenheim was too controversial to find many imitators, and the National Museum of Western Art may have been just too far away. In any event, with a few exceptions—like I. M. Pei's Everson Museum of Art in Syracuse, New York (1968), in which balconies and catwalks opening to a central space follow Le Corbusier's example—by the mid-1970s neutral white boxes—among them, Philip Johnson and John Burgee's Neuberger Museum at Purchase, New York (1972), and Edward Larrabee Barnes's Dallas Museum of Art (1983)—had become the norm for museum galleries (see Chapter 2). Reaction against these "ghetto spaces," as Brian O'Doherty called them, together with the vastly expanded scale of much painting and sculpture, led, as we have seen, to the use of alternative spaces for art and reinterpretations of Modernism (see Chapters 4 and 5).

One of these was Hans Hollein's Städtisches Museum Abteiberg at Mönchengladbach, Germany (1982), on which the architect worked for ten years with Johannes Cladders, the museum's director, to create galleries related to the kind of art to be exhibited. Cladders believes that museums have the potential to resolve the autonomy of art and architecture, and he worked to this end with Hollein. The resulting galleries include curvilinear walls, a ramp,

a bridge and side and top lighting, as well as different kinds of artificial light, which create a variety of moods—or environments—so appropriate to the displays that the spaces seem to have been custom-designed for them, even though this was not the case.

A cloverleaf plan frees circulation between the Abteiberg's galleries, which are situated in a series of cubes that cascades down a hillside paralleled by an active pedestrian path from the town's main street to the gardens below. Hollein's spaces, conducive to a lively interplay between art and architecture, and his placement of the museum squarely within the urban fabric, were important steps toward a new museum typology.

Städtisches Museum Abteiberg, Mönchengladbach, by Hans Hollein (1982).

← Gallery.

↓ Site plan.

At about the same time a renewed interest in historical allusion reached maturity in the work of James Stirling and Michael Wilford, notably with their Neue Staatsgalerie in Stuttgart (1984), and in museum designs by Venturi, Scott Brown and Associates (see Chapter 5). The Classical details of these galleries, many in enfilades, act as a visual context for art of different periods, as the columns and beams of industrial loft spaces do for contemporary art.

Now several architects—each with his own distinct vocabulary—including Peter Eisenman, Wolf Prix, Rem Koolhaas, Daniel Libeskind and Frank Gehry, have created what will be referred to here as the new museum (new in design as well as age). The new museum is intended to show work by artists who are responding to the

spaces or existing art that can interact with the spaces in a dialogue that goes beyond the contextualism of classic or postmodern architecture. As radically different from modern movable walls that floated in open space as the latter were from the fixed enfilades of Classical galleries, the new museum relates to a definition of environmental art formulated by the critic and curator Germano Celant: "when an artist uses space not as a 'bed' for his work, but as an integral part of it." Examples of this intimate relationship between art and architecture exist from prehistoric cave paintings to the present.

Until the 20th century museum buildings were dictated by architectural styles rather than by changes in art. The advent of abstraction led to a rethinking of the means by which to present this new art form to the public. Beginning in the 1920s installation design addressed the problem in ways that relate to current architecture. In this respect, El Lissitzky and Frederick Kiesler, notably, tried to break away from the conventional box.

Repudiating the "eternal passivity of museum art," El Lissitzky developed alternative viewing conditions, starting with his Proun Room at the 1923 Berlin Art Exhibition, where abstract wall reliefs were connected with long slats meant to lead the viewer from one work to another. Three years later, at the request of Alexander Dorner, the artist built in the Hanover Landesmuseum the Abstract Cabinet, identified by Alfred Barr as "probably the most famous single room of twentieth century art in the world." In it, walls were effectively dematerialized by narrow perpendicular slats painted white on one side and black on the other; the slats changed color as the viewer moved by them. Additionally, the manipulation of sliding metal panels to conceal or expose paintings enlisted the viewer's participation. El Lissitzky's use of elements resembling scaffolding for an installation at the 1929 International Exhibition of Film and Photography in Stuttgart foreshadows a similar structure at Peter Eisenman's Wexner Center (1989).

Installation at ↑
International Exhibition
of Film and Photography,
Stuttgart, by
El Lissitzky (1929).

Austrian Theater →
Exhibition (known as
Space City),
at the Exposition
internationale
des arts décoratifs
et industriels
modernes, Paris,
by Frederick
Kiesler (1925).

As El Lissitzky did, the Romanian-born Frederick Kiesler used techniques from the theater, with which his installation designs were long identified; to these he added ideas from film and commercial display. All of his methods were aimed at involving the viewer's participation in an integral environment. Kiesler first demonstrated his theory of three-dimensional motion in continuous space in Vienna in 1924, using cantilevers and displays that were tilted or placed at right angles to one another for "The Art of the Theater in Austria." The following year he anticipated El Lissitzky's Stuttgart design with his installation for the Austrian Theater show at the Paris Exposition internationale des arts décoratifs et industriels modernes (in 1926 the installation was mounted in New York). For it, struts held horizontal and vertical plywood panels that appeared to float in space against blackened walls and ceilings. Kiesler's most dramatic and best-known installation was his 1942 Art of This Century Gallery for Peggy Guggenheim in New York City. Unframed abstract paintings and sculptures were hung from ropes in one room; in another, Surrealist paintings were affixed to supports protruding from concave walls. Individual lighting for each painting varied in harmony with audio effects that simulated an approaching train.

The late-20th-century's explosion of art forms, such as site-specific, installation, conceptual, video and performance art, also necessitates a different kind of space, a different environment from the one in which paint on canvas and traditional sculpture are shown. The new museum was introduced in 1989 by Frank Gehry's Vitra Design Museum in Weil am Rhein, Germany, and Peter Eisenman's Wexner Center for the Arts at Ohio State University in Columbus, Ohio. Quite different stylistically, the two buildings are examples of highly articulated architecture where the contents are an integral part.

It is no coincidence that Eisenman and the other architects discussed here were included in the Museum of Modern Art's "Deconstructivist Architecture" exhibition (1988). Despite their differing philosophies and aesthetics, their work harks back to ways in which Russian Constructivist architecture of the 1920s and 1930s broke the rules of classical composition. To paraphrase Mark Wigley's catalog for the exhibition, Constructivism broke down the condition of enclosure so that form followed deformation instead of function. Each in its distinct way, the new museums incorporate recurring themes: skewed, irregular geometries; the absence of hierarchies within a unified whole; and the displacement of structure.

WEXNER CENTER FOR THE ARTS

Ohio State University, Columbus, Ohio

by Eisenman Architects, with Trott and Beam
1989

140,000 square feet

12,000 square feet of exhibition space

$43 million

Exterior. →

Ground-floor plan. ↓

Peter Eisenman calls his Wexner Center for the Arts, consisting most conspicuously of scaffolding and landscaping, a "non-building." The scaffolding—a metaphor for a building constantly under construction—is a white steel framework that runs in part between brick towers reminiscent of an armory that occupied the site until its destruction by fire in 1958. The structure itself has a curtain wall of different types of glass, with some metal siding and limestone cladding. Raised sandstone "plinths" containing wildflowers and grasses, designed with landscape architect Laurie Olin, allude to Ohio Indian mounds. These large, waist-high planting areas at the Wexner's northeast and northwest sides alternate with the differently proportioned brick towers and the scaffolding to create a mirage of a building—now you see it, now you don't. Eminently appropriate to its constrained site, the Wexner, with its ephemeral quality, corresponds to the new breed of nonmonumental museums placed within a pedestrian pathway.

Faced with a choice of sites, Eisenman took the risk of opting for an awkward, leftover space between the Mershon Auditorium to the east and Weigel Hall to the west. The structure is organized along a diagonal originating in the city's historic grid that enters the campus at 15th Avenue and passes beside its central oval and across the end of its football stadium. Twisting the grids of city and campus, the Wexner succeeds best as urban design, effectively linking with

N

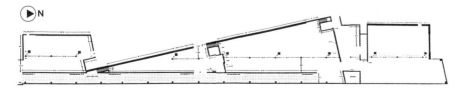

← Interior spine with
view to galleries.
Joseph Kosuth's *Ex Libris,
Columbus (for W.B.)*
attached to beam.

the 1880s campus by Frederick Law Olmsted and with adjacent buildings to create a new entrance for the university.

In 1983, when Eisenman won the competition for the project, he was better
known for his complex theories than for his built work, which then consisted of
a few small houses that were experiments in the superposition of grids and the
problem of multiple scales. The last of these experiments before he went on to
a different methodology, the Wexner incorporates two colliding structural grids
that are expressed in the white exterior framework (which resembles a Sol
LeWitt sculpture); they are recalled throughout the building's exposed beams,
columns, window mullions, floor patterns, light fixtures and just about everything else with a visible surface. The 516-foot-long scaffold provides an architectural kaleidoscope of changing perspectives; within, its outlines mingle with
those of the window mullions.

The Wexner has no central space. Like Eisenman's two subsequent buildings, the Columbus Convention Center (1993) and the Aronoff Center for Design
and Art in Cincinnati (1996), it is organized along an interior spine, which at the
Wexner ramps up gradually from basement to grade level as it runs from south
to north. Three galleries are located at ground level; below is a fourth gallery,
275-seat film and video theater, black box theater, library, café, bookstore,
storage and support systems. Offices are placed in the towers. The spine and
three main-level galleries constitute the Wexner's principal spaces. The first
two galleries are triangular; surprisingly, the third, "experimental" gallery is
rectangular and the most traditional of the three. Three minuscule stairways
are squeezed into the far corners of the wedge-shaped galleries: two provide

Gallery. ↑

alternatives to the ramp access; the third dead-ends with a view to the space below. Intended to break down the building's hierarchy, whimsical gestures like these mini-stairs together with many small, apparently functionless interstitial spaces are among the Wexner's most appealing characteristics.

Lively spatial effects occur in the circulation areas, to which the galleries do not live up. The excitement of the main stairway's square, truncated columns, which stop in midair, and of the spine's broken beams and collision of grids, is not matched by galleries, in which floor and ceiling grids present strong competition for what is being shown. The canvas canopy designed by Arata Isozaki for a Louis Kahn exhibition at the Wexner provided such welcome relief from the ceiling's visual confusion that the museum staff unanimously decided to retain it for three subsequent installations. The floor's distracting changes from granite to wood must be particularly disturbing for artists who work on the ground. The fact that the area's largest wall is glass drastically reduces the surfaces on which art can be hung: paintings on panels added to this wall are compromised by views of exterior activity and, again, by the pervasive grids.

The Wexner Center was conceived amid the early 1980s flush of enthusiasm for new contemporary art forms. Its primary purpose was to provide a testing ground for experimental art and media, with an emphasis on the avant-garde and art in process: four studios were to be used by visiting artists who would work in direct response to the museum's architecture. The Wexner has fulfilled this intention by inspiring several remarkable artworks that could only have been done here. Among them are Maya Lin's *Groundswell*, 46 tons of shattered glass that form sensual, undulating mounds in three "residual" spaces on the building's exterior, and Joseph Kosuth's *Ex Libris, Columbus (for W.B.)*, a neon text attached to one of several horizontal beams that intersect the galleries. On the other hand, conventional art can be exhibited in these spaces only by means of costly custom-made panels to accommodate it. Like most museum spaces, the Wexner works best with the kind of display for which it was designed—in this case, installation art made specifically for it.

OLD MASTER GALLERY, GRONINGER MUSEUM

Groningen, the Netherlands

by **Coop Himmelblau**

1994

9,690 square feet

6,730 square feet of exhibition space

$2 million

← Exterior.

At the Groninger Museum the Vienna–Los Angeles firm of Coop Himmelblau takes the concept of nonhierarchical space far beyond the Wexner Center. Despite its innovations the Wexner retains the conventional idea of galleries in a linear sequence, whereas Wolf Prix and Helmut Swiczinsky, principals of Coop Himmelblau, have reinvented the open, universal space of Mies.

When the museum planners were unable to reach an agreement with Frank Stella regarding his proposal for a gallery (see Chapter 4), Prix had just completed the Video Clip Folly, an audio/video pavilion for an event organized by Groninger director Frans Haks. The pavilion's jagged steel plates and strips were in a different style from existing designs for other parts of the museum (see Chapter 6) and thus conformed to Haks and Alessandro Mendini's wish for diversity. Retaining Stella's decision to create the only daylit galleries within the complex, Prix and Swiczinsky used wildly tilting rust-colored steel plates alternating with laminated glass for a structure that looks as if it is coming apart at the seams. The space within is punctuated by stairs, bridges, ramps and

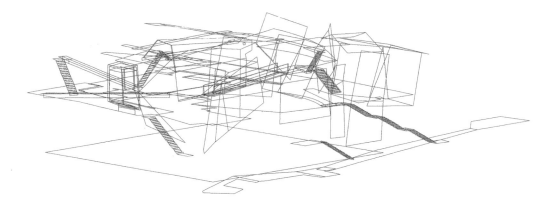

Axonometric plan, ↑
circulation space.

Galleries. →

platforms; it provides overhead glimpses of the sky and underfoot views to the canal in which the museum islets sit, together with an infinite number of exhibition viewing points.

Among the sources for the design, Prix cites the Picasso Museum in Paris (see Chapter 3) and the firm's project for a studio/museum for the German painter Anselm Kiefer. In both, ramps and stairs give the spectator different views of the work, thereby helping, in the architect's words, "to liberate art from the museum."

Prix emphasizes the importance of chance in his designs because of his willingness to pursue computer variables; these allowed him also to use the preliminary sketch for the Groninger for a museum installation and a stage set. For the museum a blueprint of a model was laid over the original drawing to produce a digitalized design model. This model was sent to Holland by modem, and the pavilion was constructed there by the same shipbuilders who had put together the Video Clip Folly (thereby realizing, Prix notes, Le Corbusier's prediction that in the future buildings would be constructed like ships). The sketch served yet another purpose: it was applied in tar, a quasi-indestructible material, to steel plates both inside and outside the pavilion, which will eventually rust and disappear. Thus the tar plan will be the only record of this most interesting of the Groninger pavilions.

Prix's adjustable sunscreens and his system of white exhibition placards suspended from the ceiling were not ready for the museum's inauguration. Consequently, large, mostly freestanding contemporary objects were substituted for the Old Masters intended for the gallery. This art was in perfect harmony with the space—an ideal realization of the museum as environmental art. Completion of the installation system eventually allowed the hanging of traditional paintings, with results that are open to question. Generically, the new museum requires creative curating: Prix compares his Groninger space with an organ, observing that "you can't play it easily." Its dynamic quality could complement any kind of object, if properly installed; the extra effort would seem worthwhile.

KUNSTHAL, ROTTERDAM

**Rotterdam,
the Netherlands**

by Rem Koolhaas/O.M.A.

1993

75,310 square feet

34,320 square feet of exhibition space

$12.25 million

↑ View from
the west:
auditorium at
left, restaurant
underneath,
road parallel to
Maasboulevard.

In stark contrast with the expressive exteriors of the Wexner Center and the
Coop Himmelblau pavilion, Rem Koolhaas's Kunsthal in Rotterdam is an outwardly simple quasi-Miesian box. It differs further in that it is not a museum but
a place for performances as well as for exhibitions that will range from automo-
biles to fine art. Yet, for all the apparent dissimilarities, the Kunsthal shares with
the Eisenman and Prix museums Constructivist roots and an unsettling reversal
of architectural norms.

Head of the Rotterdam-based Office for Metropolitan Architecture (O.M.A.),
Koolhaas is both an architect and an urban planner, with a stated preference for
the latter. In his words, "Architecture limits and exhausts possibilities; urbanism
generates potentials and keeps them open." The Kunsthal, like O.M.A.'s subsequent project for the Tate Museum's Bankside competition (one of six finalists),
is urbanistic in the priority it gives to circulation, which takes the form of a
continuous path through the building. Progression along this path is like the
unfolding of a film narrative, a comparison that Koolhaas—who began his
professional life as a journalist and screenplay writer—encourages with his presentations of grainy, black-and-white photographs and excessive, sequential
illustrations in his 1995 book *S,M,L,XL.* As in the case of what Le Corbusier
called a "promenade architecturale," the building reveals its meaning fully only
as one progresses through it.

Each of the Kunsthal's four facades is distinct: perversely, materials that one
would usually expect to be at the top—the glass and steel of the garden and a
side facade—are surmounted by a robust masonry box; likewise, the glazed main
facade is crowned by a sturdy orange I-beam that functions like a Venturian billboard facade in its signaling of the entrance. The building's presence on the busy,
multilane Maasboulevard is further heralded by a tall, steel-framed service tower
covered in plastic siding and illuminated from within. The boulevard runs along
the top of a fifteen-foot-high dike, at the bottom of which is a two-lane road and,

beyond it, a museum park. Koolhaas's genius lay in his ability to put these potentially problematic conditions to good use. Entered from the boulevard, the Kunsthal spans the lower road and creates direct access to the park via a wide outdoor ramp that bisects the building. Large picture windows at one side of the ramp provide views into the lower hall; opposite them, a corrugated plastic wall contains the entrance doors to the auditorium, restaurant (also with its own separate, park entrance) and exhibition spaces. Once inside the building, the visitor is led through its different levels and layers—of walls, partitions and screens with varying degrees of transparency—by means of a ramp that joins the auditorium and three exhibition halls. In the process interior and exterior ramps interweave at times; their glass walls allow views from one to the other. These unsettling circulation areas incorporate what Koolhaas refers to as the city's "culture of congestion" and give the excitement he feels is needed to contrast with the serenity of the exhibition halls.

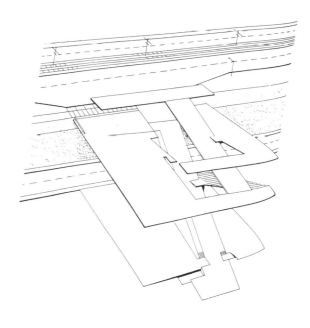

Not everyone would call these halls serene. Only one (Hall 1, on the park level) is rectangular; its black ceiling, randomly patterned with neon lights, is supported by columns of oak and chestnut tree trunks, suggesting a transition from the adjacent park. The ceiling of a small space beside Hall 1 is a see through metal grid that also serves as the floor of the gallery above it. On the next level, a second large exhibition space (Hall 2) is topped by translucent undulating glass laced with orange structural trusses. While an Andy Warhol exhibition installed on panels in Hall 2 was energized by the luminescent ceiling, some artists consider it intrusive; the open floor grid has been criticized for the same reason. Above is Hall 3, a black box across from which run lush plantings on an exterior slope. This roof garden distorts the rectangularity of Hall 3, and its footprint affects the entries at ground level and to Hall 2.

↑ Isometric drawing.

← Hall 1.

← Hall 2.

The unusually rich experience of the Kunsthal's architecture is in part due to elements like the shaped ceiling and the trusses that interplay with the exhibits to form a complete environment. Additionally, Koolhaas's mix of clear glass and corrugated plastic sheeting incorporating neon lights creates remarkable lighting effects, as does the translucent ceiling. Circulation not only provides unmistakable orientation but is also dynamic—one has the feeling of being literally propelled from one space to another. No museum fatigue here.

As with the Wexner Center, a director was not in place when the Kunsthal was being designed. With no precise directives as to the art they would exhibit, both buildings present problems for some work. Koolhaas says that had the Kunsthal been a museum, he would have designed it differently to accommodate specific works of art. But he emphasizes that all his work is "an oscillation between specificity and indeterminacy." Whatever its flaws, the Kunsthal's unique and surprising spaces encourage a fresh vision of what they contain.

THE JEWISH MUSEUM EXTENSION

Berlin, Germany

by **Daniel Libeskind**

1998

over 107,640 square feet

102,260 square feet of exhibition space

$65 million

Of the five architects discussed in this chapter, Daniel Libeskind is the youngest both in age and in experience; he was 43 years old in 1989 when he won the competition for the Jewish Museum in Berlin, which will be his first realized building. Born in Poland of political dissident parents, Libeskind moved to the United States in 1960 and subsequently became head of the architecture department at Detroit's Cranbrook Academy of Art.

Besides being an architectural theorist, Libeskind is something of a philosopher. His explanation of the Jewish Museum's competition design concept has been widely published:

> The official name of the project is the "Extension of the Berlin Museum with the Jewish Museum Department," but I have called it "Between the Lines." I call it this because it is a project about two lines of thinking, organization and relationship. One is a straight line, but broken into many fragments; the other is a tortuous line, but continuing infinitely. These two lines develop architecturally and programmatically through a limited but definite dialogue. They also fall apart, become disengaged, and are seen as separated. In this way, they expose a void that runs through this museum and through Architecture— a discontinuous void.

Rising through the building's three levels in a skylit structural rib, the void, or empty space, between the fragmented straight walls is the heart of the concept. It represents absence—all that, because of the Holocaust, is lost to Berlin and to civilization in general. Likened to a thunderbolt, the zigzagging exhibition spaces are repeatedly traversed by the straight, 13-foot-wide void structure. The design relates to Libeskind's 1988 composition *Line of Fire* and to his later Felix-Nussbaum-Haus (see Chapter 3), self-references that are a constant in his work. To reduce construction costs from the original $120 million, the competition design was simplified; most notably, its canted exterior walls were straightened.

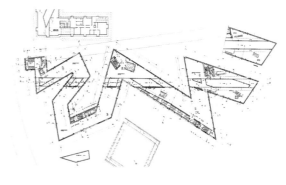

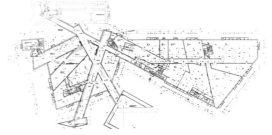

↑ Plans.
TOP: **Second floor with galleries.**
BOTTOM: **Underground floor.**

Commenting on the connection between Jewish tradition and German culture, Libeskind says that the Jewish Museum Department must be integrated with the Berlin Museum but at the same time remain independent. This is why the buildings' junction is subterranean, in the architect's words "preserving this contradicting autonomy of both on the surface, while binding the two together in depth." The city's pre-1871 history is addressed in the Berlin Museum, which is located on the Lindenstrasse near the Rondell, formerly a famous Baroque inter-section; the extension contains the Jewish Museum, devoted to religious and community history together with a continuation of Berlin history from 1871 to the present, the theatrical and graphic design departments, a lecture hall, spaces for changing exhibitions and service areas. The new wing sits beside the 18th-century building, projecting slightly beyond the latter's stone street facade. Its zinc cladding—a variation of Gehry's use of metal—relates to the galvanized sheet metal of nearby roofs and would not in itself be surprising were it not for the building's unusual form. Its startling asymmetry is made even more dramatic by unframed window openings that appear to be slashed at random into its facades. The Jewish Museum is entered underground from the existing institution and immediately confronts the visitor with crossed axes that present three alternatives: a long stair to the exhibition areas, the steeply raked E. T. A. Hoffmann Garden outside or the Holocaust Tower.

Detail of exterior. ↑

Exterior, with → E. T. A. Hoffmann Garden at center.

Libeskind cites four sources of inspiration. First, there was the history of German Jews in Berlin: plotting connections between the addresses of famous Jewish intellectuals who lived near the museum produced the window slashes. Another inspiration came from Arnold Schoenberg's unfinished opera *Moses and Aaron,* based on the contrast between the expressed and the ineffable. A third factor in his conceptualizing was provided by the *Gedenkbuch,* the German government's record of the Jewish population deported from Berlin together with their presumed places of death. Finally, descriptions in Walter Benjamin's 1928 book of general reflections, *One-Way Street,* played a part.

These are compelling ideas, but no amount of theorizing prepares for the experience of Libeskind's building. From the moment one enters, there is a feeling of dislocation: the multiple axes; the steep, monumental main stair crisscrossed by oblique girders overhead; the tortured, slanted asymmetrical wall incisions through which light beams splice the interiors; and acoustics that amplify the slightest sound. All are threatening. Passage through the narrow concrete bridges that span the skylit voids is profoundly moving. Glimpses of the voids through small openings in the bridges' walls evoke the 16th-century Kabbalah concept of *Tsimtsum*—God's withdrawal into himself in order to make creation possible—something the scholar Gershom Scholem calls "a primordial exile, or self-banishment."

Thus the Jewish Museum provides a strong psychological, as well as a new formal environment. As Frank Gehry notes of Libeskind, "You feel his anger about the Holocaust in this building." Libeskind's spaces are so imbued with a sense of the Jewish experience in Germany that the art they will display must necessarily be enriched by them. The museum's program is expected to include works of art related to, and forming a continuum with, the museum's historical presentations. An example is Edvard Munch's portrait of Walter Rathenau, a German-Jewish statesman who was assassinated by nationalists in 1922. For art that will be viewed as documentation as well as for its aesthetic value, Libeskind envisages dramatic installations: vitrines and partitions that can accommodate scales varying from small documents to the room-size *Kaiser Panorama*, a 19th-century "step-in" perspectival painting of Berlin. Like James Ingo Freed's Holocaust Memorial Museum in Washington, D.C., the Jewish Museum goes beyond what we think of as a museum to become a monument of mourning. Whereas Freed's building incorporates literal references to aspects of the Holocaust experience, Libeskind's allusions are indirect, his forms unprecedented.

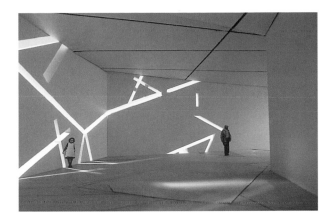

↑ TOP: Gallery. Model.
BOTTOM: Main stairway.

← Void with bridges.

THE VITRA DESIGN MUSEUM

**Weil am Rhein,
Germany**
by **Frank O. Gehry
& Associates
1989**

9,900 square feet

7,000 square feet of exhibition space

$10 million

← Exterior with entry.

A native of Toronto residing in Los Angeles, Frank Gehry has been identified with southern California since he started his practice there in 1962. His friendship and extensive collaboration with first local and then international artists has been an important influence on his work. The catwalks, balconies and platforms in the house he designed in Malibu for the geometric abstractionist artist Ron Davis (1972) anticipated current interest in giving artists the means to interact with their art and foreshadowed aspects of his later museums.

For years Gehry had used his designs for art installations to try out ideas he later applied to architecture. His signature unpainted metal siding and plywood first appeared in an exhibition of the Los Angeles pop artist Billy Al Bengston (1968). More important, his first construction of the fish form, which became a major theme of his oeuvre, was as the setting for an exhibition of new products by the Italian fashion conglomerate GFT (Gruppo Finanziario Tessile) in Florence (1986). Gehry attributes to this installation the beginning of his interest in new forms that could take the place of historical decoration. He states: "I was interested in a sense of movement as a replacement for the decorative vocabulary of cornices, moldings and other details that architects in the nineteenth century and before could rely on to humanize space." Gehry's interest in traditional details is part of his overall relationship to classical architecture with which—unlike other architects of the new museum—he never loses touch. For the Vitra, he used an architectural vocabulary based on his observation of moving fish to meld discrete elements—like those of his Winton Guesthouse (1986)—into a single unit. The Vitra Design Museum is to Gehry's Frederick R. Weisman Art Museum in Minneapolis and Bilbao Guggenheim what his exhibition installations were to his subsequent architecture: an initial, small-scale statement that he later developed and refined.

The museum is set at the edge of a field; its white stucco walls and expressive forms relate to the entrance of the furniture factory across the street, also designed by Gehry. The two-level building provides a jewel-like setting for what was intended to be private exhibition spaces for a collection of innovative 19th- and 20th-century furniture, a library and storage. When it became apparent that the museum would have to be available to the public, the library was turned into an exhibition area and a small ground-floor space was given over to a café. Three galleries, two on the first floor, one on the second, open into one another by means of two curved staircases and a double-height central space. Curved cruci-form beams, short spans of which break free of the ceiling in a dialogue with bal-conies and interior windows, anticipate the larger flying beams at the Bilbao Guggenheim. There are no windows to the exterior, but interiors are flooded with natural light that penetrates shaped skylights placed strategically through the building. Inspired by Rudolf Steiner's second Goetheanum in Dornach (1928) and by Le Corbusier's Chapel of Notre Dame-du-Haut at Ronchamp (1955), Gehry's use of diffused and reflected light equals that of the Swiss-French archi-tect. Within the three galleries—each different in scale and with varieties of nat-ural illumination—every object comes alive in play with complex forms and light. It is no surprise that white boxlike settings for historical objects made to be seen in diversified interiors seem bland when compared with Vitra's, as in the case of Richard Meier's Museum für Kunsthandwerk in Frankfurt.

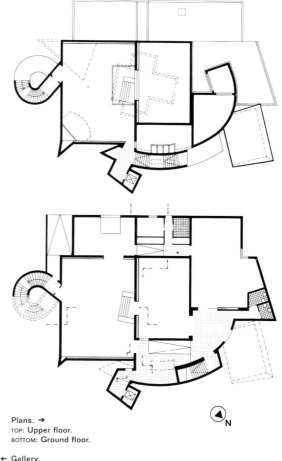

Plans. →
TOP: **Upper floor.**
BOTTOM: **Ground floor.**

← **Gallery.**

THE FREDERICK R. WEISMAN ART MUSEUM

University of Minnesota, Minneapolis, Minnesota

by **Frank O. Gehry & Associates**

1993

47,300 square feet

12,000 square feet of exhibition space

$15 million

In Minneapolis Gehry adapted Vitra's sculptural design for his first art museum (he applied it to the University of Toledo's Center for the Visual Arts in the same year). The Frederick R. Weisman Art Museum (WAM) houses the University of Minnesota's early-20th-century collection of American art together with contemporary works bequeathed by the California entrepreneur Frederick R. Weisman, a university alumnus who contributed $3.5 million toward the building's total cost. The museum sits on a bluff overlooking the Mississippi River and downtown Minneapolis, beside the Washington Avenue Bridge that links the campus's two parts. Galleries are on the third level of the four-story building, with offices above and two levels of parking and storage below. The WAM's dramatically faceted, stainless-steel facade looks west toward the river, leaving a bare-bones brick box to face the central mall quadrangle.

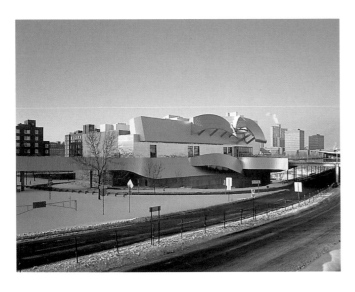

Brick facades: facing campus, ↑ at left, and promenade, at center.

Western, river facade. ➔

Gehry has been criticized for his apparent indifference to the university's Cass Gilbert plan and Georgian architecture, but originally three of the museum's facades, including those facing the campus and the promenade, between the bridge and the mall, were to have been faceted. When budget restrictions allowed only one important facade, Gehry placed it initially at the east, facing the campus, then shifted its orientation in response to the advice of local planners. They argued for the building's enhancement of the riverbank (an important part of an extensive metropolitan park system), where the metallic facade could distract from the cumbersome Washington Avenue Bridge. While cars enter at the west, the main pedestrian entrance is on a campus walkway from which passersby can look into the galleries through the museum's large picture windows. Two cloudlike, curved metal canopies—one above the entrance, one over the windows—signal the museum's presence. Teak-framed windows at the end of a spine running the length of the museum and in the office tower look to the river and beyond, further tying the building to its site.

Galleries occupy the southeast area of the third level, part of which is taken up by a black-

box auditorium that opens to the adjacent lobby for special events. The WAM's diverse program, including changing exhibitions, curatorial training and display of the permanent collection, required flexibility, so all the interior walls are movable or temporary. Spaces are partially defined by massive structural trusses that span the galleries. The 16-foot-high peripheral walls for hanging are topped by 6-foot-high lighting coves. Four sculptural skylight wells rise to 55 feet and efficiently allow maximum light to penetrate through the smallest possible opening, a device—like that of the oculus in Rome's Pantheon—preferred by Gehry in all of his museums to overall skylights. Seen from the side, the wells' billowing forms appear to be as complex as Baroque sculpture, so it is surprising to realize that they are almost symmetrical. Despite its box shape, the New York architect Alexander Gorlin considers the museum's interior baroque because "it is sculpted out of light." Without this sculpting element, when the skylights are closed the lofty rectilinear spaces lose some of their vitality, but when animated by daylight, they establish a lively and supportive setting. For the Bilbao Guggenheim Gehry has developed the Minneapolis museum's facade facets from cubism's three-dimensionality to freestanding expressionist sculpture.

← TOP: Gallery.
BOTTOM: Plan of gallery level.

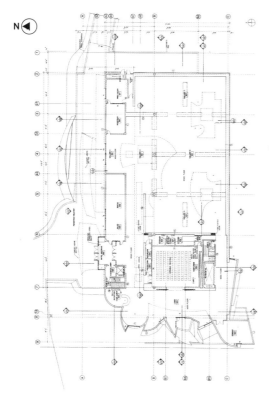

THE GUGGENHEIM MUSEUM, BILBAO

Bilbao, Spain

by Frank O. Gehry & Associates

1997

256,000 square feet

112,000 square feet of exhibition space

$100 million

← Northern, river facade.

As surprising as the Bilbao Guggenheim's extravagant forms is the impression the structure gives of always having dominated this urban landscape. Nothing about the building is alien. The curvilinear shapes of the "flower," Gehry's interpretation of the traditional museum dome, evoke the flora of the lush Basque countryside: the building's sophisticated surface materials are as at home here as Gehry's studs and chain link were in his early work in southern California. Puckered in what is known as an "oil can" surface, the titanium cladding recalls the city's steel factories; limestone from the southeast of Spain echoes the university buildings across the river; and the office building's stucco surface—painted bright blue rather than the more prevalent earth colors of existing buildings—relates to the region's historical architecture. (Commonly used in aeronautics, titanium, an unusual building material, was chosen by Gehry because its shimmering gray responds to different lights and it appears to ripple in the wind. Only one-third of a millimeter thick, it is more durable than stone.) The whole complex sits within a large reflecting pool that further integrates it with its setting on the south bank of the Nervión River.

Like the Weisman Museum, the Bilbao Guggenheim occupies a riverside site beside a bridge. But whereas in Minneapolis the Weisman stops demurely beside the Washington Avenue Bridge, the Bilbao museum embraces the La Salve Bridge, sweeping exuberantly under and above it to what Gehry calls

the "high-reader," the open-frame stone-and-steel tower that signals the Guggenheim's presence. If Wright's Guggenheim was intended to be centrifugal, a spiraling explosion outward, Gehry's Guggenheim is centripetal: he has turned Wright's inverted ziggurat right side up to make a modified pyramid that exerts a strong central pull. In its intimate relationship with the bridge the museum ties into the site and at the same time establishes a prominent new gateway to the city at the center of a cultural triangle made by the Fine Arts Museum, the university and the old town hall. Sited in an area that railway lines and port facilities had rendered unusable, the museum is expected to be a major factor in extending the city to the riverbank.

The Bilbao Guggenheim is part of one of the most ambitious attempts to date to associate an art museum with urban renewal. Like the Lingotto project in Turin (see Chapter 6), the $1.5 billion redevelopment of Bilbao addresses the problem of obsolete industrial facilities. More radical than Turin in displacing these facilities, Bilbao and the surrounding area is abandoning industry altogether in favor of technology and services, using the museum as a symbol of this change.

Located in the semiautonomous Basque region of northern Spain, approximately ten miles in from the Bay of Biscay, Bilbao was a major port for much of its 700-year history and, since the 19th century, a prosperous center of shipbuilding and steel and iron refining. In the last 15 years the decline of these industries has had a devastating effect on the Basque economy, which was compounded by an unwelcome notoriety from the terrorist tactics of the Euskadi ta Askatasuna (Freedom to the Basques) extremists intent on political autonomy. By making culture the symbol of Bilbao's regeneration, the government hopes to attract new business and create a tourist industry. To facilitate access, there are plans to restructure the port, rail and highway systems and to build a new airport terminal designed by the Spanish architect Santiago Calatrava. Operational since 1995 is one of the world's most elegant subway systems, by the high-tech architect Sir Norman Foster.

By the time the Basque government approached Guggenheim director Thomas Krens in 1991, Arata Isozaki's renovation of a loft building into the Soho Guggenheim had initiated Krens's concept of a series of Guggenheim museums to be designed by world-famous architects. The Soho building was part of the Guggenheim's New York expansion (see Chapter 5); with consideration of Venice, Salzburg, Vienna, Tokyo and Moscow as Guggenheim sites, Krens began a different kind of commercially based expansion. Peggy Guggenheim, Solomon's niece and the founder of her own museum in Venice, had envisioned a global network of museums controlled by the New York foundation and forming local collections. She felt that, like the parent institution in New York, other Guggenheim museums should have spectacular architecture. The Basque government's interest in creating a new museum in Bilbao fit perfectly with this concept.

Krens quickly persuaded the Basques to abandon their plan to rehabilitate an existing structure in favor of a new building that could be as important a symbol for Bilbao as the opera house is for Sydney. The Basques offered $100 million for construction plus $50 million for acquisitions, a $20 million fee to the New York Guggenheim and a subsidy of any shortfalls in revenues if the Guggenheim would oversee construction and rotate parts of its collection with, and run, the new museum. An Asian, a European and an American architect—Isozaki, Coop Himmelblau and Gehry—were asked to submit proposals for the building in a limited competition. Gehry was chosen by Krens, Carmen Jimènez, a former museum director and now a Bilbao curator, and three members of the Basque government.

Gehry attributes most of the museum's program to Krens, who traces his interest in museum design to his experience with expanding the Williams College Museum of Art. His work on the project in the mid-1980s with the late architect Charles Moore confirmed his conviction that the museum is an 18th-century concept housed in a 19th-century box, an obsolete formula that must change to accommodate art's new forms. Scale was of prime importance: instead of the 10-foot-high walls proposed by Moore, Krens wanted a variety of heights going up to 18 feet.

The director's subsequent involvement with the Mass MOCA project to convert a factory complex into a museum confirmed his belief that unprecedented large spaces are essential to today's museums. As important for Krens as exhibiting art is what he calls "architecture's subtle impact on the museum," with the "fun and surprise" it can give.

If ever architecture has provided these it is in Bilbao. In addition to the bravura of its unique forms, no detail of this extraordinary building has been treated routinely. Even working spaces have soaring, double-height areas and subtly curved window sills. Titanium and stone pass back and forth between

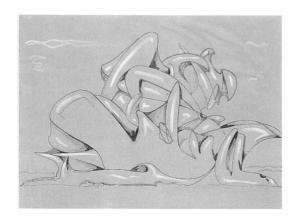

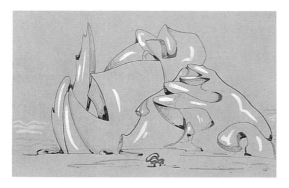

Die Häuser der Schaffenden by ↑
Hermann Finsterlin (1919).

exteriors and interiors that are separated only by abutting glass. Glass is repeatedly pulled beyond its frame in playful delight in the sensuousness of the material. An atrium column, narrow at its base, broadens to unfurl at the top like a giant banner. And these are only a few of Gehry's apparently unlimited sleights of hand.

The Bilbao Guggenheim is as long as New York City's Metropolitan Museum of Art, and considerably higher, but unlike the Met and in defiance of classical norms, this museum has no conventional entrance facade: Gehry has broken the enormous structure into differently shaped segments that relate to one another and to the site. As with the Vitra's debt to the Winton Guesthouse, the Guggenheim's sail-like forms relate to two unbuilt projects begun in 1989: the Walt Disney Concert Hall in Los Angeles (for which funding is now being completed) and the 40,000-square-foot Lewis residence (1989–95) in Cleveland; for the latter, Gehry first experimented with titanium and first used a computer to implement his design. The combination in both of these projects of curved and rectilinear forms in plan is further developed at Bilbao, where sculptural pavilions flow around two rectilinear structures containing classical galleries and the café. Shapes by the German Expressionist architect Hermann Finsterlin come to mind, but even though there is an affinity of form, this is no exploration of a given vocabulary: rather, it is the invention of a whole new language.

Aligned with a major city street, with which there will be a pedestrian connection, a ramp and broad, shallow stairs cascade *down*, in another anti-classical gesture, to the museum entrance. The entrance is tucked between the curved, metal-sheathed wall of a gallery and a lower stone wall that supports a generous terrace that allows separate access to the museum café, bookstore and 300-seat auditorium. (On the terrace, high above the entrance, is an enormous glass signage screen that should eliminate the ubiquitous museum banners.) This gradual descent in part compensates for the 20-foot grade differential between the city and the riverside. A glazed ticket vestibule, referred to as the teepee, mediates between the entryway and the dramatic 180-foot-high stone-and-plaster atrium, fronted by faceted glass and steel. Doors open within this glazed facade to a terrace on the opposite side from which installations in the reflecting pool can be viewed (the blue flames of Yves Klein's five *Fire Fountains* were the first of these). The platform is protected by a canopy supported by one of Gehry's signature tree-trunk columns.

← View of exterior from
a small street.

↓ LEFT: Atrium with elevator towers.
RIGHT: Atrium with *Soft
Shuttlecock* by Claes Oldenburg
and Coosje van Bruggen
on balcony.

Over one-and-a-half times the height of Wright's rotunda, on which its softened curvature is based, the atrium is animated by two glass-enclosed elevators and curvilinear catwalks that connect with two stairways while providing spectacular views of the river and the city and hills beyond. As with Wright's Guggenheim, the atrium is the museum's spinal cord, a central orientation area around which the galleries are organized, its energized space in constant dialogue with the calmer gallery spaces. In contrast to the disjunction between atrium and galleries in Mario Botta's Museum of Modern Art in San Francisco (see Chapter 2), here they are organically related.

Gehry associates three images with the atrium's design. Initially, thinking it would be used for multimedia art, he envisioned a rock quarry—the same metaphor Wright applied to his Wisconsin home and studio Taliesin, where "space is broken down with blocks of walls and terraces to allow individual and overall viewing." When Krens decided that the atrium should be enjoyed primarily as architecture, the dominant image became Fritz Lang's expressionist film *Metropolis* (1926), which, in turn, was derived from futurist visions of architecture, especially those of Antonio Sant'Elia, who in 1914 forecast that the street would:

> plunge stories deep into the earth, gathering up the traffic
> of the metropolis connected for necessary transfers to metal
> cat-walks and high-speed conveyor belts.

The Italian architect wanted to bring the elevator out of hiding to "swarm up the facades like serpents of glass and iron." In Gehry's atrium both visions are realized.

Now that his building is completed, Gehry sees a third affinity: between the atrium's shapes and Brancusi sculpture. *Endless Column* and *Bird* come to mind, as does the surrealistic *Woman with Her Throat Cut* for the atrium's crowning "flower," especially when seen from above. Still, it is the reference to *Metropolis* that is most evident: the atrium's enormous scale contributes to the dizzying effect of its transparent and opaque leaning towers, which rise next to stone walls within the transparent enclosure. Beside these heroic forms, people on the catwalks are dwarfed, but in spite of its scale, distances are manageable: the atrium is encompassed quickly and galleries flow easily into one another. This grand central space is welcoming both to visitors and to art: small alcoves within its walls are used as exhibition spaces and its balconies allow the draping of large pieces such as Claes Oldenburg and Coosje van Bruggen's *Soft Shuttlecock*.

"Heroic" also describes the museum's largest, ground-level gallery: bigger than a football field, the boat gallery is 450 feet long and over 80 feet at its widest, with a ceiling that soars far above the 23-foot-high walls. An access floor contains the technology for electronic art and performances. As with all the galleries, its Sheetrock walls are covered with smooth white plaster; its polished concrete floor is the same as in the other sculptural galleries (the rectilinear galleries have resin-finished floors of local ashwood laid in unusually wide strips).

For Krens "scale makes the building," but he qualifies this statement by specifying "scale that is inspiring, not overwhelming." And this huge space could be overwhelming if it were not for the human dimension provided by the sensuous bowing out of the gallery's walls: barely perceptible on the north, river side; slightly deeper for almost half of the south side, where the wall splits open and is glazed in one of several glass links that provide glimpses of other parts of the museum and the city. Additionally, changes in ceiling height and details such as curved flying ceiling beams, carefully placed skylights and a balcony above the entrance make the space less intimidating. For the architect Thom Mayne the building's ambitious size is the key to its success. He states:

> The fish is gone, the scales are there . . . this is all about one thing . . . Gehry started with chain-link, he disregarded details but kept discipline, now the raw steel and off-the-shelf railings really start to work as textural quality.

Before art was installed in it, however, even Gehry was fearful that this enormous, uninterrupted gallery could appear scaleless and he urged the erection of two short stubwalls. For the inaugural exhibition, "The Guggenheim and the Art of This Century," these fears proved only in part founded. Three monumental sculptures—Robert Morris's 16-by-30-foot painted plywood and masonite walk-in *Labyrinth*, Richard Serra's 103-by-18.75-by-13-foot Cor-Ten steel *Snake* and Oldenburg's 40-foot-long *Knife Ship* in wood covered with vinyl

Boat gallery, view toward →
entrance.
FAR LEFT: *One Hundred and
Fifty Multi-Colored Marilyns*
by Andy Warhol.
CENTER: *Snake*.
FAR RIGHT: *Reef* by Carl Andre.

with motorized oars and knife blades—had no trouble holding the space in a strong dialogue with each other. Placed as it was at the gallery's skylit far end, where the space narrows slightly and the ceiling is lower, *Knife Ship* filled the area in the best possible way—seeming ready to burst out of it. Other pieces—among them, Lawrence Weiner's wall painting *Reduced* and Carl Andre's pink Styrofoam *Reef*—were equally at home here. Only large canvases hung on the walls—even Andy Warhol's *Sixty-Three White Mona Lisas* (6.75 by 35.5 feet)—appeared dwarfed by the gallery.

Seven nonlinear galleries, each with its own distinct spatial qualities, including ceilings that vary from 13 to 65 feet in height, skylights (protected by adjustable blinds), mezzanines and different lighting systems, will serve contemporary artists. In these galleries some walls are curved (one so subtly that at close range it appears flat), and some have ceiling trusses flying through and catwalks for lighting. In many of them views from one space to another are Piranesian in their complexity and beauty.

Conforming to Krens's conviction that today's museum should abandon the idea of an encyclopedic collection for in-depth exhibitions of a few artists, each of these seven galleries is occupied by the work of one or, at most, two individuals. As in the case of Hans Hollein's Museum Abteiberg at Mönchengladbach, the galleries were not designed for individual works but for the *kinds* of art that would occupy them, and for what Krens calls "an internal rhythm between the spaces." Gehry attributes his museum designs to conversations over time with Daniel Buren and other artists:

> They made me realize that the stature of a building in the community could make it equally as important as other buildings, therefore it should not be a neutral box.

TOP: Sculptural gallery; → untitled installation by Jenny Holzer. CENTER. Curved space within large northern gallery; *Terremoto* by Joseph Beuys. BOTTOM: Sculptural space within large southern gallery; *Humans* by Christian Boltanski.

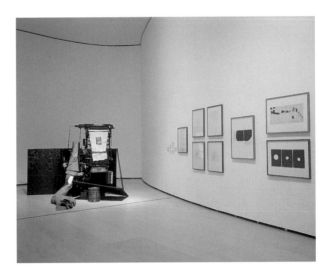

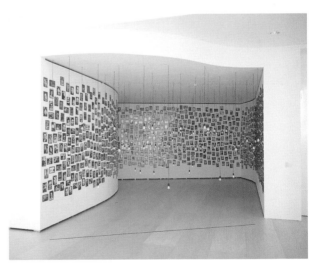

The curved walls of the double-height gallery for Jenny Holzer's red-and-blue electronic LED sign columns gently inflect the ends of the piece and its shadows. Pleased with the result, the artist says, "I considered doing something the room did for me." Walls scooped out in two other galleries make cavelike spaces that also complement the art in them. The architecture allows the viewer to circle Joseph Beuys's freestanding, multifaceted *Terremoto* while affording a protective semienclosure for it; the contoured surfaces on which Christian Boltanski placed hundreds of photographs for *Humans,* a retrospective vision of his career, give them a complexity they do not have in rectilinear installations.

The dramatic individualized spaces flow around what Gehry terms the "stodgy galleries": two levels of three consecutive 50-foot-square, skylit rooms reserved for Modern art. These serenely classical galleries are designed so that daylight from each of the upper vaulted rooms penetrates a central square opening in its floor to the space below, giving even the three second-level galleries some natural light. On the top level, at Krens's request, the balustrades originally planned to surround these openings were

Classical galleries. ↑
TOP: Upper level.
BOTTOM: Lower level.

Sections. ↓
TOP: East-west through boat
gallery and atrium.
BOTTOM: North-south through
atrium and classical galleries.

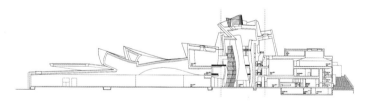

enlarged to make hanging walls. They result in rooms shaped like square doughnuts that work well for the art but effectively block the enfilade of the three galleries. The classical rooms are positioned so as to facilitate comparisons with work in the adjoining, sculptural spaces. Thus, midcentury Abstract Expressionists like Mark Rothko and Jackson Pollock are shown in the first rooms as the source for later artists like Sol LeWitt and Anselm Kiefer, each of whom has his own gallery. "Nothing comes from nowhere," Gehry says. "I was comforted by discovering the linkages, and I think other people are too." Besides the six classical galleries, five other larger spaces are rectilinear. In each there are variations in shape, ceiling treatment and light; occasional windows make the city a constant presence.

Curators and artists have responded enthusiastically to the new museum. Karen Meyerhoff, the Guggenheim's director of exhibitions and collection management and design, notes that "art can be placed within the spaces without being dictated to by square walls . . . the building is so strong that it frees the artwork." Serra calls it "the best museum of this century." He points out that the mammoth ground-floor gallery has "the neutrality of an industrial space." Coosje van Bruggen feels that at Bilbao Gehry has designed an ideal variety of spaces— "not overwhelming, not monumentalized in the wrong way"—that will do justice to a small drawing as well as to a huge installation. And Ellsworth Kelly notes that "twentieth-century artists have given us so much and no museum has caught up to it. This is a beginning."

The Bilbao Guggenheim effectively points to a new kind of museum. Its sculptural galleries are among the most evocative forms ever made, and they offer an architectural context for contemporary art equivalent to what many artists and critics have demanded for centuries. Here, Gehry's architecture of movement has produced flowing forms that appear as film

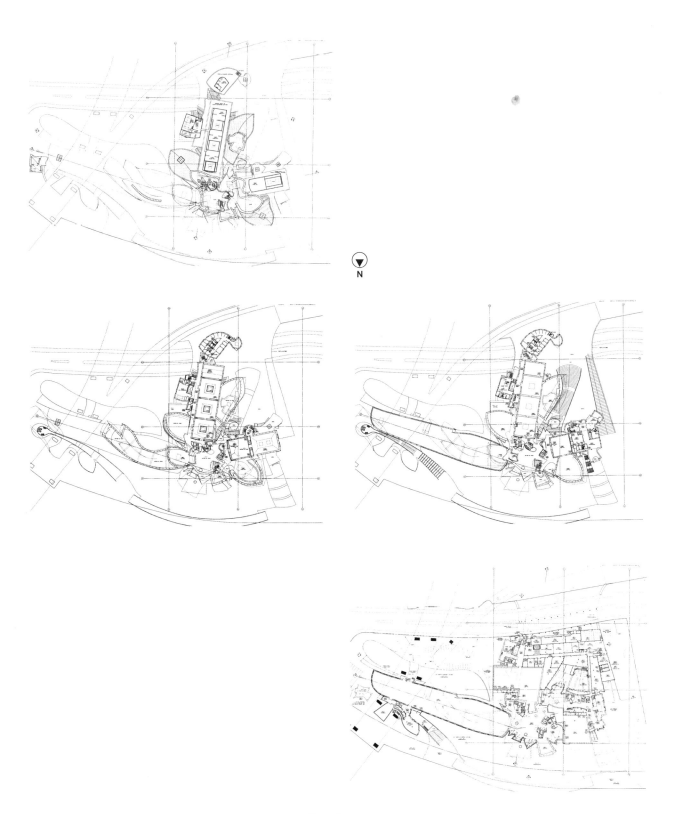

N

Plans. ↑
TOP: **Fourth floor.**
CENTER LEFT: **Third floor.**
CENTER RIGHT: **Second floor.**
BOTTOM: **First floor.**

stills: motion caught and made definitive at a particular moment. The result finally restores what Paul Valéry referred to as "the mother"—architecture—to "the orphans"—painting and sculpture. In addition, spatial complexity—rectilinear, loftlike and sculptural—introduces a new inclusiveness. Up until now, most museums have acknowledged a single attitude toward viewing art: Wolf Prix's interactive Groninger pavilion and Peter Zumthor's minimal Kunsthaus (see Chapter 2) represent opposite poles of such attitudes. Even Wright's Guggenheim offered only one option. Already this is starting to change, as those architects committed to a more conservative vocabulary are also including spaces that are more responsive to contemporary art, such as Botta's loftlike top gallery at San Francisco and Meier's circular and Peanut galleries at Barcelona. To date, Gehry is alone in achieving this diversity so skillfully and on such a grand scale.

Gehry compares construction of the Bilbao museum with "berthing the Queen Mary in a Volkswagen parking lot." What allowed the architect to build futuristic forms confined until now to paper or film is his unusual use of the computer. Many architects rely on electronic technology, most commonly to develop construction documents and client presentations. Some give the computer a conceptual role in design. Not Gehry, who has little patience with electronic technology, except what he enlists for the building process to eliminate costly intermediary steps between design and construction.

Instead, Gehry employs CATIA, a program developed to design the Mirage jet by the French aerospace firm Dassault, to translate through a digitizing wand his handcrafted paper-and-wood models into three-dimensional wire-frame computer models that combine with multidisciplinary programs to provide a structural analysis. These data control a robotic milling machine capable of sculpting any material on any number of axes. Gehry first encountered CATIA in 1990 in connection with the large fish sculpture he had designed for Barcelona's Olympic Village; the same method was applied to the undulating cladding for his Walt Disney Concert Hall project and to the curvilinear forms of both his bus shelter in Hanover, Germany (1994) and his "Fred and Ginger" office building in Prague (1996). For Bilbao CATIA indicated that Gehry's early competition model of horizontal concrete blocks with sail-like metal shapes floating above them required a steel-framed structure.

The fact that Gehry's discovery of CATIA did not come in time to be used for the Weisman Museum provides an insight into the ways in which the computer is now a factor in realizing his designs. The formal differences between the Weisman's faceted west facade and the Bilbao Guggenheim are in part due to CATIA's ability to free architecture from Euclidean geometries. To illustrate the difference, David De Long draws a parallel with Alvar Aalto's single curve and Charles Eames's double-curve "potato chip," which the architects applied to their respective chair designs. For De Long, Gehry is revolutionizing the process whereby the structural concept of a building traditionally dictated its form; freed of the potential problems of structure, the architect is now able to work more like a sculptor. What was a dream for Frank Stella a few years ago (see Chapter 4) Gehry has made a reality.

This freeing of form from structure is not without modern precedents. Le Corbusier's chapel at Ronchamp, conceived as a lightweight steel frame with a thin-skin surface, was, in fact, created by a thick, rubble-filled concrete wall and sprayed-on concrete. Aalto's curvilinear buildings display a similar autonomy of form and structure. Gehry describes his structure as serving images and spaces, making the building's interior fit into the exterior "like the old 'poché,' where they don't quite meet."

To accomplish this in his 408,000-square-foot Samsung Museum of Modern Art project in Seoul, South Korea, Gehry has taken even further his vision of architectonic motion: stainless steel and glass are molded into what the architect describes as "shapes that are almost in a liquid state, like a waterfall"; indeed, they are inspired by the mountains and cascades of the Korean landscape as depicted in traditional ink paintings. These forms are expressed only on some of the 25-to-30-foot-high ceilings of the otherwise strictly rectilinear galleries requested by the client. The galleries are arranged in a nine-story spiral (six above grade, three below) that opens each space to daylight from occasional partings in the metal panels for windows and skylights. Light wells, balconies and other openings allow views between the different levels; ramps, escalators and stairs are located between the outer skin and the gallery walls. (Unavailability of the necessary real estate has halted the project.)

In several ways the Bilbao Guggenheim recalls issues raised over a century and a half ago for one of the first and most influential purpose-built museums: the Altes Museum in Berlin (1830) by Karl Friedrich Schinkel, early 19th-century Germany's leading architect. Both museums arose from the need for a new civic

↓ Samsung Museum
of Modern Art,
Seoul, unbuilt project.
TOP: Model.
BOTTOM: Section.

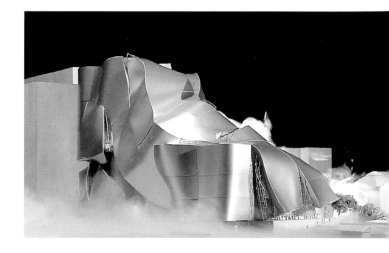

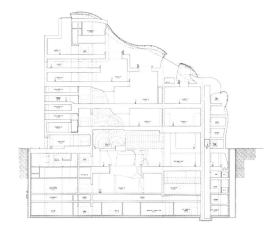

image to mark the end of political and economic turmoil: the Napoleonic Wars in Prussia, Basque terrorism and industrial decline in Bilbao. Both were part of a new beginning, entailing urban renewal for a historic city where a museum is the major feature of a newly developed area: in Berlin a filled-in canal, in Bilbao the obsolete port facilities. And both raised the issue of container versus content.

Defending his museum's sophisticated design, Schinkel expressed his intention to "first delight, then instruct." He fought efforts to downplay the building's architecture, insisting that it was as important as the art it would house. Like today's new museum architects, Schinkel called for a "higher unity" of art and architecture, with "as many relationships as possible." The scholar Douglas Crimp notes that the architect's position agreed with the aesthetic system that had been recently formulated by Hegel, who decried "venerating works of art as divine and worshiping them." The Altes Museum established unparalleled precedents for museum buildings for 150 years after its completion; Bilbao may prove to be equally influential. In one respect, however, the Berlin/Bilbao comparison breaks down: in a 20th-century democracy Gehry's control is a long way from that exerted by a reigning monarch's official building counsel.

The Bilbao Guggenheim sits at the eastern tip of an almost mile-long stretch of riverfront with a conference and concert hall by the Spanish architects Federico Soriano and Delores Palacios at the far end and a multiuse complex planned by Cesar Pelli at the center. Gehry is less concerned about the proximity of two projected office towers than he is about what he calls the "sweetie-pie" park envisioned by the municipality that would seriously compromise his stated intention to position the museum squarely in the middle of the city. From the beginning Gehry favored the riverside site because of its tough, industrial character, in dialogue with which his design was created. Designed by Pelli's wife, the landscape architect Diana Balmori, the soft setting would interrupt this dialogue. By the same token Gehry feels that Calatrava's new footbridge upstream from the museum is too "pretty" for the riverfront's strong character. Considering Gehry's sensitive response to the locale, it is regrettable that he wasn't given the opportunity to design the urban plan for it.

Gehry is not alone in his criticism of Bilbao's overall renewal plan. Several Spanish architects object to what they refer to as a self-referential, piecemeal strategy that may prove more beneficial to corporate interests than to the people for whom the various projects are supposedly being built. And Pelli compares Bilbao's problems with those of New Haven, Connecticut, where he resides: in the 1950s and 1960s massive government spending failed to create permanent jobs there. The Guggenheim's ability to attract an estimated half million visitors annually is inevitably connected to the success of Bilbao's grand scheme. In a formula standard for most American museums, and increasingly being adapted in Europe, private and corporate funding will supplement the museum's income.

Another imponderable is Krens's global concept. Departing from Peggy Guggenheim's idea of a controlling head institution, Krens envisions "one museum comprised of discontinuous museum spaces." For him Bilbao is not a subservient satellite revolving around New York but one of many cross-fertilizing museum "constellations," each with its own identity. An advantage of this system is Bilbao's proportionate increase in exhibition space relative to service space. The usual museum ratio between exhibition and other museum functions is one-to-two; at Bilbao, because there is no duplication of storage, conservation, curators or other essential factors, it is one-to-one. Says Krens, "I can run a larger facility with a smaller staff than anyone else." With two museums in New York, one each in Venice, Bilbao and Berlin and negotiations for other locations underway, Krens already has more ready-made venues for his exhibitions than any other museum.

Some artists and curators have attacked Krens's idea of a globalized museum because it increases the transportation of art, exposing it to potential damage and often depriving it of an artist-designated setting. Donald Judd was a prime exponent of this position (see Chapter 4). Political critics call the Guggenheim formula cultural imperialism and openly express their resentment of the priority it will give to international, and especially American, artists, a particularly sore point for the fiercely independent Basques. Others question the amount of government money being spent on building and maintaining the museum and the effectiveness of avant-garde art as a cultural catalyst in this region.

Krens's concept, and the building itself, may prove to have shortcomings, but they are unimportant when compared with the introduction of museum architecture that is as revolutionary as Wright's Guggenheim and Piano and Rogers' Pompidou. Together, these three museums now constitute later-20th-century landmarks of this building type. The architects of several recent museums (the Groninger, for example) have attempted to resolve the contentious container versus content conflict by including different kinds of space to accommodate various art forms; only at Bilbao are such disparate spaces brought together into a synthetic whole. Gehry's invention of new forms, and his plurality of forms, provide a model for future museum architecture that must now be taken into account.

The new museum attempts to make art once again a vibrant part of life and a powerful aesthetic experience rather than a didactic tool or a remote object of veneration. One of the first 20th-century architects to try this, Frederick Kiesler, collaborated from the beginning of his career with Marcel Duchamp. Both men were preoccupied with questions of human perception and its relation to art. Kiesler shared Duchamp's conviction that "it is the viewers who make the paintings" and designed his installations to encourage that process. The viewer's active participation in experiencing art and the interaction of art with its setting are two related problems that architects have grappled with throughout this century. Among them, Kiesler and El Lissitzky in the 1920s, Wright, Le Corbusier, Scarpa and Albini in midcentury and now the new museum architects have used architectonic theatricality as an important element in their resolution of this issue.

One of the most significant shared traits of these museums is the idea that they can become a catalyst for new art. It is hoped that artists will respond to the challenge of innovative architectural forms with work that relates directly to them. Maya Lin's *Groundswell* at the Wexner Center and works by Sol LeWitt, Daniel Buren and Richard Serra among others at the Bilbao Guggenheim bear out this intention. For the first time a 20th-century building type looks back to the kind of dynamic between disciplines that flourished in earlier eras in the way, for example, that Bernini's *Saint Teresa in Ecstasy* combines sculpture, painting techniques and architecture in a single environment.

The fractured forms of these museums also exert a strong dynamic. The "complexity and contradiction" taken as a model by Robert Venturi for the mid-1960s could be replaced today with "chaos and confusion." In the three decades since Venturi's plea for a postmodern vision, art—in a reflection of society's increasing fragmentation—has eschewed traditional classification by trends, schools or even the distinction between disciplines. Unlike sanctuaries of art that exclude these contemporary realities, the structures discussed in this chapter incorporate them; in the case of Libeskind's Jewish Museum, encompassing allusions to past events as well. Instead of countering the existing condition—as the Getty's "order" attempts to do with the disorder of Los Angeles—they embrace it to capture the spirit of the times.

With few exceptions the new museums function more as *Kunsthallen* for temporary exhibitions than as institutions for the collection and preservation of art. Storage is minimal and the perennial problem of expansion moot: in several cases, siting renders the buildings virtually unexpandable. Apart from Koolhaas's exhibition hall, however, the architecture of these museums differs radically from that of the *Kunsthalle* in that it addresses specific types of art. Until now the *Kunsthalle* did not have the same close identification with a community as did the traditional museum. The new museum's extraordinarily distinctive architecture—as site-specific as art so designated—promises to go a long way toward erasing the distinction. Whereas museums have always identified with their collections—the Louvre is the *Mona Lisa*, MoMA is *Les Demoiselles d'Avignon*—the new museum is identified with its architecture: the dominant image is the container rather than the contents.

AFTERWORD

It's cheap. It's fast. It offers great shopping, tempting food and a place to hang out. And visitors can even enjoy the art. *New York Times*, 1997

If recent years have witnessed the upstaging of art by museum architecture and amenities, the future may see the disappearance of original art objects altogether. One hundred million people visited art museums in the United States in 1996, and attendance in Europe was proportionately high: while such phenomenal success is a reassurance of vitality, it is also a threat to the museum's most basic mandate of preserving the objects it owns and exhibits. Already in the 1920s the extraordinary popularity of drawings like Dürer's *Rabbit* in Vienna's Albertina necessitated the substitution of facsimiles; continuous exposure has destroyed perishable works on paper and has menaced other art forms. Konrad Oberhuber, the Albertina's director, notes that "from the beginning it was clear that while preferring the original, the public chose to see the reproduction of a famous drawing to an authentic work with which it was unfamiliar. A current exhibition of little-known original drawings has failed to attract the crowds that come to see masterpieces in facsimile."

Not only did viewers often prefer copies to originals, they usually could not tell the difference. With a contest he organized for an exhibition titled "Original and Facsimile" in Hanover in 1929, Alexander Dorner (whose museum's Abstract Cabinet was discussed in Chapter 7) demonstrated that even specialists were unable to distinguish between the high-quality reproductions and the drawings, pastels and watercolors by Old Master and contemporary artists hung next to them.

In the same manner today, far more people—300,000 annually—visit a replica of the prehistoric Lascaux caves in France's Dordogne than once visited the real caves. (That site was closed when deterioration of the wall paintings alerted the regional government to the danger of exposing them.) In their place an underground reinforced-concrete copy was opened in 1983: irregular, cavelike walls were simulated by sculptors, and artists approximated the 17,000-year-old drawings. A similar concept is being applied to Spain's prehistoric Altamira caves, for which a building containing a museum, a replica and a research center designed by Juan Navarro Baldeweg will be completed in 1999. To a greater extent than at Lascaux II, Baldeweg wants the public to be aware that the re-creation is an illusion. A classic Modernist with a special interest in framing structures within their sites, he has framed the mouth of his cave with a contemporary portal that clearly signals the artificiality of the replica.

The toll taken by Pompeii's nearly two million visitors in 1996—more than for any other public museum or historic place in Italy—has prompted the idea of Pompeii II.

↑ Lascaux II, France. Monique Peytral duplicating wall paintings in cave replica (1983).

↓ Altamira Museum complex, Spain, by Juan Navarro Baldeweg (1999).
TOP: Model.
BOTTOM: Section, with cave replica within new museum.

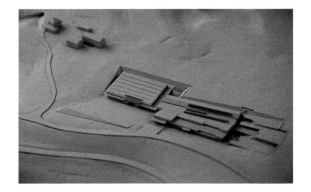

This theme park based on the ancient city—with mockups of the houses and gardens and tours led by guides in Roman dress—would divert crowds away from the archaeological remains in order to prevent further damage to them. Experts insist that information provided by the re-creation would make it more meaningful to visitors for whom the actual ruins are indecipherable.

Even apart from the threat of deterioration, reproductions are sometimes considered more desirable, as demonstrated by two outdoor museums designed by Tadao Ando in which great masterpieces around the world—from da Vinci's *Last Supper* to one of Monet's *Water Lilies*—are replicated full scale or larger on ceramic panels. The Garden of Fine Arts in Osaka (1990) was built as part of an International Garden and Greenery Exposition, with the replicas demonstrating new ceramic technology. In Kyoto a similar concept was realized next to a botanical garden in 1994. The museums offer an outdoor experience of art that could not otherwise be seen in these locales; in choosing the subject matter, the client, like visitors to the Albertina, preferred copies of famous works to lesser-known originals. For both structures Ando further explored the kind of processional spaces that figure in several of his earlier works. Ramps in the two gardens, combined with bridges in Kyoto (where there is also a series of waterfalls), provide a variety of viewing perspectives that would well serve the original art in other museums the architect has designed (see Chapter 1).

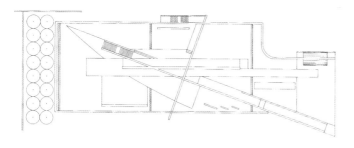

The Garden of Fine Arts, Kyoto, by Tadao Ando (1994). TOP: Views of the museum. BOTTOM: Ground plan.

There is a long-standing tradition of respect for an established canon, even if it can be known only through copies. Leonardo da Vinci, for example, advised students to train their eye by copying drawings of art rather than working from the art itself. A Renaissance treatise on painting recommended that "casts of the finest statues in Rome" be the models for students to learn from; Rubens advocated the use of his own drawings of "the best sculptures" in avoiding the mediocre.

The practice of replicating great works of art is an old one that often produced copies held in the same esteem as the originals. As early as the 5th century B.C. the Greeks duplicated rare cult statues, and many Greek works are, in turn, known today only through Roman copies. The Renaissance fascination with ancient art produced a veritable industry of reproduction, whose output was valued both on its aesthetic merits and as a teaching exemplar. So eager was Francis I of France to have copies of Rome's most famous Classical statues for his château's park at Fontainebleau that he commissioned plaster casts of all of them. The practice—occasionally supplemented by bronze and marble copies—was followed by Louis XIV for Versailles and by ruling monarchs and aristocratic collectors throughout Europe. (Famous works were also liberally reinterpreted in gold and gems—for jewelry—porcelain, ceramics and other materials.) In the 18th century many galleries eschewed original art altogether in favor of contemporary copies of Classical sculpture. And the 19th century saw Viollet-le-Duc's founding, as a didactic tool, of the Musée de Sculpture Comparée in Paris (1882), which was devoted to copies of sculpture. (In 1937 the museum was renovated and reopened as the Musée des Monuments Français.)

↑ Musée des Monuments Français, Paris, renovation by Jacques Carlu, Louis Boileau and Léon Azéma (1937). Gallery.

Graphic representation in the form of prints supplemented three-dimensional reproduction after 1500, and within a hundred years, publications of Classical masterpieces grouped according to size and symmetry were prefiguring André Malraux's 1947 book *Museum Without Walls* (*Le Musée Imaginaire*). The implications of photography for art had been explored by the German philosopher Walter Benjamin in his widely read 1936 essay "The Work of Art in the Age of Mechanical Reproduction." While both men mused on the implications of photography and film as new art forms, Malraux addressed photographic replication primarily as a means to enlarge the scope of art studies by showing an entire style, or an artist's oeuvre, in a book. Additionally, his conviction that great art transcends its context was served by photographs that isolated the object on the page. Had he lived to see the current revolution in electronic technology, Malraux would surely have endorsed the Internet as the true "museum without walls."

Artequín, Santiago, → Chile (1993), in Chilean pavilion for 1889 International Exposition, Paris, by Henri Picq. Exterior.

Indisputably, the enormous potential of today's technology surpasses all previous modes of reproduction. Whereas in the 19th century museums routinely exhibited reproductions for comparative purposes, museums now incorporate Micro galleries offering computerized images of art along with extensive information about it. Among many capabilities, a museum's computer database can include objects from other institutions as well as from its own collections, and works can be compared according to chronology or theme. Often Micro galleries have more visitors than do the permanent collections. In at least one case—Artequín in Santiago, Chile (1993)—a museum has been created exclusively for photographic replicas and interactive computers; this alternative was adopted in the absence of a collection or the means to exhibit important art.

CD-ROMs, some of which are interactive, show the world's great art collections in high-quality reproduction. In contrast to the abstraction of an object on the printed page, a Virtual-Reality Modeling Language environment with goggles and gloves allows users to navigate through a three-dimensional gallery, as for example the Louvre's stroll through rooms of French painting. The appropriate program and hardware can achieve the same sense of immersion in an increasing number of formats.

The finite capacity of closed-circuit programs and CD-ROMs is surpassed by the superior capacity and capability of the Internet. David Ross, director of the Whitney Museum of American Art, compares the CD-ROM to a single book, whereas he likens the World Wide Web to a network of all the libraries in the world. Almost every museum in existence, from the smallest, most remote institution to the largest, most central one is represented on the Internet, where a site like the WebMuseum network can deliver over 10 million documents from around the world and has 200,000 visitors a week. The ease with which this massive storehouse of information can be tapped puts into question the museum's structure: by offering a vast number of options for viewers to choose from, the computer challenges the museum's authority in determining relative merit and, ultimately, in shaping art history. Like visitors to a Renaissance cabinet of curiosities, users of a museum Web site are free to draw their own conclusions rather than accept those of a curator (although there is still a place for the guidance of museum professionals). The video artist Bill Viola remarks that the television screen, formerly considered a "window to the world," has become a "revolving door: circulating objects to your private space and extending them out beyond it." Viola notes that whereas formerly a painting's value lay in its uniqueness, now the potential profit from digital rights places its value in commercial usage.

Besides its reproductive capacity the Internet can also convey original art, with computer artists transmitting their work in the medium in which it was created. The result is not a replication but a work as authentic as paint on canvas, and like an oil painting it is not easily transferred to other media: obtaining a high-quality print of a digital image is as complex as reproducing a painting electronically. When offered the means to enter Web art through hypertext, viewers themselves can alter the work, thus greatly expanding Duchamp's notion of art needing a viewer to complete it.

The implications for collaborative creation of this sort are manifold, as are those of the public's potential empowerment by means of the new technology. Whereas the standard global networks of television and cable are tightly controlled and belong to an economics of scarcity, the Internet is uncontrolled and is part of an economics of abundance. Open to anyone who wants to set up his or her own site, it is the great leveler, and an unknown artist and a powerful corporation have addresses of equal weight. Known primarily as a video artist, Nam June Paik anticipated this possibility in a 1973 lithograph in which he asks how soon artists would have their own television channels. It remains to be seen whether this revolutionary potential will be realized to a greater extent than was the promise of community-access channels for cable television.

To a generation brought up on computers, electronic pixilated art is more accessible than conventional art forms. In its "American Canvas" report (1997), the National Endowment for the Arts found that many look with suspicion at what they perceive as an intimidating and incomprehensible "arts world," whereas the Web offers them "the very attributes—participation, interactivity, collaboration—that are so conspicuously absent from the more traditional media."

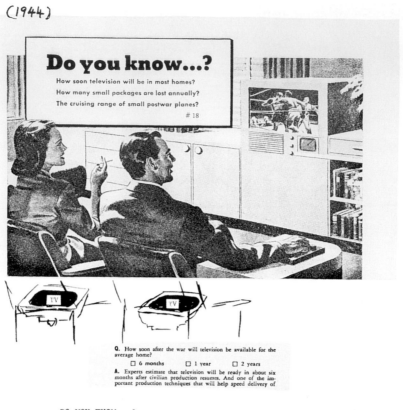

(1944)

Do you know...?

How soon television will be in most homes?
How many small packages are lost annually?
The cruising range of small postwar planes?

#18

Q. How soon after the war will television be available for the average home?

☐ 6 months   ☐ 1 year   ☐ 2 years

A. Experts estimate that television will be ready in about six months after civilian production resumes. And one of the important production techniques that will help speed delivery of

```
DO YOU KNOW...?

     How soon TV-chair will be available in most museums ?

     How soon artist will have their own TV channels ?

     How soon wall to wall TV for video-art will be installed
          in most homes ?


A new design for TV-chair
                              (dedicated to the great
                               communication-artist Ray
                               Johnson)
```

← *TV Chair* by Nam June Paik (1973). Offset lithograph.

Moreover, electronic technology is redefining, with a structure of its own, the context for art that a museum supplies: an intellectual framework equivalent to architecture yet unconfined to a physical place. The Austrian media artist and scholar Peter Weibel describes the new virtual architecture "not as the art of space but a form of time, a locational discourse that has become dislocational." Physically, the monitor allows a uniquely individual experience, a private one-on-one relationship between viewer and viewed comparable to that of a confessional, says David Ross. With a single click viewers can pop in and out of various sites, creating their own museums.

If art can now penetrate the lives of people around the world without the intermediary of museums, video art has in its own way erased institutional boundaries by establishing a new relationship with the container. Made for churches or civic buildings, the art that was exhibited in the first public museums bore no relationship to them. By the early 19th century some large-scale painting seemed intended primarily for museum display —a purpose artists have retained to the present. In the 1960s, however, artists advanced a step by actually working in museums as they would in their studios, using the gallery as part of their art: Richard Serra did this for *Splashing* by throwing molten lead at the intersection of wall and floor. In addition to circumventing the museum with taped work that can be viewed at home, some video art now pushes beyond existing dynamics between art and architecture by exploding the space it occupies: Viola describes the phenomenon as "turning solid into gas so that the whole room becomes the domain of the artist." Often more like music than plastic art, an audio-visual piece can defy both museum space and practices such as chronological placement and labeling.

The electronic reproductions in Bill Gates's home—where famous paintings are called up on large computer screens embedded in the walls or on flat screens propped on painters' easels—further a concept expressed almost 80 years ago by Frederick Kiesler: the replacement of paintings hanging on walls by a "telemuseum" whose sensitized panels would receive images broadcast from museums worldwide. Far from rendering the museum obsolete, the computer is enabling it to achieve a distinct individuality.

In its mirroring of the entire information world, electronic communication frees the museum from what now seem like naive attempts at universality. The computer is today's cabinet of curiosities: it can actually provide the cosmology the *Wunderkammer* strove to re-create; it can be truly encyclopedic in the sense that the Louvre and the Metropolitan Museum were intended to be. Just as novel forms of knowledge and categorization in the late 16th century replaced an earlier culture of curiosity, today's technology has replaced the 18th-century idea of an encyclopedic museum (and computerized video is the new art form that photography and film were for Walter Benjamin). By making information available on the computer, museums are liberated from these former constraints: with no need to be all-encompassing, their architecture can relate to specialized collections, and there is no longer a reason to expand physically. Repeatedly, the preceding pages have testified to the success of museums whose architecture is attuned to such individuality, and to the relative failure of those uncommitted to specific art forms.

When asked why there are no computers at the Whitney, Ross, who with three Web sites for his institution is among those most profoundly committed to the role of electronics, replies: "Because you don't eat the menu instead of the food." Says Konrad Oberhuber, "Every reproductive medium conveys only information and not art; the overwhelming experience of art cannot be had with facsimiles or with virtual reality." Suzanne Pagé, director of the Musée d'Art Moderne de la Ville de Paris, sees uniformity as a greater threat than the computer: to maintain their vitality, she insists, museums must have "une singularité irréductible."

In a world that has become increasingly virtual, the museum is an important refuge of reality, making both its contents and their relation to architecture more important than ever before. Viewing Peter Märkli's Hans Josephsohn museum on a monitor cannot capture the sensations, sights and smells that are part of a visit to this concrete box in a Swiss meadow. The same can be said of all the great museums discussed here: the experience of seeing original art in the unique spaces designed by Renzo Piano, Richard Rogers, Frank Gehry and others cannot be duplicated. Conversely, art's availability via the computer makes its viewing in bland, inappropriate architecture—or in settings that confuse authentic and replica (to wit, the Metropolitan Museum's 19th-Century Painting and Sculpture Galleries)— all the more unacceptable.

The wide range of scale, style and content in many contemporary museums is a truer measure of their vitality as cultural institutions than attendance figures that obscure the failure of many museum-goers to actually visit the art. In the same way that history is no longer represented as a single path through major movements—the linear, or "conveyor belt," approach—museum architecture can conform to no rules. When properly designed, new museums should be as varied as the virtual reality that complements them, as varied as the art they contain.

The Crossing by Bill ➔
Viola (1996).
Detail, video/sound
installation.

Notes

Unless otherwise indicated, all quotes and related information are from interviews the author conducted between December 1994 and January 1998.

Preface

8: "museumification"—Jean-Pierre Keller, *Tinguely et le Mystère de la roue manquante* (Geneva: Zoé, 1992), 185.

9: "architecturalized nature"—See line note p. 43.

10: *Wings That Don't Fly*—This chapter title was mentioned by the author to Rem Koolhaas, who used it in his 1997 charrette presentation to MoMA. Because the presentation remained unpublished, no source was given, and Paul Goldberger unwittingly attributed the phrase to Koolhaas in his article "The Modern Made New," *New Yorker*, 8 December 1997, 118–19.

11: "taking a high C in music"—Frank Lloyd Wright in *Frank Lloyd Wright: The Guggenheim Correspondence*, ed. Bruce Brooks Pfeiffer (Fresno: Press at California State University; Carbondale: Southern Illinois University Press, 1986), 248.

12: "graveyards"—See line note p. 47.

12: While 5,000 museums—Magaly Cabral, "Global Museum," in *New Strategies for Communication in Museums*, Proceedings of ICOM/CECA 1996, ed. Hadwig Kräutler (Vienna: WUV Universitäts-Verlag, 1997), 119–21.

12: In the United States—Allan Schwartzman, "Art vs. Architecture," *Architecture*, December 1997.

12: In France—*Le Monde*, 15 January 1997, 23.

12: Just as the World Trade Center—based on Paul Goldberger, "Landmark Kitsch," *New Yorker*, 18 August 1997, 38–40.

Chapter 1

14: Referred to as galleries—Mark Girouard, *Life in the English Country House* (New Haven: Yale University Press, 1978), 100–101; Rosalys Coope, "The Gallery in England: Names and Meanings," *Architectural History* 27 (1984): 446–55.

15: Whereas the small study—Krzysztof Pomian, *Collectors and Curiosities* (Cambridge: Cambridge University Press, 1990), 47.

15: The cabinet of curiosities—Anthony Alan Shelton, "Cabinets of Transgression: Renaissance Collections and the Incorporation of the New World," in *The Cultures of Collecting*, ed. John Elsner and Roger Cardinal (Melbourne: Melbourne University Press, 1994).

15: "entertain and amuse"—Eliška Fučíková, "The Collection of Rudolf II at Prague: Cabinet of Curiosity or Scientific Museum?," in *The Origins of Museums: The Cabinet of Curiosities in Sixteenth- and Seventeenth-Century Europe*, ed. Oliver Impey and Arthur MacGregor (Oxford: Clarendon Press, 1985).

15: Exhibits randomly juxtaposed—Giuseppi Olmi, "Science—Honour—Metaphor: Italian Cabinets of the Sixteenth and Seventeenth Centuries," in Impey and MacGregor, *The Origins of Museums*.

15: Art, however, remained for some time—John Dixon Hunt, "Curiosities to Adorn Cabinets and Gardens," in Impey and MacGregor, *The Origins of Museums*.

15: One of the first to do so—Elizabeth Scheicher, "The Collection of Archduke Ferdinand II at Schloss Ambras: Its Purpose, Composition and Evolution," in Impey and MacGregor, *The Origins of Museums*.

15: Besides the additional space—Thomas Da Costa Kaufmann, *Court Cloister and City: The Art and Culture of Central Europe 1450–1800* (Chicago: University of Chicago Press, 1995), 172–73.

16: "Museums are essentially compromises"—Lawrence Alloway and John Coplans, "Talking with William Rubin: The Museum Concept is Not Infinitely Expandable," *Artforum*, October 1974, 51–57.

17: "The great things are those you discover"—Peter C. Papademetriou, "The Responsive Box," *Progressive Architecture*, May 1987, 87–96.

18: "Big museums are a bore."—Francine du Plessix, "Philip Johnson Goes Underground," *Art in America*, July/August 1966, 89–97.

18: "a cross between"—du Plessix, "Philip Johnson," 89.

18: "so that it would be springy"—Franz Schulze, *Philip Johnson: Life and Work* (New York: Knopf, 1994), 290.

19: "one of the most artfully intricate"—John Coolidge, *Patrons and Architects: Designing Art Museums in the Twentieth Century* (Fort Worth: University of Texas Press, 1989), 17.

19: "each sculpture should"—John Morris Dixon, "Sculpture Under Glass," *Architectural Forum*, December 1970, 23–24.

20: This was exactly how Dominique de Menil—Rosamond Bernier, "A Gift of Vision," *House & Garden*, July 1987, 121–25, 180–82.

20: Conceived with her house in mind—Dominique de Menil, "The Menil Collection and Museum," *A+U*, November 1987, 62–63.

21: Its single-story—John Pastier, "Simplicity of Form, Ingenuity in the Use of Light," *Architecture*, May 1987, 84–91.

21: By calling the area her "treasure chamber"—Reyner Banham, "In the Neighborhood of Art," *Art in America*, June 1987, 124–29.

21: "living light"—Banham, "In the Neighborhood of Art," 129.

22: Each of the massive, fixed, 40-foot-long leaves—Pastier, "Simplicity of Form," 89.

22: The less cohesive grouping—Kay Larson, "Chez Dominique," *New York*, 13 July 1987, 52–53.

23: *"luxe, calme, et volupté"*—Mildred F. Schmertz, "Renzo Piano's Fondation Beyeler," *Architectural Digest*, October 1997, 94–96, 102–6.

23: "Without a good client"—Schmertz, "Renzo Piano's Fondation Beyeler," 96.

24: Indeed, the legacy of Erasmus—Hans Christoph Ackerman, "Basel's Cabinets of Art and Curiosities in the 16th and 17th Centuries," in Impey and MacGregor, *The Origins of Museums.*

25: The museum's walls—Florian Vischer, interview by Mildred F. Schmertz, Basel, 27 June 1997.

25: "the collection governed the forming of space"—Schmertz, "Renzo Piano's Fondation Beyeler," 102.

27: The twelve new pavilions—See *Erwin Heerich, Museum Insel Hombroich,* ed. Christine Spiegel (Stuttgart: Hatje, 1996).

30: For many years Ambasz has taken his inspiration—Peter Buchanan, "Return to Mother Earth," *Daidalos,* 15 June 1993, 50–61.

30: a configuration similar to Frank Lloyd Wright's—Buchanan, "Return to Mother Earth," 57.

32: Their use of raw, industrial materials—Jayne Merkel, "Architecture of Dislocation: The L.A. School," *Art in America,* February 1994, 32–41.

32: "high-tech Japanese tea house"—Merkel, "Architecture of Dislocation," 38.

34: Gordon used light—Paula Rice Jackson, "British Design," *Interiors,* March 1987, 142–46.

37: "raw, obscene and nightmarishly immense"—Peter de Jonge, "The Rubells in Miami," *Bazaar,* February 1997, 207–9, 223.

38: "anonymous architecture"—Herzog & de Meuron in Cynthia Davidson, "An Interview with Herzog & de Meuron," *ANY* 13 (1996): 48–59.

38: The building consists of—Peter Rumpf, "Kunst aus der Kiste," *Bauwelt,* 29 January 1993, 180–87; see also Jacques Lucan, Veit Loers and Helmut Federle, *Herzog & de Meuron Sammlung Goetz* (Stuttgart: Hatje, 1995).

41: With changes in light—"Herzog & de Meuron in Conversation with *ARCH+,*" *ARCH+,* December 1995, 116.

41: Herzog and de Meuron's emphasis on surface—Alain Guiheux, "De l'architecture de H&deM," in Rémy Zaugg, *Herzog & de Meuron, une exposition* (Paris: Editions du Centre Pompidou, 1995), 113–31.

41: In reality, it derives from—Gerhard Mack, *Herzog & de Meuron 1989–1991: The Complete Works,* vol. 2 (Boston: Birkhäuser, 1996), 15.

43: "an architecturalized nature"—Tadao Ando, "From the Church on the Water to the Church of the Light," in Francesco Dal Co, *Tadao Ando: Complete Works* (London: Phaidon Press, 1994), 455.

44: "a museum should be"—Father Marie Alain Couturier in Renzo Piano interview, *A+U,* March 1989, 70–71.

Chapter 2

46: The noted historian—Nikolaus Pevsner, *A History of Building Types* (Princeton: Princeton University Press, 1976), 111.

46: 1683—*Oxford English Dictionary* (Oxford: Oxford University Press, 1971), compact edition, 1880.

46: Among the first of many rulers—Thomas Da Costa Kaufmann, *Court Cloister and City: The Art and Culture of Central Europe 1450–1800* (Chicago: University of Chicago Press, 1995), 444.

46: and in Paris in 1750—Andrew McClellan, *Inventing the Louvre: Art, Politics, and Invention of the Modern Museum in Eighteenth-Century Paris* (Cambridge: Cambridge University Press, 1994), 13–14, 49.

47: J.-N.-L. Durand—Helen Searing, *New American Art Museums* (exh. cat., New York: Whitney Museum of American Art; Berkeley: University of California Press, 1982), 15.

47: The Wadsworth Athenaeum—Searing, *New American Art Museums,* 26.

47: Museum attendance in the 1850s—Daniel J. Sherman, *Worthy Monuments: Art Museums and the Politics of Culture in Nineteenth-Century France* (Cambridge: Harvard University Press, 1989), 130.

47: "waxen desert, which resembles a temple and a salon, a graveyard"—Quatremère de Quincy in Marc Fumaroli, "What Does the Future Hold for Museums?," *Masterworks from the Musée des Beaux Arts, Lille* (exh. cat., New York: Metropolitan Museum of Art, 1992), 285.

48: "cemeteries"—F. T. Marinetti, "The Founding and Manifesto of Futurism 1909," in *Futurist Manifestos,* ed. Umbro Apollonio (New York: Viking Press, 1973), 22.

48: "We no longer want"—El Lissitzky, "Proun Room, Great Berlin Art Exhibition, 1923," in *El Lissitzky: Life, Letters, Texts,* ed. Sophie Lissitzky-Küppers (London: Thames and Hudson, 1968), 365.

48: "the only true museum"—Le Corbusier, *The Decorative Art of Today* (Cambridge: MIT Press, 1987), 15.

48: "Painting and sculpture . . . are orphans."—Paul Valéry, "Le Problème des Musées," *Oeuvres II* (Paris: Gallimard, 1960), 1293.

48: "artificially lighted world"—Trevor Thomas, "Impressions of the Museum of Modern Art, New York," *Museums Journal,* August 1941, 98–101.

49: "the white cube"—Brian O'Doherty, *Inside the White Cube: The Ideology of the Gallery Space* (San Francisco: Lapis Press, 1986).

49: "timeless, limbolike gallery"—O'Doherty, *Inside the White Cube,* 15.

49: "Just as images of saints"—Carol Duncan, *Civilizing Rituals: Inside Public Art Museums* (London and New York: Routledge, 1995), 110.

50: "high walls"—George Baselitz, "Four Walls and Light From Above or No Painting on the Wall," *Kunstforum International* 34 (1979): 162.

50: In their original state—"The Museum of Modern Art," *Museums Journal,* August 1941, 93–97.

61: "a space dedicated to"—Allan Temko, "Art and Soul," *San Francisco Focus,* January 1995, 2–10.

62: Rather, it was his skillful handling—Jack Lane, then director, San Francisco Museum of Modern Art, interview by author, San Francisco, California, 26 March 1996.

62: Three structural columns—Lane, interview.

63: "a great Art Deco department store"—Herbert Muschamp, "An Emporium for Art Rises in the West," *New York Times*, 12 February 1995, 34.

66: In a process—Xavier Costa, "Large-Scale Barcelona: The City and its Architecture after the Olympics," *Practices* 3–4 (1995): 58–63.

66: Barcelona undertook plans—Marisa Bartolucci, "Barcelona," *Metropolis*, July/August 1996, 61–64, 94–95.

66: Barcelona's then mayor, Pasqual Maragall— Interview by author, New York City, 17 September 1996.

70: light-filled slots—Kenneth Frampton, "Richard Meier in Europe: Recent Work," *Casabella*, December 1990, 4–20, 61.

70: A similar situation—Peter Cannon-Brookes, "Frankfurt and Atlanta: Richard Meier as a Designer of Museums," *International Journal of Museum Management and Curatorship* 5 (1985): 39–63.

71: At the Frankfurt museum—Arnulf Herbst, telephone interview by author, fall 1996.

71: Despite the cost of MACBA—Juli Capella, "Barcelone et Richard Meier," *Architecture d'Aujourd'hui*, December 1995, 40–41.

Chapter 3

74: The homes and studios—Jeffrey M. Muller, *Rubens: The Artist as Collector* (Princeton: Princeton University Press, 1989), 30, 71, Thomas Da Costa Kaufmann, *Court Cloister and City: The Art and Culture of Central Europe 1450–1800* (Chicago: University of Chicago Press, 1995), 444.

75: One of the first monographic museums—Francis Haskell, "The Artist and the Museum," *New York Review of Books*, 3 December 1987, 38–42. The following history of monographic museums is based on this article.

75: The possibility that—Giuseppe Pavanello, "Gipsoteca," in *Antonio Canova*, ed. Giuseppe Pavanello and Giandomenico Romanelli (exh. cat., Venice: Museo Correo, 1992), 361–69.

76: It was the first—David Finn, *Canova* (New York: Abbeville, 1983), 270.

76: Bindesbøll added—Lisbet Balslev Jørgensen, "Thorvaldsen's Museum, a National Monument," *Apollo*, September 1972, 24–31.

76: The artist wanted—Lisbet Balslev Jørgensen, "Thorvaldsen's Museum: A Display of Life and Art, 1848–1984," *International Journal of Museum Management and Curatorship* 3 (1984): 237–50.

76: In 1862—Maïté Roux, "The Story of a 'Single Parent' Museum: Gustave Moreau, Artist and Megalomaniac?," *Museum* 44, no. 2 (1992): 122–23.

78: The success of Simounet's project—Sylvia Lavin, "Viewpoint," *Interiors*, September 1988, 21, 23, 25, 27.

79: The visitor is guided—Jean-François Pousse, "Hôtel Salé, l'architecture apprivoise Picasso," *Techniques et Architecture*, October/November 1986, 74–78.

79: "unraveling thread"—Martin Meade, "Picasso Palais: Picasso Museum, Paris," *Architectural Review*, July 1986, 20–25.

80: The Andy Warhol Foundation—Avis Berman, "The Right Place: The Founding of the Andy Warhol Museum," *The Andy Warhol Museum*, ed. Callie Angell (Pittsburgh: Andy Warhol Museum, 1994), 17–38.

80: "for something as untried"—Berman, "The Right Place," 35.

80: The bridge's aluminum leaf—Brooks Adams, "Industrial-Strength Warhol," *Art in America*, September 1994, 70–77.

82: Buddhist awakening—David Bonetti, "'The Spirit of Purest Zen,'" *San Francisco Examiner*, 5 April 1995, C1, C5.

84: Its architect is a theoretician—Martin Steinmann and Beat Wismer, "Laisser la porte ouverte pendant la journée, A propos de la maison destinée aux oeuvres de Josephsohn à Giornico TI," *Faces* 26 (1992–93): 8–14; see also *Stiftung La Congiunta, Peter Märkli—Haus für Reliefs und Halbfiguren des Bildhauers Hans Josephsohn*, ed. Christine Spiegel (Stuttgart: Hatje, 1994).

84: Without base, crown or windows—"Peter Märkli," *Architecture d'Aujourd'hui*, June 1995, 104–5.

89: in the two nearby farmhouses—The houses were seen by the author only in pictures: Nicholas Fox Weber, "The Kirchner Museum and Residences," *Architectural Digest*, March 1996, 68.

89: Annette Gigon began her career—Dorothea Huber, "De la neige sur le toit, le Musée Kirchner à Davos," *Faces* 26 (1992–93): 15–19.

90: Tinguely lived—Pontus Hulten, *Jean Tinguely* (exh. cat., Paris: Centre Georges Pompidou, 1988), 13.

90: La Verrerie—Jill Johnston, "Report from Basel: Rebel's Memorial," *Art in America*, March 1997, 44–47.

90: "museumification"—See line note p. 8.

90: The museum was initiated by Paul Sacher—Margrit Hahnloser-Ingold, "Paul Sacher–Jean Tinguely," in *Letters from Jean Tinguely to Paul Sacher and Common Friends*, ed. Margrit Hahnloser-Ingold (Berne: Benteli, 1996), 11–38.

94: The sculptor had stipulated—Germain Viatte, "Une longue marche pour l'atelier de Constantin Brancusi," *Constantin Brancusi 1876–1957* (exh. cat., Paris: Centre Georges Pompidou, 1995), 13–18.

96: In the last decade—Pepe Karmel, "Felix Nussbaum at the Jewish Museum," *Art in America*, July 1985, 136–37.

Chapter 4

102: The founding by Louis XVIII—Francis Haskell, "The Artist and the Museum," *New York Review of Books*, 3 December 1987, 38–42.

102: Far more popular than museums—Gérard Monnier, *L'Art et ses institutions en France, de la Révolution à nos jours* (Paris: Gallimard, 1995), 122–49.

103: When in 1855 the jury—Kathleen Adler, *Manet* (London: Phaidon/Oxford, 1986), 98.

103: Other artists have addressed the museum—The following discussion is inspired by A. A. Bronson and Peggy Gale, eds., *Museums by Artists* (Toronto: Art Metropole, 1983).

104: The Boîte-en-Valise—Unless otherwise indicated the following description is based on Ecke Bonk, *Marcel Duchamp, The Box in a Valise, de ou par MARCEL DUCHAMP ou RROSE SELAVY* (New York: Rizzoli, 1989).

105: "replaces the museum's authority"—Dalia Judovitz, *unpacking Duchamp: art in transit* (Berkeley: University of California Press, 1995), 149.

106: "I'm the *Mouse*"—Claes Oldenburg in Martin Friedman, *Claes Oldenburg* (exh. cat., Minneapolis: Walker Art Center, 1975), 25.

106: the phallic gun—Barbara Rose, *Claes Oldenburg* (New York: Museum of Modern Art, 1979), 56.

107: "somewhere between that of a small scale panorama"—Coosje van Bruggen, *Claes Oldenburg: Mouse Museum/Ray Gun Wing* (exh. cat., Cologne: Museum Ludwig, 1979), 5.

108: "museum of popular objects"—van Bruggen, *Claes Oldenburg*, 50.

108: Four years later—See Claes Oldenburg, *The Mouse Museum, The Ray Gun Wing, Two Collections/Two Buildings* (exh. cat., Chicago: Museum of Contemporary Art, 1977).

109: "managers of consciousness"—Hans Haacke, "Museums, Managers of Consciousness," in *Hans Haacke: Unfinished Business*, ed. Brian Wallis (Cambridge: MIT Press, 1986), 60–72.

109: Among the first—Phil Patton, "Other Voices, Other Rooms: The Rise of the Alternative Space," *Art in America*, July/August 1977, 80–87.

109: Located in a wide variety—See Helen Searing, "The Brillo Box in the Warehouse: Museums of Contemporary Art and Industrial Conversions," in *The Andy Warhol Museum* (Pittsburgh: Andy Warhol Museum; New York: Distributed Art Publishers, 1994), 39–66.

113: "having culture without culture having any effect"—Donald Judd, "Nie wieder Krieg," in *Donald Judd, Architektur* (exh. cat., Vienna: Museum für Angewandtekunst, 1991), 13.

113: "everything which I've done has already disappeared"—Donald Judd in Rudi Fuchs, "Das Ideale Museum, Eine Kunst-Siedlung in der Texanischen Wüste," in *Donald Judd, Architektur*, 66–70.

113: "The better new work"—Michael Fried, "Art and Objecthood," *Artforum*, June 1967, 12–25.

114: "In one relief . . . "—Donald Judd, "Symmetry," in *Donald Judd, Architektur*, ed. Marianne Stockebrand (Stuttgart: Edition Cantz, 1992), 190–92.

114: First used in the 19th century—The discussion of cross-mullioned windows is based on the author's conversation with Vincent J. Scully Jr., Fall 1997.

116: art as an experience, not an object—Barbara Rose, *American Art Since 1900* (New York: Praeger, 1975), 223.

118: "The unbelievable combination of estrangement"—Robert Storr, "An Interview with Ilya Kabakov," *Art in America*, January 1995, 60–69, 125.

119: "will to form"—Kenneth Frampton, *Modern Architecture: A Critical History* (New York: Oxford University Press, 1980), 116.

119: "What we build"—Peter Rice, "Lecture at the Architectural League of New York on February 7, 1994," in *Frank Stella: A Vision for Public Art* (Tokyo: Tankosha, 1994), 139–40.

119: William Rubin refers to Stella's involvement—William Rubin, *Frank Stella* (exh. cat., New York: Museum of Modern Art, 1970), 45–46.

120: The artist's design combined—Frank Stella, "Broadsides," in *Frank Stella: A Vision for Public Art*, 136–40.

124: Real estate developers and passionate collectors—See Rolf and Erika Hoffmann, *Kunsthalle Dresden—a project Architecture: Frank Stella* (Cologne: Rolf and Erika Hoffmann publishers, distributed by Walther König, 1996).

126: The German press—"Buntes Ding im Park," *Der Spiegel*, 19 August 1991, 197.

130: "I am nature"—Jackson Pollock in Ellen G. Landau, *Jackson Pollock* (New York: Harry N. Abrams, 1989), 168.

130: "It was a very sunny day"—Robert Barnes and Simon Pummell, "Architectur e Art, a film about paper buildings," unpublished manuscript, 1991, 27.

131: Mies's creation of columnless space—Franz Schulze, "Museum for a Small City, 1942," in *The Mies van der Rohe Archive, XIII*, ed. Franz Schulze and George E. Danforth (New York: Garland, 1992), 68–74.

132: "from the four sides" . . . "literally be *in*"—Jackson Pollock in Landau, *Jackson Pollock*, 168.

132: "In its treatment of paintings as walls"—Arthur Drexler, "Unframed Space; a Museum for Jackson Pollack's [sic] Paintings," *Interiors*, January 1950, 90.

133: An episode in the dialogue—David Moos, "Name Change (1972)," in Patrick Ireland, *Gestures: Instead of an Autobiography* (exh. cat., Youngstown, Ohio: Butler Institute of American Art, 1994), 30–33.

135: Novak points out—Barbara Novak, "Piero in Ireland (1957)," in Patrick Ireland, *Gestures*, 6.

Chapter 5

139: "Many became caught up in a frenzy of growth"—Paul Goldberger, "Doesn't Anybody Want This Job?," *New York Times*, 26 June 1994, II:1.

140: between $500 million and $600 million—Arthur Rosenblatt, telephone interview by author, 7 January 1998.

140: "a building spacious"—Morrison H. Heckscher, "The Metropolitan Museum of Art, An Architectural History," *Metropolitan Museum of Art Bulletin*, Summer 1995, 5. The following history of the Metropolitan Museum is based on this publication.

141: "speak for itself"—Rudolf Wittkower, "Mass Culture vs. Intimate Contemplation," *Art News*, January 1970, 31–32.

141: "mazelike" . . . "spatial complexity"—Philippe de Montebello in Hecksher, "The Metropolitan Museum of Art," 40.

141: "a setting appropriate to its archaeological character"—D.M., "Lower Nubia to Upper Fifth Avenue," *Progressive Architecture*, November 1978, 22–23.

141: "I had to find an architect!"—Thomas Hoving in William Marlin, "The Metropolitan Museum as Amended," *AIA Journal*, May 1981, 28–41.

142: But the strong vertical emphasis—Bernhard Leitner, "A Master Plan: The Met Plans its Second Century," *Artforum*, October 1970, 64–68.

143: The Lehman interiors—Ada Louise Huxtable, "Wrong but Impeccable," *Progressive Architecture*, August 1975, 60–63.

143: "greenhouse aesthetic"—Helen Searing, *New American Art Museums* (exh. cat., New York: Whitney Museum of American Art; Berkeley: University of California Press, 1982), 61.

144: Unfortunately, the hall's south wall—Marlin, "The Metropolitan Museum," 36.

144: "look down on"—Nelson Rockefeller in Marlin, "The Metropolitan Museum," 36.

145: "ninety-nine percent of all collectors"—de Montebello in Grace Glueck, "The Met Makes Its Move Into the 20th Century," *New York Times*, 18 January 1987, II:1, 20.

145: "opaque in its organization"—Joseph Giovannini, "On the New 20th-Century Wing at the Metropolitan," *Artforum*, April 1987, 8–9.

145: Predicated by their relationship—"MMA—Wallace Wing for Twentieth-Century Art," *A+U*, April 1988, 120–27.

146: "When shown in"—William Rubin, "When Museums Overpower Their Art," *New York Times*, 12 April 1987, II:31, 34.

146: "we re-created the past we wished we had had"—Gary Tinterow, *The New 19th-Century European Painting and Sculpture Galleries* (New York: Metropolitan Museum of Art, 1993), 27.

147: "it ought to have been"—Umberto Eco, "Travels in Hyperreality," in *Travels in Hyperreality* (San Diego, New York, London: Harcourt Brace, 1986), 32.

147: The Metropolitan's continuous growth—Ashton Hawkins, interviews by author, New York City, May 1997 and January 1998.

148: Barr wanted to "metabolically" discard—Kirk Varnedoe, "The Evolving Torpedo: Changing Ideas of the Collection of Painting and Sculpture of the Museum of Modern Art," in *The Museum of Modern Art at Mid-Century: Continuity and Change*, ed. John Elderfield (New York: Museum of Modern Art, 1995), 12–73.

148: What began in the 1930s as a revolutionary institution—Helaine Ruth Messer, "MoMA: Museum in Search of an Image," Ph.D. thesis, Columbia University, 1979.

148: "It will reopen firmly established"—Tom Wolfe, "M.O.M.A. Opens Her Arms Again," *New York Herald Tribune Sunday Magazine*, 24 May 1964, 11–13, 55.

149: "installations display the synoptic gospel"—Calvin Tomkins, "The Art World: Agora," *New Yorker*, 15 October 1984, 126–33.

149: "What can you challenge in a Temple?"—Rem Koolhaas, "Charrette," Museum of Modern Art, New York, 17–19 February 1997.

149: Among the several proposals—Robert A. M. Stern, Gregory Gilmartin and Thomas Mellins, *New York 1930: Architecture and Urbanism between the Two World Wars* (New York: Rizzoli, 1987), 142ff.

151: When interest in a new building revived—Rona Roob, "1936: The Museum Selects an Architect," *Archives of American Art Journal* 1 (1983): 22–31.

151: But as Howe's biographer—Robert A. M. Stern, *George Howe: Toward a Modern American Architecture* (New Haven: Yale University Press, 1975), 106.

151: "a watered [down] version"—Philip Johnson, MoMA Oral History transcript, 1991, 134.

151: Within eight years—"MoMA Expansion Announced," *New York Herald Tribune*, 9 February 1947, 42.

152: When framed by dark brownstones—Paul Goldberger, "A Wistful Ode to a Museum That Once Was," *New York Times*, 11 June 1989, II:35.

152: In 1959 MoMA trustee Nelson Rockefeller—Russell Lynes, *Good Old Modern: An Intimate Portrait of the Museum of Modern Art* (New York: Atheneum, 1973), 391–93.

152: The plans for an eight-story wing—Robert A. M. Stern, Thomas Mellins and David Fishman, *New York 1960: Architecture and Urbanism between the Second World War and the Bicentennial* (New York: The Monacelli Press, 1995), 480–82.

152: Within a year Johnson's scheme was relaunched—Rona Roob chronology, MoMA archive.

154: From the time it reopened—Thomas B. Hess, "MoMA and the Towering Limbo," *New York Magazine*, 15 March 1976, 78, 81.

154: Within four years of the East Wing addition—Rona Roob chronology, MoMA archive.

154: Basically, Elliott's complex plan was threefold—Suzanne Stephens, "MoMA's Castle in the Air," *Artforum*, Summer 1976, 28–31.

154: An intricate tax-exemption scheme—Suzanne Stephens, "Trust for Cultural Resources Legislation: Implications for Urban Design," *Connecticut Law Review* 3 (Spring 1978): 605–19.

155: "dubious undertaking"—Ada Louise Huxtable, "A Dubious Survival Plan for the Modern," *New York Times*, 7 August 1977, II:1, 20.

155: As well as criticizing the tower's impact—Huxtable, "A Dubious Survival Plan," II:1, 20.

155: Johnson, who had been working—Rona Roob chronology, MoMA archive.

155: By the time of Pelli's selection—Cesar Pelli, MoMA Oral History transcript, March 1994, 28.

155: "It wasn't an opportunity"—Richard Weinstein, MoMA Oral History transcript, June 1994, 64.

156: An exception to the rule—Koolhaas, "Charrette," 187.

156: "the cheapest of any major museum ever built"—Pelli, MoMA Oral History transcript, 20.

156: Within ten years of its completion—*Museum of Modern Art Annual Report,* 1993–94.

158: For the first time in its history—Peter Reed, "The Space and the Frame: Philip Johnson as the Museum's Architect," in *Studies in Modern Art 6,* ed. John Elderfield (New York: Harry N. Abrams, 1998), 70–103.

159: In the late 1970s—Richard Koch, MoMA Oral History transcript, 147–48.

159: As the only proposal—Herbert Muschamp, "Make the Modern Modern? How Very Rash!," *New York Times,* 15 June 1997, II:31.

160: "core" . . . "satellite" . . . "hotbed of experimentation"—Bernard Tschumi, charrette entry, "Toward the New Museum of Modern Art: Sketchbooks by Ten Artists," exhibition at MoMA, 3 May–7 October 1997.

160: In presenting Taniguchi's winning entry—Glenn Lowry, MoMA staff conference, 9 December 1997.

161: "throughout its history"—Charrette program, Museum of Modern Art, 17–19 February 1997, 4.

162: soon after excavation—*Frank Lloyd Wright: The Guggenheim Correspondence,* ed. Bruce Brooks Pfeiffer (Fresno: Press at California State University; Carbondale: Southern Illinois University Press, 1986), 242.

162: "the most beautiful building in America"—Emily Genauer in Peter Blake, "The Guggenheim: Museum or Monument?," *Architectural Forum,* December 1959, 86–97.

162: Gwathmey Siegel proposed an 11-story tower—Mildred Schmertz, "Wright Revamped," *Architecture,* August 1992, 34–41.

162: The Guggenheim Museum was produced—The following account of the museum's history is based on Neil Levine, "The Guggenheim Museum's Logic of Inversion," chapter 10 of *The Architecture of Frank Lloyd Wright* (Princeton: Princeton University Press, 1996), 299–364.

163: "order creating order"—Hilla Rebay in Levine, "Logic of Inversion," 299.

163: Neil Levine quotes Rebay's description—Levine, "Logic of Inversion," 315.

163: "the substitution of passive reception"—Levine, "Logic of Inversion," 315.

163: "Modern Gallery"—Levine, "Logic of Inversion," 327–36.

163: "the alpha and omega"—Albert Gleizes in Levine, "Logic of Inversion," 480 n.12.

164: Levine points out—Levine, "Logic of Inversion," 343.

164: "rectilinear frame of reference"—*Frank Lloyd Wright: The Guggenheim Correspondence,* 281.

164: Working with Josep Lluís Sert—Henry-Russell Hitchcock, "Notes of a Traveller: Wright and Kahn," *Zodiac* (Milan) 6 (1960): 15–21.

164: As late as 1958—*Frank Lloyd Wright: The Guggenheim Correspondence,* 255.

164: "make the picture more natural to the sweep"—*Frank Lloyd Wright: The Guggenheim Correspondence,* 281.

164: "the most ill-considered and defacing alteration"—Martin Filler, "Wright Wronged," *House & Garden,* February 1986, 42, 44, 46, 48.

164: "that gave negative emphasis"—Filler, "Wright Wronged," 43.

165: "just plain wrong"—William Marlin, "Laying Off the Guggenheim Museum," statement submitted to 25 June 1986 hearing before New York City Board of Standards and Appeals.

165: In 1986—Douglas C. McGill, "Guggenheim Plan Debated at Hearing," *New York Times,* 26 June 1986, C17.

166: Ironically, Thomas Krens—Grace Glueck, "Guggenheim Plans SoHo Branch for Offices and Art Exhibitions," *New York Times,* 18 April 1991, C15, C22.

167: "When the first atomic bomb"—"The Modern Gallery," *Architectural Forum,* January 1946, 82–88.

167: "a consistent, organic whole . . ."—Aline B. Saarinen, "Tour with Mr. Wright," *New York Times Magazine,* 22 September 1957, 22–23, 69–70.

168: "For the first time"—Frank Lloyd Wright, "The Guggenheim Museum Memorial," *Architectural Record,* May 1958, 182–90.

168: "unique physical condition"—New York City Board of Standards and Appeals, Resolution 20, October 1987, 2.

168: "the continuous and sequential exhibition"—New York City Board of Standards and Appeals, Resolution 20, 2.

168: "Art may be sacred"—Ada Louise Huxtable, "Creeping Gigantism in Manhattan," *New York Times,* 22 March 1987, II:1, 36.

169: Even though Graves—Roger Kimball, "Michael Graves Tackles the Whitney," *Architectural Record,* October 1985, 113–15.

170: Ten years later—Carol Vogel, "$14 Million Expansion Planned by the Whitney," *New York Times,* 20 September 1995, C14.

170: "almost imperceptible"—"On the Drawing Boards," *Oculus,* November 1995, 3.

170: "We thought we were making"—Flora Biddle, interview by author, New York City, 9 August 1990.

171: Le Grand Louvre—Dimensions and design credits were provided by Pei Cobb Freed & Partners. See also *Le Grand Louvre, Histoire d'un projet,* ed. Dominique Bezombes with Catherine Bergeron (Paris: Le Moniteur, 1994), 204, 211.

171: The controversy—Susan R. Stein, "French Ferociously Debate the Pei Pyramid at the Louvre," *Architecture*, May 1985, 25, 31–34, 40, 46.

171: The pyramid was only the top of the iceberg—Timothy W. Ryback, "From Villain to Hero: I. M. Pei's Louvre Odyssey," *Art News*, Summer 1995, 99–102.

172: The critic Charles Jencks—Charles Jencks, "Symbolism and Blasphemies," *Art & Design*, September 1985, 42–44.

172: Indeed, announcement of Pei's 71-foot-high—Henri Mercillon, "Contre le Grand Louvre," *Connaissance des Arts*, April 1985, 48–51.

172: The scholar Antoine Schnapper—Antoine Schnapper, interview by author, Paris, 29 June 1997. See also Bruno Foucart, Sebastien Loste, Antoine Schnapper, *Paris Mystifié* (Paris: Juilliard, 1985).

173: French building codes—Charlotte Ellis, "An Ace Pyramid," *Blueprint*, May 1989, 34.

174: Upon discovering its mistake—Patricia Mounier, Grand Louvre, Communications Department, interview by author, Paris, 2 June 1997.

175: Like the Metropolitan Museum—Grand Louvre, aile Richelieu, press release, 18 November 1993, 77.

176: The advantage of a real-life context—Pierre Schneider, *les dialogues du Louvre* (Paris: Adam Biro, 1991), 11–13.

177: Had it not been—Patricia Cummings Loud, *The Art Museums of Louis I. Kahn* (Durham, N.C.: Duke University Press, 1989), 54–56.

177: Buckminster Fuller—Loud, *The Art Museums of Louis I. Kahn*, 68–69.

177: Building codes—"Louis Kahn's Hollow Concrete Floor for Yale's Design Lab," *Architectural Forum*, November 1952, 148–49.

177: In addition, the architect's insertion—Loud, *The Art Museums of Louis I. Kahn*, 84.

178: "Much of this vitality"—Vincent J. Scully, "Art Gallery and Design Center, Yale University, New Haven," *Museum* (Unesco) 9 (1956): 101–13.

178: To display art—George A. Sanderson, "Art Gallery and Design Center: New Haven, Connecticut," *Progressive Architecture*, May 1954, 88–101.

178: Here, too, Kahn's intended openness—Sasha M. Newman, curator of contemporary art, Yale University Art Gallery (1987–95), interview by author, New York City, summer 1997.

179: The old gallery is a U-shaped building—James Stirling, "Design Philosophy and Recent Work," in *James Stirling Michael Wilford and Associates* (New York: St. Martin's, 1990), 9.

179: Like those for the two prior Modern art museum competitions—Alan Colquhoun, "Architecture as a Continuous Text," *ANY*, September/October 1993, 18–19.

179: "place of popular entertainment"—James Stirling, "The Monumentally Informal," *Neue Staatsgalerie und Kammertheater Stuttgart* (Stuttgart: Staatliches Hochbauamt 1, 1984).

180: Inside the building—James Stirling, "The Monumental Tradition," *Perspecta* 16 (1980): 33–39.

180: "precarious" and "fragile" . . . "evasive"—Francesco Dal Co, "The Melancholy Experience of Contemporaneity," *ANY*, September/October 1993, 26–29.

180: "the central pantheon"—Stirling, "Design Philosophy," 8.

182: William Wilkins's design—This and the following background of the Sainsbury Wing commission are based on Colin Amery, *A Celebration of Art and Architecture* (London: National Gallery, 1991).

182: "a monstrous carbuncle"—Amery, *A Celebration of Art and Architecture*, 49.

182: Their Corinthian pilasters—John Morris Dixon, "Learning from London," *Progressive Architecture*, August 1991, 80–87.

185: "soft" . . . "as the speech balloons"—Stanislaus von Moos, "Body Language and Artifice," *A+U*, July 1990, 121–30.

185: In designing the galleries—Robert Venturi, "From Invention to Convention in Architecture," *RSA Journal*, January 1988, 89–103.

186: The Spanish architect and teacher—José Rafael Moneo, "Discussing Today's Architectural Principles," lecture delivered at the Architectural Association, London, 14 November 1996.

186: The Beck Building—The background of the Museum of Fine Arts is based on "The Museum of Fine Arts, Houston: An Architectural History, 1924–1986," *Houston Museum of Fine Arts Bulletin*, April 1992.

186: The Venturi office—Peter C. Papademetriou, "Loose Fit: The Houston Museum District," *Cite*, Spring 1996, 8–15.

187: "a regular, outwardly closed structure"—Moneo, "Discussing Today's Architectural Principles."

Chapter 6

190: "not about explaining but dreaming, excitement"—Pontus Hulten in Calvin Tomkins, "A Good Monster," *New Yorker*, 16 January 1978, 37–67.

190: Already in the early 1920s—Yve Alain Bois, interview by author, New York City, 29 March 1997.

191: In a 1967 interview—Annette Michelson, "The Museum World," *Arts Yearbook* 9 (1967): 84–92.

191: "Theme parks . . . "—Margaret J. King, "Theme Park Thesis," *Museum News*, September/October 1990, 60–62.

191: the ramp of New York's Guggenheim—P.N., "After the Guggenheim," *Lotus International* 85 (1995): 44–45.

191: Krens's frequent references to "the museum industry"—Rosalind Krauss, "The Cultural Logic of the Late Capitalist Museum," *October* 54 (Fall 1990): 3–17.

191: And in a recent lecture—Glenn Lowry, "Building the Future: Some Observations on Art, Architecture and the Museum of Modern Art," lecture at MoMA, 22 October 1997.

192: Astronomical attendance figures—Gary O. Larson, *American Canvas*, NEA Report, 1997, 43.

192: The English architect Colin St. John Wilson—Colin St. John Wilson, "James Stirling: In Memoriam," *Architectural Review,* December 1992, 18–20.

193: "a light-flooded cathedral"—John Coolidge, *Patrons and Architects: Designing Art Museums in the Twentieth Century* (Fort Worth: University of Texas Press, 1989), 43.

193: Piano and Rogers ensured excitement—Antoine Picon, "Interview with Renzo Piano and Richard Rogers," foreword to *Du Plateau Beaubourg au Centre Georges Pompidou, Renzo Piano and Richard Rogers* (Paris: Centre Georges Pompidou, 1987), 9–44.

193: "Museums are no longer"—Pontus Hulten, "Toutes les Muses, Le Musée de Demain," *L'ARC* 63 (1975): 4–5.

193: But its sources—William J. R. Curtis, *Modern Architecture Since 1900* (London: Phaidon Press, 1996), 600.

193: "loud, aggressive and tempestuous"—Paul Greenhalgh, "Education, Entertainment and Politics: Lessons from the Great International Exhibitions," in *The New Museology,* ed. Peter Vergo (London: Reaktion Books, 1989), 74–98.

194: When in 1969 the market was moved—Annette Michelson, "Beaubourg: The Museum in the Era of Late Capitalism," *Artforum,* April 1975, 62–67.

196: Shortly after Piano and Rogers won—Michael Davies, Laurie Abbott and Alan Stanton, "An Inside View," *Architectural Design* 47, no. 2 (1977): n.p.

197: what could be more permanent—Michael Gibson, "Visages Multiples," *Connaissance des Arts,* May 1986, 66–79.

198: Nineteen percent—Alan Riding, "At 20, Pompidou Center Seeks a Lift," *New York Times,* 1 February 1997, A9.

198: attendance at two-to-three-month exhibitions— Figures supplied by the director's office, Centre Georges Pompidou, 24 September 1997.

199: The original factory—Marcia E. Vetrocq, "Fast Track Art Center Opens in Turin," *Art in America,* September 1989, 35.

200. Conservation measures—Peter Buchanan, "Reviving Lingotto," *Architectural Review,* November 1996, 62–67.

200: The press shop—Peter Buchanan "Lingotto Factory Renovation, Turin," in *Renzo Piano Building Workshop,* vol. 2 (London: Phaidon, 1995), 150–67.

203: "room of miracles"—Alessandro Mendini, "Fragmenten," in *Atelier Mendini, een visuele utopie,* ed. Raffaella Poletti (Milan: Fabbri, 1994), 15–25.

203: "a poetic moment"—Marijke Martin and Cor Wagenaar, "A Design for a New Groninger Museum," in *Groninger Museum,* ed. Marijke Martin, Cor Wagenaar and Annette Welkamp (Groningen: Groninger Museum, 1996), 71–118.

203: A search committee—Wijnand Galema, "Fun Park or Cultural Palace? The Story of a Remarkable Museum Site," in *Groninger Museum,* 53–69.

204: A café portico—Bohdan Paczowski, "Hans Hollein," *Architecture d'Aujourd'hui,* February 1992, 116–21.

206: "fog banks or clouds"—Martin and Wagenaar, "Design for a New Groninger Museum," 105.

208: "try and bring a little bit of order"—Richard Meier, "The Getty Trust and the Process of Patronage, Interviews," *Harvard Architecture Review* 6 (1987): 122–31.

208: the Getty's conservative mandate—George E. Marcus, "The Production of European High Culture in Los Angeles: The J. Paul Getty Trust as Artificial Curiosity," *Cultural Anthropology,* August 1990, 314–30.

209: Kurt Forster—Kurt W. Forster, "A Citadel for Los Angeles and an Alhambra for the Arts," *A+U,* November 1992 (Special Issue), 6–14.

209: but it is as protected—Diane Ghirardo, "Invisible Acropolis," *Architectural Review,* June 1990, 93–95.

209: The villa's sprawl—Colin Rowe and Fred Koetter, *Collage City* (Cambridge: MIT Press, 1978), 86–117.

209: The resulting difficulties—Richard Meier, *Building the Getty* (New York: Knopf, 1997), 137.

211: Uppermost in their minds—William Lacy, Ada Louise Huxtable, Kurt W. Forster, Stephen Rountree, telephone interviews by author, 4, 5, 6 and 13 March 1997, respectively.

212: Correa attributes the inspiration—Charles Correa, "India: From a Philosophy of Ages, Architecture for Today," *Museum* 4 (1989): 223–29.

212: Meier's comparison—Meier, *Building the Getty,* 167.

216: "atmosphere rooms"—Samuel Cauman, *The Living Museum: Experiences of an Art Historian and Museum Director—Alexander Dorner* (New York: New York University Press, 1958), 88.

217: $8 million worth of landscaping from a man who knew nothing about plants—Lawrence Weschler, "When Fountainheads Collide," *New Yorker,* 8 December 1997, 60–70.

217: "must visit"—Patricia Ward Biederman and Doug Smith, "The New Getty Center Rises Above the Masses," *Los Angeles Times,* 10 October 1994, A21.

217: mixed signals—Thomas F. Reese, "The Architectural Politics of the Getty Center for the Arts," *Lotus International* 85 (1995): 6–43.

217: "examples of the conjunction"—Umberto Eco, "Travels in Hyperreality," in *Travels in Hyperreality* (San Diego, New York, London: Harcourt Brace, 1986), 1–58.

218: "a source of entertainment"—William Marlin, "A Building of Paris," *Architectural Record,* February 1978, 103–14.

218: "a more intensely urban experience"—Kurt Forster quoted in Jennifer Taylor, "Art, Architecture and Los Angeles," *Design Book Review* 31 (1994): 67–73.

218: much as the 19th-century opera house did—Jürgen Paul, "The Art Museum as a Palace of Aesthetics: The Neue Staatsgalerie in Stuttgart by James Stirling and Some Considerations Concerning the Cultural Function of an Art Museum," in *Tribute to Lotte Brand Philip, Art Historian and Detective,* ed. William W. Clark, Colin Eisler, William S. Heckscher, Barbara G. Lane (New York: Abaris Books, 1985), 133–43.

218: the three-month Cézanne exhibition—Tom Csaszar, "Spectacular Record-Breaking Sold-Out Smash-Hit Blockbuster Supershow!," *New Art Examiner*, December 1996/January 1997, 22–27.

218: Disney is in turn—Edwin McDowell, "Tourists Respond to Lure of Culture," *New York Times*, 24 April 1997, D1, 3.

Chapter 7

221: "the missionary position"—Joseph Giovannini, "More Than One Way to See Art," *New York Times*, 13 November 1994, II:48.

221: Yet another aspect—John Coolidge, *Patrons and Architects: Designing Art Museums in the Twentieth Century* (Fort Worth: University of Texas Press, 1989), 49.

222: Like the earlier pavilions—Coolidge, *Patrons and Architects*, 49.

223: "when an artist uses space"—Germano Celant, "Artspaces," *Studio International* 190 (1975): 114–23.

224: "eternal passivity of museum art"—El Lissitzky, "New Russian Art: A Lecture (1922)," in *El Lissitzky: Life, Letters, Texts*, ed. Sophie Lissitzky-Küppers (London: Thames and Hudson, 1968), 335.

224: "probably the most famous single room"—Samuel Cauman, *The Living Museum: Experiences of an Art Historian and Museum Director—Alexander Dorner* (New York: New York University Press, 1958), 108.

224: El Lissitzky's use of elements—Kurt W. Forster, "Shrine? Emporium? Theater? Reflections on Two Decades of American Museum Building," *Zodiac* 6 (March/August 1991): 30–73.

224: As El Lissitzky did—Christoph Grunenberg, "Espaces Spectaculaires: l'art de l'installation selon Frederick Kiesler," in *Frederick Kiesler, Artiste-Architecte* (exh. cat., Paris: Centre Georges Pompidou, 1996), 103–18; Cynthia Goodman, "The Art of Revolutionary Display Techniques," in *Frederick Kiesler*, ed. Lisa Phillips (exh. cat., New York: Whitney Museum of American Art, 1989), 57–84.

224: Kiesler first demonstrated—Dieter Bogner, "Kiesler and the European Avant-Garde," in Phillips, *Frederick Kiesler*, 46–55.

225: To paraphrase Mark Wigley's catalog—Mark Wigley, *Deconstructivist Architecture* (exh. cat., New York: Museum of Modern Art, 1988), 19.

226: "non-building"—Ellen Posner, "A $43 Million Dollar Arts Center Opens—Minus the Art," *Wall Street Journal*, 14 December 1989, A20.

227: The last of these experiments—Alejandro Zaera-Polo, "A Conversation with Peter Eisenman," *El Croquis* 83 (1997): 6–20.

228: The canvas canopy—Sherry Geldin, director, Wexner Center for the Arts, interview by author, Columbus, Ohio, 26 July 1995.

228: conventional art can be exhibited—Geldin interview.

233: Once inside the building—"Popular Culture," *Blueprint*, January 1993, 19.

235: "The official name of the project"—Daniel Libeskind, "Between the Lines," in *Daniel Libeskind, Extension to the Berlin Museum with Jewish Museum Department*, ed. Kristin Feireiss (Berlin: Ernst, 1992), 57–67.

236: Commenting on the connection—Libeskind, "Between the Lines," 63–65.

236: Libeskind cites from sources—Libeskind, "Between the Lines," n.p.

239: "a primordial exile, or self-banishment"—Gershom Scholem, *On the Kabbalah and Its Symbolism* (New York: Schocken Books, 1996), 111.

240: The catwalks, balconies and platforms—Mildred Friedman, "Fast Food," in *The Architecture of Frank Gehry*, ed. Mildred Friedman (exh. cat., New York: Rizzoli, 1986).

242: When budget restrictions—William Morrish, program director, Design Center, American Urban Landscape, University of Minnesota, interview by author, Minneapolis, Minnesota, 20 July 1996.

247: Peggy Guggenheim—Alessandro Rocca, "From the Spiral to the Web," *Lotus International* 85 (1995): 47–74.

247: The Basques offered—Figures supplied by the director's office, Guggenheim Museum, New York.

250: "plunge stories deep"—Antonio Sant'Elia in Reyner Banham, *Theory and Design in the First Machine Age* (New York: Praeger, 1960), 129.

250: "swarm up the facades"—Sant'Elia in Banham, *Theory and Design*, 129.

256: Paul Valéry—See line note p. 48.

256: Instead, Gehry employs CATIA—Raul A. Barreneche, "Gehry's Guggenheim," *Architecture*, September 1996, 177–79; James Glymph, telephone interview by author, 24 January 1997.

258: "first delight, then instruct"—Karl Friedrich Schinkel in Douglas Crimp, "The End of Art and the Origin of the Museum," *Art Journal* (Winter 1987): 261–66.

258: "higher unity" . . . "as many relationships as possible"—Schinkel in Crimp, "The End of Art," 264.

258: "venerating works of art"—Hegel in Crimp, "The End of Art," 265.

258: Several Spanish architects—Javiar Salazar, "Industriekrise und Stadterneuerung in Bilbao," *Werk, Bauen + Wohnen* 12 (1996): 6–17.

259: Political critics—Joseba Zulaika, "The Seduction of Bilbao," *Architecture*, December 1997, 60–63.

259: Others question—Zulaika, "Seduction," 61–62.

260: "it is the viewers"—Marcel Duchamp (author's translation) in Dieter Daniels, "Points d'interférence entre Frederick Kiesler et Marcel Duchamp," in *Frederick Kiesler, Artiste-Architecte* 119–30.

Afterword

262: "It's cheap. It's fast."—Judith H. Dobrzynski, "Glory Days for the Art Museum," *New York Times*, 5 October 1997, II:1, 44.

262: 100 million people—Dobrzynski, "Glory Days," II:1.

262: Already in the 1920s—Konrad Oberhuber, director, Albertina Museum, telephone interview by author, 27 November 1997.

263: With a contest he organized—Joan Ockman, "The Road Not Taken: Alexander Dorner's Way Beyond Art," in *Autonomy and Ideology: Positioning an Avant-Garde in America* (New York: The Monacelli Press, 1997), 80–112.

263: In the same manner today—Office of Tourism, Dordogne, September 1997.

263: In their place—Daniel Debaye, "Lascaux II: une reproduction pour l'an 2000," *Vieilles Maisons Françaises*, July 1982, 26–27.

263: To a greater extent—See Rojo de Castro, "Conversation with Juan Navarro Baldeweg," *El Croquis* 73 (1995): 6–25.

263: The toll taken by Pompeii's—Frederika Randall, "The Mobile Guide: The Latest Days of Pompeii," *Wall Street Journal*, 6 February 1997, A12.

264: For both structures—Francesco Dal Co, *Tadao Ando: Complete Works* (London: Phaidon, 1995), 410.

264: Leonardo da Vinci—Jeffrey M. Muller, *Rubens: The Artist as Collector* (Princeton: Princeton University Press, 1989), 67.

264: "casts of the finest statues in Rome"—Francis Haskell and Nicholas Penny, *Taste and the Antique* (New Haven: Yale University Press, 1981), 16.

264: "the best sculptures"—Muller, *Rubens*, 67.

264: As early as the 5th century B.C.—Andrew Stewart, *Greek Sculpture*, vol. 1 (New Haven: Yale University Press, 1990), 24–25.

265: So eager was Francis I—Haskell and Penny, *Taste and the Antique*, 2.

265: The practice—Haskell and Penny, *Taste and the Antique*, 31ff, 79.

265: Famous Works—Haskell and Penny, *Taste and the Antique*, 93–98.

265: In the 18th century many galleries—Haskell and Penny, *Taste and the Antique*, 79–91.

265: graphic representation—Haskell and Penny, *Taste and the Antique*, 41.

266: David Ross—Unless otherwise indicated the following discussion of the Internet is based on David Ross, interviews by author, 9 December 1997 and 5, 22 and 28 January 1998.

266: the WebMuseum network—As reported on WebMuseum network, http://sunsite.unc.edu/wm, 23 September 1997.

266: The ease with which—Eleanor Heartney, "Re Museums: Lights on Nobody Home," *Art in America*, September 1995, 39–43.

266: Like visitors to a Renaissance cabinet—Heartney, "Re Museums," 40.

268: "arts world" . . . "the very attributes"—Gary O. Larson, "American Canvas" (NEA, 1997), 13, 115.

268: an intellectual framework—Bill Viola, telephone interview by author, 31 December 1997.

268: "not as the art of space"—Peter Weibel, "The Museum of the Future," in *New Strategies for Communication in Museums*, Proceedings of ICOM/CECA 1996, ed. Hadwig Kräutler (Vienna: WUV Universitäts-Verlag, 1997), 35–39.

269: In the 1960s—Nicholas Serota, *Experience or Interpretation: The Dilemma of Museums of Modern Art* (New York: Thames and Hudson, 1997), 33–36.

269: "telemuseum"—Cynthia Goodman, "The Art of Revolutionary Display Techniques," in *Frederick Kiesler*, ed. Lisa Phillips (exh. cat., New York: Whitney Museum of American Art, 1989), 57–84.

269: culture of curiosity—Martin Prösler, "Museums and Globalization," in *Theorizing Museums*, ed. Sharon Macdonald and Gordon Fyfe (Cambridge: Blackwell, 1996), 21–44.

270: In a world—Martin Weil, letter to the author, 25 July 1995.

270: the failure of many museum-goers—Dobrzynski, "Glory Days," II:44.

Illustration Credits

Unless otherwise indicated, all plans, sections, isometrics and photographs of models and buildings are courtesy of the architects. The square footages given were provided by the architects and are in some cases approximate.

Aker/Zvonkovic: 186
Alinari Archives/Art Resource, N.Y.: 75
Alinari Archives/George Tatge: 133, 134
© 1998 Artists Rights Society (ARS), New York/ADAGP, Paris/FLC: 222 (top)
Courtesy of Artequín: 266
Avery Architectural and Fine Arts Library, Columbia University in the City of New York: 149, 180

Richard Barnes: 31
Richard Barnes/Esto: 61, 63, 64
Bitter Bredt Fotografie, Berlin: 236, 237, 238, 239 (bottom)
Tom Bonner © The J. Paul Getty Trust: 214 (bottom), 216 (bottom)
Brandenburgisches Landesamt für Denkmalpflege, Meßbildarchiv: 15 (top)
Steven Brooke: 112
Richard Bryant/Arcaid: 77 (top)

Lluis Casals: 67
Courtesy of Centro Galego de Arte Contemporánea, Santiago de Compostela: 68
M. Chassat/Louvre: 173 (top right)
Courtesy of Chinati Foundation: 113
Sophie Chivet/Mission Interministérielle aux Grands Travaux: 265

Robert Damora: 157 (top)
Michel Denancé: 23, 25, 94, 95
Chris Duisberg/Studio Libeskind: 96
By permission of the Trustees of Dulwich Picture Gallery: 185

Todd Eberle: 36, 115, 116, 117, 142 (bottom)

Ferrero-Labat/*Explorer*: 263 (top)
Alain Fleischer/Courtesy of Gae Aulenti Architect: 198
Scott Frances/Esto: 69, 70
Scott Frances/Esto © The J. Paul Getty Trust: 209, 210, 213, 214 (top), 216 (top)
Yukio Futagawa: 195

Steven Gerrard & Eric Schall/Studio Libeskind: 239 (top)

Bob Goedewaagen: 232, 234
Paula Goldman/Courtesy of Museum of Contemporary Art: 110
Alexander Gorlin: 246
Solomon R. Guggenheim Museum, New York. Exterior view ca. 1964–65. Photo by Robert E. Mates © Solomon R. Guggenheim Foundation, New York: 165
Solomon R. Guggenheim Museum, New York. Exterior view, 1991. Photo by David Heald © Solomon R. Guggenheim Foundation, New York: 166
Solomon R. Guggenheim Museum, New York. Exhibition gallery view from "Masterpieces from the Permanent Collection" (Tower Five). June–September 1992, Guggenheim Museum, New York. Photo by David Heald © Solomon R. Guggenheim Foundation, New York: 168
Solomon R. Guggenheim Museum, New York. Guggenheim Museum Bilbao, 1997. (Exterior and Interior Views.) Photos by David Heald © Solomon R. Guggenheim Foundation, New York: 249 (bottom left/right), 251, 252, 253 (middle/bottom), 254 (top)
Solomon R. Guggenheim Museum, New York. Guggenheim Museum Bilbao, 1997. Photos by Erika Barahona Ede © Solomon R. Guggenheim Foundation, New York: 253 (top), 254 (bottom)

Courtesy of Verlag Gerd Hatje: 248
Heinrich Helfenstein: 87, 88, 89, 111
Lucien Hervé: 221 (bottom), 222
Hickey-Robertson, Cy Twombly Gallery, Courtesy of the Menil Collection, Houston: 82, 83
Hickey-Robertson, The Menil Collection, Houston: 21, 22
Courtesy of Rolf and Erika Hoffmann: 125 (top)
Studio Hans Hollein/Sina Baniahmad: 204
Ariel Huber/Studio Libeskind: 97
Franz Hubmann, Vienna: 223
Timothy Hursley: 249 (top)

Andres Jaque: 263 (bottom)
Donald Judd, *100 Untitled Works in Mill Aluminum*, 1982–86, installation at Chinati Foundation. © Estate of Donald Judd/Licensed by VAGA, New York, N.Y. Photos by Todd Eberle: 116, 117 (top)

© 1977 Louis I. Kahn Collection, University of Pennsylvania and the Pennsylvania Historical and Museum Commission: 178
Courtesy of Robert Kahn Architect: 127
Angelo Kaunat: 99
John Kernick: 170
Österreichische Friedrich und Lillian Kiesler-Privatstiftung: 225
Kunsthaus Bregenz, Adolf Bereuter: 58 (bottom), 60 (middle/bottom)
Kunsthaus Bregenz, Hélène Binet: 57 (top)
Kunsthaus Bregenz, Ignacio Martinez: 57 (bottom), 58 (top)

Materiale di Archivio—Lingotto Srl: 200, 201

Guy Marineau: 175
Peter Mauss/Esto: 240, 241
Norman McGrath: 18, 19, 126
The Metropolitan Museum of Art, New York. *Autumn Rhythm (Number 30)* by Jackson Pollock. Courtesy of the Metropolitan Museum of Art/George A. Hearn Fund. Photograph by Todd Eberle: 145 (bottom)
The Metropolitan Museum of Art, New York. Main Entrance of Fifth Avenue Facade of the Metropolitan Museum of Art. Photographed September 1968. The Metropolitan Museum of Art: 142 (top)
The Metropolitan Museum of Art, New York. Museum Views—Exteriors. 20th C., 1995. Aerial view of the Museum from the northeast. The Metropolitan Museum of Art: 143
The Metropolitan Museum of Art, New York. Museum Views—Interiors. Gallery Views—European. The Nineteenth-Century European Paintings and Sculpture Galleries. View #6. (Shown on the cover of 1993 publication on the galleries.) The Metropolitan Museum of Art: 146
Grant Mudford: 32, 33
Museum of Modern Art, New York. Installation view of the exhibition "Painting and Sculpture from the Museum Collection." The Museum of Modern Art, New York. May 1964. Photograph © 1998 The Museum of Modern Art, New York: 48 (top)

Museum of Modern Art, New York. Mies van der Rohe, Ludwig. Museum for a small city. 1942. Plan. Pencil on illustration board, 30" x 40" (76.2 x 101.6 cm). The Museum of Modern Art, New York. Gift of the architect. Photograph © 1998 The Museum of Modern Art, New York: 48 (bottom)

Museum of Modern Art, New York. Stella, Frank, with Earl Childress, Robert Kahn Architects, Nageli and Vallebuona Architekten. Kunsthalle, Project. Dresden, Germany. 1992. Stainless steel, 9" x 60¾" x 42" (22.9 x 154.3 x 106.7 cm). The Museum of Modern Art, New York. Gift of Frank Stella: 125 (bottom right)

Museum of Modern Art, New York. Goodwin, Philip, and Stone, Edward D. The Museum of Modern Art, New York. 1939. Facade. Photograph by Andreas Feininger, Courtesy of the Museum of Modern Art, New York: 150 (top left)

Museum of Modern Art, New York. Installation view of the exhibition "Art in Our Time." The Museum of Modern Art, New York. May 10 through September 30, 1939. Photograph © 1997 The Museum of Modern Art, New York: 150 (bottom left/right)

Museum of Modern Art, New York. Johnson, Philip. 21 West 53rd Street Extension (Grace Rainey Rogers Memorial Annex) to the Museum of Modern Art, New York (1953). Photographic Archives, The Museum of Modern Art, New York. Photograph by Alexandre Georges, Courtesy the Museum of Modern Art, New York: 151

Museum of Modern Art, New York. Installation view of the exhibition "Selections from the Permanent Collection: Painting and Sculpture." The Museum of Modern Art, New York. May 17, 1984—continuing. Photograph © The Museum of Modern Art, New York: 153, 158

Museum of Modern Art, New York. 1992. Lobby. Photograph © 1997 The Museum of Modern Art, New York: 157 (bottom)

Museum of Modern Art, New York. View of the the Museum of Modern Art's Main Hall facing Sculpture Garden. Summer 1964. Photograph by Alexandre Georges. © 1997 The Museum of Modern Art, New York: 157 (middle)

Museum of Modern Art, New York. David Allison/The Museum of Modern Art, New York: 160

Pino Musi, Como: 62, 90, 91, 93

The National Museum of Western Art, Tokyo: 221 (top)

Artworks © Claes Oldenburg/ Photograph © Hans Biezen: 107

Artworks © Claes Oldenburg/ Photograph © Helaine Messer: 106, 108

Nam June Paik. *TV Chair*, 1973, offset lithograph. Courtesy of Carl Solway Gallery, Cincinnati, Ohio. Photograph by Cal Kowal: 267

Paschall/Taylor: 169

Kira Perov: 271

Courtesy Renzo Piano Building Workshop: 197

Sydney Pollack: 245

Collection of the Pollock-Krasner House and Study Center, East Hampton, N.Y. Peter Blake, "ideal museum" for Jackson Pollock's work, 1949. Original model lost. Replica fabricated by Patrick Bodden, with sculptures by Susan Tamulevich, 1993–94. Made possible by a grant from the Graham Foundation for Advanced Studies in the Fine Arts. Photograph by Jeff Heatley: 130, 131

Jock Pottle/Esto: 123

Réunion des Musées Nationaux: 78, 171, 174

Réunion des Musées Nationaux/Caroline Rose: 173 (top left)

Ralph Richter/Architekturphoto: 205, 206, 207, 229, 231

Christian Richters: 84, 85

Tomas Riehle: 27

Cervin Robinson: 155

Paul Rocheleau: 80, 81

Brian Rose: 144, 145 (top)

Rubell Family Collection, Miami: 37

© 1989 by Schirmer/Mosel München: 104

Shinkenchiku-Sha: 264

Steven Sloman: 121 (bottom right), 125 (bottom left/right)

Margherita Spiluttini: 39, 40

Staatsgalerie Stuttgart: 179, 181

John Stoel: 121 (top and bottom left)

Ezra Stoller © Esto: 167, 220

Thorvaldsens Museum: 77 (bottom)

Thyssen-Bornemisza Collection: 15 (bottom)

James Turrell. Performing Lightworks, Kunsthaus Bregenz, 1997. Photo: Gruppe S. F. & H., Bregenz: 60 (top)

Courtesy of Lauretta Vinciarelli: 114

Matt Wargo: 183, 184

Hans Werlemann: 233

Wexner Center for the Arts, The Ohio State University, Columbus, Ohio. Photo: Kevin Fitzsimons: 226, 227

Wexner Center for the Arts, The Ohio State University, Columbus, Ohio. *The body and the object: Ann Hamilton, 1984–1996*. Installation view, May 18–August 4, 1996. Photo: Richard K. Loesch: 228.

Joshua White/Frank O. Gehry and Associates: 257

Stephen White (London): 35

Don F. Wong: 242, 243, 244

Courtesy of Yale University Art Gallery: 177

Index